Gender, Drink and Drugs

Cross-Cultural Perspectives on Women

General Editors: Shirley Ardener and Jackie Waldren,
for The Centre for Cross-Cultural Research on Women, University of Oxford

Gender, Drink and Drugs

Edited by
Maryon McDonald

BERG

Oxford • New York

First published in 1994 by
Berg
Editorial offices:
150 Cowley Road, Oxford, OX4 1JJ, UK
70 Washington Square South, New York, NY 10012, USA

Paperback edition reprinted in 1977

© Maryon McDonald 1994, 1997

Berg is the imprint of Oxford International Publishers Ltd.

Library of Congress Cataloging-in-Publication Data
Gender, drink, and drugs / edited by Maryon McDonald. – 1st ed.
    p. cm. – (Cross-cultural perspectives on women ; v. 10)
    Includes bibliographical references and index.
    ISBN 0-85496-719-2 (cloth). – ISBN 0-85496-867-9 (pbk).
    1. Women–Alcohol use–Cross-cultural studies.   2. Women-Drug
use–Cross-cultural studies.   3. Drinking of alcoholic beverages-
 Cross-cultural studies.   4. Drug abuse–Cross-cultural studies.
 I. McDonald. Maryon.   II. Series.
 HV5137.G46 1994   93-33151
 362.29´12´082-dc20   CIP

British Library Cataloguing-in-Publication Data
Gender, Drink and Drugs. –
(Cross-cultural Perspectives on Women Series)
    I. McDonald, Maryon

The cover illustration courtesy of Camden Graphics and the Mary Evans
Picture Library.

ISBN 0-85496-719-2 (cloth)
        0-85496-867-9 (paper)

Printed in the United Kingdom by WBC Book Manufacturers,
Mid-Glamorgan.

TO COLIN AND HANNAH

Contents

Acknowledgements

The discussions which led to this volume first began some time ago, in a workshop at Queen Elizabeth House, Oxford, in December 1987. I am grateful to all the participants in that original workshop, and especially to Shirley Ardener, Director of Queen Elizabeth House's Centre for Cross-Cultural Research on Women, who made our discussions possible. I am grateful to Alain Cerclé, Jenny Littlewood and Geoff Hunt for their contributions to the debate; and to Joselyn and George Ross for their subsequent help and forbearance.

I owe a special debt to discussions with my professional colleagues in the Department of Human Sciences, Brunel University, and especially to Ronnie Frankenberg and Ian Robinson. The reflections and ethnographic projects of Georgina Holmes, Vibhavari Patel and Andy Ashenhurst, undergraduates in that Department, have also offered important bases for critical discussion, and I am endebted to the many wise and witty students enrolled on the Department's Medical Anthropology M.Sc., all of whom it has been a great pleasure to teach. I give special thanks, too, to Peter Richards, general practitioner, who has never failed to offer critical advice. It is advice that I have not always been able to follow.

M. McD.

Introduction
A Social-Anthropological View of Gender, Drink and Drugs

Maryon McDonald

The title of this volume includes three topics – gender, drink and drugs – which can, each in its own right, make claims on social attention.

Over the last decade or so, 'gender' has become commonplace in book titles. Its popularity has been due, in part, to a realisation that women had been relatively invisible in social-science texts prior to the 1970s, and to a growth of feminisms of various kinds which have since tended to push women-centred issues to the fore. Gender, however, is not just about women or about women's roles. There are more fundamental issues at stake. Gender is about the various ways in which notions of 'man' and 'woman' are constructed.

Drink and drugs are issues which regularly claim the headlines. 'Alcoholism', for example, is said to be a veritable 'epidemic' which ruins the lives of individual victims. 'Drugs', on the other hand, are in themselves evil substances, and 'war' has been declared on them. Such ideas are now very common. Put together gender, drink and drugs, and we seemingly have a powerfully charged volume. However, one of the aims of this volume is to take away some of the unreflecting excitement that these issues have generated. We need to stand back a little and ask what all the fuss is about.

In saying this, I am not ignoring or denying the serious problems which drink and drugs obviously pose. The point of this book, however, is to try to add to our understanding of how problems arise. In an important sense, a problem does not exist until perceived and defined as such. We have to begin, therefore, by trying very briefly to understand how and why alcohol and drugs came to be seen as problems.

Evil Substances and Sick People

The idea that alcohol was a problem arose in specific circumstances. In the US, for example, a wider availability and increased consumption of spirits in the late eighteenth and nineteenth centuries, together with new social relations accompanying increased industrialisation, meant that drunkenness, which was not considered a major problem previously, became perceived as a serious threat to the economic and moral order. Drink and drunkenness, the lawless western frontier, waves of new immigrants, and new jobs and values challenging established modes of difference and respect, all became associated. In these circumstances, decreased consumption and the conspicuous avoidance of alcohol offered important means of social distinction, means by which statements of moral and social superiority could be made or reasserted. Abstinence became a 'ticket of admission into respectability' and was associated with self-control, industriousness and thrift, qualities both indicating religious adherence and deemed to accompany prosperity (Gusfield 1963; Heather and Robertson 1989).

The evils of alcohol were given confirmation over the same period by the idea that what had previously been known as 'habitual drunkenness' was in fact a disease[1]. This idea, developed principally by medical doctors in the US and in Britain, was in accordance with the development of a mode of thought (sometimes known as 'positivism') which suggested that the methods of natural science could be used in explanations of human behaviour. Human beings afflicted with the disease of habitual drunkenness behaved as they did because they could not do otherwise. This 'scientific' understanding also produced the term 'alcoholism', used from the mid-nineteenth century onwards as a general name for the disease which alcohol produced, and it became linked with new notions of 'psychosis' in psychiatry's developing taxonomies. 'Alcoholism' became, for some, an important paradigm of mental illness. Its credibility was sustained by the important invention, in the nineteenth century, of the notion of 'addiction'[2]. This idea, developed in the US initially, was closely tied in with Protestant notions of self-control. 'Addicts' were supposed to have a disease of the will, unable to control themselves, experiencing a 'craving' for alcohol. The notion of a state of addiction, invented for alcohol some seventy years before being applied to opium, later coloured and dominated understandings of 'drugs', imbuing them with an autonomous capacity for evil. It is still the case that the imputed 'addictiveness' of a substance holds a persuasive congruence with the degree of religious and political fear of it, and the capacity for evil attributed to it. The nineteenth-century Temperance Movement in the US undoubtedly helped to create an image of alcohol as a singularly powerful substance. The moral, religious, political and legal spotlights turned on alcohol in such a way that it appeared, of itself, capable of producing social effects of all kinds. These effects were deemed to be largely bad. Later on, with the repeal of Prohibition and the founding of Alcoholics Anonymous in the 1930s, the emphasis shifted a little. The source of addiction was not simply the substance itself – meaning that anyone touching alcohol could develop an involuntary craving – but instead it became a question of the vulnerability of a few individuals (Heather and Robertson 1989:34). Alcohol was now legal, if regulated, but not everyone became addicted or alcoholic as had once been predicted. It was therefore not the substance but a minority of users, bad or unfortunate, who now came into focus (Christie and Bruun 1969). At the same time, the powers and evils once attributed to alcohol *per se* were attributed to other substances – 'drugs' – and these substances have remained so empowered in supportive concordance with the requirements of illegality.

In Britain and in parts of Continental Europe, drunkards or 'inebriates' were also medicalized into alcoholics and addicts. However, the medical and political investments were slightly different from those in the US, and there was never any comparable move towards legal prohibition. In nineteenth-century Britain, for example, elements of disease theory in relation to alcohol had been around for some time, but it was a particular congruence of factors which brought such ideas to prominence and gave them credibility. Amongst these, evangelical and Temperance interests, the growing status and prestige of the medical profession and the expansion of psychiatry with the increase in asylums, all allowed and encouraged a medicalisation of areas previously understood in various ways as morally deviant – from poverty to homosexuality to alcoholism (Conrad and Schneider (eds) 1980; Berridge 1990; Porter 1985). This was the beginning of what many theorists have since seen as 'medical imperialism' (cf. Heather and Robertson 1989:146). However well-intentioned and humanitarian in ambition, such medicalisation is now deemed to have served well not only the interests of churchmen and the State, but also the expansionist ambitions and self-defining interests of the medical profession, and the 'apparently objective and value-free rationale of science provided a legitimation of contemporary social and economic relationships' (Berridge 1990:999).

In late nineteenth- and early twentieth-century Britain, a combination of hereditarian ideas with the assumptions and preoccupations of the public health and sanitary reform movements, produced convictions about mental hygiene in which poor human stock and ill-health might be eradicated for the sake of economic and industrial efficiency. Alcoholism, along with venereal disease and tuberculosis, was discussed in synonymy with concerns about racial degeneracy and national decline. The natural science formulation of social problems was an important feature of the professionalising strategies of a range of middle-class groupings at the time, and the education and reform of the lower classes, through various eugenicist means, were serious concerns for nation and Empire alike (see Jones 1986; Searle 1976 and Berridge 1990:chapter 3). Such views were not confined to Britain (see, for example, Nye 1984 on France, and McDonald, chapter 4 in this volume). In the 1930s, new eugenicist methods in Germany – involving the compulsory sterilisation of incurable alcoholics – seemed to reinvigorate flagging argument in Britain.

It was from a combination of Temperance preoccupations with eugenics and hereditarian, degenerationist debates that alcohol and drug research was eventually launched (Berridge 1990). Moral and political perceptions of danger allowed and encouraged the establishment of a pharmacology of harm. Without these perceptions, the developing edifice of pharmacological and biochemical studies of alcohol and 'drugs' might never have been constructed; certainly, without the moral and political fears, neither physicalist nor psychologistic perceptions of danger, disease or dependency would ever have been so persuasive.

An important early feature of the moral and political perceptions of danger which eventually created the space for such edifices of scientised addiction – edifices later housing a range of disease theories from notions of simple pharmacological compulsion to constructions of an 'alcoholic (or addictive) personality' – was the fact that it was groups perceived to be essentially different or threatening to the established social majority who were visibly consuming alcohol. In general, the more the working classes (or 'Negroes', Catholics, Irish immigrants, and so on) were seen to drink, the more drink and drinking became defined as a problem; but the more the middle classes were themselves felt to have drinking problems, the more these problems became amoralistically defined.

This has been especially true of the US, but many features of the story are not dissimilar for parts of Europe, including Britain (see Johnson 1973, Berridge 1990). Moral culpability gave way – ideally – to scientific causality. Medicine and related professions (notably psychology) could seemingly take away the blame.

The development of coherent disease theories of alcoholism did not mean immediately that moral condemnation or penal attitudes disappeared. Not only was implicit moral condemnation necessary for medicalisation to take place, but the two sets of ideas have continued to coexist quite explicitly in some areas (Room 1983). Early 'treatment', moreover, often involved near-penal segregation in an asylum. However, when the disease model was deliberately and carefully revived after the Second World War – largely through the work of Jellinek at Yale in the US – it was in order to rescue alcoholics from continuing moral and legal condemnation. People who seemed compelled to drink were not bad, it was emphasised, but ill. Well-known critics of such disease theories have since been happy to allow that the 'main object of the exercise was to keep the alcoholic out of gaol and get him or her into treatment' (Heather and Robertson 1989:45). The reinvention of the idea that alcoholism was a disease – whether this was now understood as *pre-existing* physical abnormality, mental illness or psychopathology, or as a disease of addiction or dependence which was a *consequence* of drinking – may have been well-intentioned but the idea was not allowed to survive undisturbed.

Important criticisms were voiced from within the growing social sciences, especially from the 1960s onwards. (For some of these criticisms, see Room 1983, and Heather and Robertson 1989.) There have also been carefully argued criticisms from philosophy and legal studies (for example, Fingarette 1983). The invention of alcohol as both a problem and a 'disease' has been seen to be culturally and historically specific. Disease theories have been shown to be contradicted, in their own terms, by much available evidence. Their claims, it has been argued, are not matters of some abstract 'science', but are legal, political and social claims linking all alcohol issues to the professional interests of medicine. Many related criticisms have been part of the concern about the 'medicalisation of deviance' which was strongly expressed in the 1960s and 1970s (Conrad and Schneider 1980). The key assumptions of disease theorists' claims (see Room 1983 for a summary) have now been largely discredited. The idea that alcoholism meant irreversibility, with abstinence the only cure, had the capacity for a while to generate debates, largely with psychologists, about whether or not 'controlled drinking' was possible, but more recent discussion about the cultural context of both drinking and its problematisation would now make many of these debates seem arcane. There has been a general retreat from disease theories and from the simplicities of notions of physical dependence. The World Health Organisation has moved from its 1950s assertions about disease and addiction towards such seemingly safe formulations as 'alcohol-related problems' (Room 1983, 1985), and others have talked of 'problem drinking' (notably Heather and Robertson 1989). Such reformulations are important. They both take account of, and create the space for, differences in modes of drinking and disparities in modes of defining a 'problem'. Widely acknowledged leaders in the field of medical studies of alcoholism and addiction made a last-ditch stand in the late 1970s to retain an interestingly tautological, disease-like 'alcohol dependence syndrome'. This, however, was not simply a physical or biological state but a 'psychobiological reality' (Edwards and Grant (eds) 1977; Edwards et al. (eds) 1983; Edwards 1984). There have been many attempts to reach out for something other than the physical, pharmacological or biochemical, and 'psycho-' seems to be a favourite and easy sleight by which to conjure up images of a new paradigm. In many such formulations the 'psycho-' seems to be inserted, however, merely to get theorists off the hook. It is generally not elaborated and when it is, it commonly turns out to be interestingly but unselfconsciously culture-bound and of unwittingly limited utility.

Griffiths Edwards was one of the rare medical practitioners who actively participated, from the 1970s onwards, in attempts to get the medical profession to grasp something other than their own, sometimes self-serving, definitions of alcoholism, addiction or dependence (see Berridge 1990). Substance-users' own perceptions, it was suggested, had somehow to be taken into account. Edwards has also posed some interesting questions about the whole notion and role of 'withdrawal symptoms' (Edwards 1990), which had become an important and traditional part of the disease package. A 'craving' or compulsion to drink alcohol bears only a fragile relationship to a situation that pharmacology or medicine might describe. Pharmacologists, physicians and consumers alike learn to organise certain events into 'withdrawal', with symptoms that can be classified and diagnosed or narrated. Diagnosis is inevitably cultural, and, at a very basic level for the craving consumer, there is a requirement for the substance taken to be perceived as making him or her feel better. The compulsion, whether for pharmacologist, diagnostician or consumer, is a heavily overladen cultural perception.

Understandings of 'addiction' as physical dependence or a disease-like condition have tended to take refuge in the domain of substances known as 'drugs' – a classification which alcohol has legally escaped. Understandings of addiction first worked out for alcohol were transposed to drugs, where – with considerable political and moral encouragement – they tended to stay. However, with new social-science understandings of the way in which the notion of addiction developed, and studies of the social use of drugs, questions have been posed about the nature of addiction in the realm of these substances also. One modern book on 'psychopharmacology' feels able to include several statements about the 'naïvety' of pharmacologically-based understandings of addiction, and in a chapter on the 'hard' drug heroin, we learn that 'sufficient evidence from other sources has gradually accumulated to indicate that any satisfactory model of addiction will have to take into account a range of known social factors which completely outweigh the pharmacological aspects of the use of heroin'. (Cochrane 1984:127) The pharmacological power of drugs is no longer a satisfactory explanation of their use. The capacities officially attributed to a substance stem, in priority, from moral and political preoccupations (cf. Thom in this volume), and many of the preoccupations which shaped understandings of alcohol were simply transposed to other substances.

In the late nineteenth century, the Temperance Movement, emanating from the US, influenced attitudes to substances other than alcohol. Opium was already in the spotlight in drives against opiate use in China and amongst Chinese workers in the US. There was also an anti-opium movement in Britain which opposed the opium trade in the Far East. By the end of the nineteenth century, habitual opium use had become, on the model of habitual drinking, a disease (Berridge 1979, 1989). In discussing opium addicts at this time, medical doctors in Britain felt they were talking mostly about their own colleagues or about people of the higher social classes. Such cases warranted understanding and 'treatment'. In the US, the use of opium was more popular and, by the same token, it seemed both more threatening and to demand a tougher moral and penal response. Under the combined pressures of the anti-opium and Temperance movements, the Harrison Act was passed in the US in 1914, effectively outlawing the medical prescribing of opiates to opium-eaters, or 'addicts' as they now were (and often equipped with hypodermics). This legislation helped to create and sustain a criminal black market. Drug control in the US became henceforth a penal matter. Prohibition, for alcohol and opiates alike, set a pattern of criminal activity and stark associations of deviance which 'drugs' have yet to shrug off, and which laid the foundations for the self-serving and self-perpetuating credibility of declarations and redeclarations of 'war' from the voices of law and order.

In Britain in the early years of this century, the fight was more between the medical profession and the Home Office over who should control the consumption of opiates. In the early years of the nineteenth century, it had been concern about poisoning that had formed the basis for a case for drug regulation. A Poisons Bill was presented to Parliament in 1819 but failed to become law in the face of a lobby of druggists, chemists and apothecaries who did not wish their sales restricted. This lobby was professionally organised in 1841 into The Pharmaceutical Society of Great Britain. There was competition for the sale of drugs from every corner grocer, travelling vendor and market stall. The Pharmaceutical Society and the General Medical Council joined forces. The Pharmacy Act was passed in 1868, which limited the sale of certain substances to pharmacists. Opium and its preparations were in a less restrictive schedule, requiring only a properly labelled container. Sales became more closely limited to pharmacists with the 1908 Poisons and Pharmacy Act, but substances such as opium and its preparations and cocaine, for example, could still be bought providing the buyer was known or personally introduced to the pharmacist, and signed the poisons register (Stimson and Oppenheimer 1982:19–21). There was no question of a prescription, or of restrictions on possession. The notion of 'drugs' was thus taking shape in a context in which the main issues were ostensibly safety, commercial rights and profit, and the development of restricted 'professions' with training and licences.

The medical profession brought the use of opiates within their domain at the end of the nineteenth century through definitions of their habitual use as disease. Issues of self-control were important here, as they had been in the invention of addiction to alcohol. In Britain, opium addicts were apparently few and well-bred. It was nevertheless known that there was common consumption of, and self-medication by, opiates amongst the labouring classes (especially in the fens of the East of England). These people were not regarded as ill or addicted, but they did not seem to seek medical supervision.

In arguments about safety, science, moral will, national efficiency and professional expertise, ways were sought to limit certain drugs to prescription. The American-inspired movement for international narcotics control brought some support therefore from medical doctors in Britain. The First Opium Convention was signed by Britain in The Hague in 1912, under American pressure. This Convention urged greater controls, which were now as much in keeping with medical as with moral and penal arguments, and it shifted attention to include questions of possession. The First World War interrupted these discussions, and also moved the ground significantly towards moral and penal reaction. 'Drugs' now appeared – as did alcohol in the US – to be a threat to moral fibre, the war effort and army efficiency. It was rumoured, for example, that soldiers on leave were taking cocaine (Spear 1969). The Home Office therefore appropriated the drugs question in Britain, as a policing issue, and one involving matters of smuggling, security and public order.

First World War legislation effected a climate heavy with prohibition, and legal backing was now given to the requirement for a doctor's prescription. After the war, the Dangerous Drugs Acts of 1920 and 1923 extended this regime in which definitions of vice and criminality dominated, but the position of the medical doctors and the question of 'medical treatment' were left unclear. The Ministry of Health's Rolleston Committee, composed of members of the medical professions, published a report in 1926 which effectively reappropriated the drugs question for medicine. Addiction was a disease, requiring treatment. As a result of this report, doctors could again prescribe, for 'legitimate' treatment, non-progressive doses of the 'dangerous' drugs. Those whom they would treat included, they stressed, their own aberrant or addicted colleagues (Stimson and Oppenheimer 1982:26–9).

This regime has often been termed the 'British system' and contrasted with the penal regime of North America. There are clearly problems, however, in trying to draw a strong contrast between systems which rested on often congruent assumptions about the constitution of a 'problem' and the necessity of control. It is also important to note that when, in the 1960s in Britain, 'drugs' took on new shape in contexts of counter-culture and dissent, and were perceived to be consumed at popular and ethnic levels, a new moral and penal regime emerged with great ease. In a fit of moral panic and State 'legislative zeal', the parameters of what constituted an offence were greatly expanded (Stimson and Oppenheimer

1982:4ff.). Growing cannabis, for example, was brought within the bounds of criminality, and led to police manpower being used to 'raid potplants' (Young 1979). The new regime meant that treatment was moved out of the general practitioners' surgeries and into hospitals and clinics. In any case, a combination of the new legislative framework plus various recensions of the counter-culture meant that the new 'junkies' and addicts did not easily seem, to growing numbers of general practitioners, to conform to the required image and behaviour of a 'patient'. Treatment possibilities have since progressively moved back towards community services which include general practitioners' surgeries, but the general practitioners have shown some resistance to accepting people on to their lists whom they see as variously 'difficult' and 'manipulative'. Right from the time of the Rolleston Committee and associated debates, there had been similar concern on the part of medical doctors that the new 'patients' they were demanding should nevertheless accept the proper subservience to medical authority and the acquiescence expected of the sick (see Berridge 1990; Stimson and Oppenheimer 1982).

Tensions between constructions of addiction as a criminal or medical question, or as a vice or disease, have played themselves out in many debates over the last hundred years or so. In general, the two approaches go hand in hand in mutual support, with different emphases and priorities emerging as the context requires. There have recently been attempts by those working in the drugs field – rather as there have been in the alcohol field – to move away from the notion of 'addiction' and its associations, replacing this with discussion of drug 'misuse' or 'abuse', or simply 'problem drug-use'. Such terms are, however, loaded with many of the same assumptions (Berridge 1989; Levine 1984).

Cultural Diversity

Our understanding of alcohol and drugs has changed with the cultural context in which they have found their meaning. We have to include in that context the broadly politico-economic setting and the views held of and by the consumer. The cultural context constructs substance and consumer alike, the one invoking the other. For example, there was little inherently 'dangerous' about the social use of opium or opiates in Britain when established literati and the Master of Queens' College, Cambridge, were partaking liberally in the early nineteenth century. Through the American-influenced debates of the early years of the twentieth century, however, the consumer re-emerged as the 'dope fiend' possessed of a feared and insatiable craving. Emancipated women were felt to be especially susceptible (Berridge 1984:22). Then the moral and political reinvention of youth and deviance in the 1960s helped to produce the 'junkie', a social figure at once more popular and ethnic. The 'junkie' was required to carry all the fears of the social Establishment, at the same time supplying thereby an attractive medium for symbolic revolt (Burr 1984a, 1984b, 1987; Hall and Jefferson 1976).

One of the main lessons of anthropological studies that have dealt with alcohol and drugs in any way has been that a substance's meaning or reality, its capacity to attract or repel, varies according to the cultural context in which it is placed. A distinctive anthropological perspective on these issues began to emerge in the 1960s. Until then, when anthropology and other social sciences mentioned alcohol at all, they were still heavily informed by the 'disease' or 'alcoholism' paradigms which were renewed with such vigour at Yale after the Second World War (see Room 1983; Heath 1975; also Douglas (ed.) 1987: the title of this last volume, *Constructive Drinking*, was explicitly intended to distinguish it from the older problem-centred approaches).

One of the best-known anthropological statements on alcohol came, in the mid-1960s, from Mandelbaum. He made the summary and forceful statement that:

> When a man lifts a cup, it is not only the kind of drink that is in it, the amount he is likely to take, and the circumstances under which he will do the drinking that are specified in advance for him, but also whether the contents of the cup will cheer or stupefy, whether they will induce affection or aggression, quiet or unalloyed pleasure. These and many other cultural definitions attach to the drink even before it reaches the lips. (Mandelbaum 1965:282)

There are many aspects we might now, with the smartness of hindsight, wish to criticise here – including the seemingly unproblematic 'he'. Anthropological literature on drink has only recently become aware of an absence of gender consciousness (see, for example, Douglas (ed.) 1987); the easy collusion of 'he' and drink had often been ignored in the past and women's drinking either condemned outright or accepted, at face value, as somehow just not really drinking (on this point, see Gefou-Madianou (ed.) 1992).

Whether paying attention to gender or not, anthropological studies have generally underlined the wide range of cross-cultural realities involved in alcohol and its consumption, from absence to self-conscious abstinence, and from positive moral evaluation to aggressive condemnation (for some useful, critical summaries of the available literature, see Heath 1975, 1987; Room 1984, 1985). It is important to stress that what we are looking at here is different cultural realities. There is otherwise a danger of thinking that there is some culture-free substance – say 'alcohol' or 'ethanol' – and then an interesting variety of different cultural perceptions of it. Cultural perceptions become a sort of cloud hanging above the 'real' thing, and 'cultural variety' a romanticism which a more rigorous science might dispel.

One important first-stage point in anthropology is that there is no culturally innocent (or culture-free) reality. Any claims to have a privileged handle on reality, to be able to perceive an extra-cultural reality, are in themselves cultural. Medicine, biology and pharmacology are examples of discourses in which such claims to an extra-cultural reality are most commonly made. For an anthropologist, however, 'science' is a cultural idea and activity like any other (on this point, see Woolgar 1988). In stark heuristic terms, the real world is not simply 'out there' waiting to be discovered, raw and in culture-free innocence, by science; rather, science is actively constructing reality, and has persuasive means to assert what is to count as 'real'. Cultural perceptions and activities which may historically or contextually differentiate science from other activities can thereafter be added, but the first-stage conceptual point is important and its implications profound.

The anthropologist does not look to medicine, biology, pharmacology, biochemistry or physiology (and so on) to understand in any simple sense what a substance really is and does. These constructions of a substance have to be set in a wider social context, in which both reality and context are far more complex.

Some non-anthropologists might be asking themselves at this stage just what an anthropologist means by apparently reducing everything to 'culture'. Very broadly, two things are meant by stressing, as this volume does, that everything is 'cultural'. Firstly, no one has a hot line to some reality external to cultural perception. Claims to such a privileged grip on the world are themselves inevitably a function of the socio-historical context in which they are made. This does not mean that scientific claims, for example, are not right. Rather, it means that we can be aware that all such claims are made and expressed in specific socio-historical circumstances, that they are ineluctably conceptual and that we have no access to the world other than through our perceptions of it. It may seem, for instance, that medical and scientific understandings of the human body are surely culture-free; it may seem that here we must have hit on some culture-free nitty-gritty. However, anthropologists have shown that the human body (or bodies) constructed by science are inevitably functions of current predispositions, composed of and drenched in contemporary social assumptions about the world, gender included (Armstrong 1983; Lock and Gordon (eds) 1988; Martin 1989; Scheper-Hughes and Lock 1986). This is the first point then: the world is conceptually given, nature is inevitably cultural. The second point is that perceptions of the world vary across time and space. We do not now see the world as people did in the fifteenth century, for example, and a Fijian may well perceive the world differently from a French person. This second point comes a little closer to popular notions of 'culture', but we should be wary of assuming that culture difference is somehow tied to national or ethnic difference. Since the nineteenth century, that has been a common perception, but it is a priority in anthropology to draw boundaries where people draw them themselves. These may well be along national or 'ethnic' lines but such gross units of identity and difference take little account of the contextual subtleties of everyday life and their salience should not be taken for granted.

Understandings of drunkenness have underlined these two main points. The idea that drunkenness frees us from 'culture' or cultural rules is common (and has allowed drunkenness to become an excuse for wife-beating and murder: Bennett and Cook 1990:242). Alcohol does not of itself, however, determine the behaviour of the consumer. A state of drunkenness will be defined differently cross-culturally, the meaning of drunkenness varies, and the behaviour which alcohol induces is a cultural matter rather than a question of the inevitable or natural consequences of ethanol entering the bloodstream (cf. Hendry, this volume). Notions of 'arousal' or a 'disinhibitor effect' are cultural expectations attendant on drink (see Room and Collins (eds) 1983) and are part of a cultural physiology. Drunken behaviour is *learned* behaviour (see MacAndrew and Edgerton 1969 for the best-known anthropological statement of this). Drunkenness perceived as 'a function of toxically disinhibited brains operating in impulse-driven bodies' (MacAndrew and Edgerton 1969:165) should be understood, therefore, as an expression of some of the cultural assumptions of medicine. One such assumption is precisely that drink has the capacity to operate at the level of, and to reveal, a culture-free nature. This is a widespread assumption (as several of the chapters of this volume suggest) but in each case the 'nature' so revealed is itself no less cultural for that.

For those who feel that a substance such as alcohol is inherently a problem and that the substance determines behaviour, a link between alcohol and violence is common. Often this link is made because it is men who drink and it is often men, in their cultural manliness, who are allowed or expected to be violent. The association of alcohol or drunkenness with violence is not at all universal (see Heath 1975 and Hendry's chapter on Japan in this volume). Apparently riotous bouts of drinking regularly occur in some cultures without any violence. The connection of violence with drink and drunkenness seems to have been learnt, as part of a learned mode of drinking and drunken behaviour, and the two are now widely associated. As the chapters here by Toren (on Fiji), Harvey (on Peru) and Huby (on the Southern Sudan) suggest, however, this violence is not raw and random, but socially structured (cf. Heath 1975:37; Riches (ed.) 1986). MacAndrew and Edgerton (1969) long ago posed important questions about drinking and violence. They showed how American Indians, for example, who had not been consumers of alcohol prior to colonisation, were at first shocked by – and then gradually emulated – the violently drunken behaviour of white trappers and settlers. By the nineteenth century, more educated visitors from the very countries the Indians thought they were emulating actually condemned the Indians' behaviour – and the 'firewater myth' of Indian alcoholism (see Leland 1976), suggesting that Indians by nature could not handle alcohol, became firmly entrenched.

The reputation of many indigenous peoples for heavy drinking or alcoholism – of which the 'firewater myth' about North American Indians is but one example – owes much to the encounter of different cultures. In Europe, self-defining centres of civilisation have long constructed images of heavy-drinking barbarians and primitives at their frontiers (see Purcell in this volume on Ancient Greek and Roman civilisation, and McDonald on the image constructed of the 'Celts'; also Stivers 1976). Barbarians or primitives ripe for such misinterpretation have been 'discovered' both within Europe and outside it (Barker (ed.) 1985).

Within Europe, the encounter of fermented grain and grape seems regularly to have generated misunderstanding on both sides. Many modern visitors from Britain on a first visit to France have had experience of this themselves. Drinks may be offered at ten o'clock in the morning, for example. This is obviously going to be one of those days. What are we celebrating? During the midday meal, wine is served. What fun! What are we celebrating? The bars are open all afternoon, and people seem to be drinking. What a riot! What are we celebrating? Pastis is served at six o'clock. Whoopee! These people certainly know how to celebrate. More wine is served with dinner. And so on. Wine has different meanings, different realities, in the two contexts, and a festive and episodic drinking culture meets a daily drinking culture, generating a tendency to celebrate all day. This has often happened to groups of young British tourists, now renowned in France and elsewhere in Europe for their drinking and drunkenness.

Whenever grape and grain have met, there seems to have been both a mutual misunderstanding of drinking cultures and also an eventual appropriation of one mode of drinking by those accustomed to another. In the British/French example just mentioned, episodic, festive beer-drinking (British) is understood in the terms of a non-drunken, daily drinking culture (French), and takes on the appearance of moral and physical excess; and then, as if to confirm this image, wine is drunk by the visiting beer-drinkers in beer quantities, and perhaps both daily and festively too. The possibilities for compounded and mutual misunderstanding are immense.

Alcohol and its consumption are inherently cultural matters therefore. Not only are there different modes and meanings of drink, drinking and drunkenness, but also drink has the capacity to set different behavioural agendas in the definition of social time and space (distinguishing work from leisure, for example, where such a distinction exists: see Mandelbaum 1965; Gusfield 1987) and in the definition of social identity (distinguishing men from women, for example, or a certain kind of man or woman from others). A situation in which a housewife prepares a gin and tonic for her husband when he comes home from work exemplifies many of these points.

If the very meaning or reality of alcohol, the mode of consuming it, the behaviour it induces, and the definition of the substance or its consumption as problematic (or not) are matters which require, for their understanding, a grasp of the context in which they take the form they do, then it follows that 'therapy' for 'alcohol problems' works only at a cultural level and is similarly contextual in its efficacy (Bennett and Cook:244). There is no 'deeper' level of some culture-free biology or human psyche at which such therapies work. Alcoholics Anonymous, for example, owes its life to a very particular cultural and historical context, and has either been transformed elsewhere (see Hendry in this volume) or simply does not work (Heath 1975). There has been a general shift from punitive to therapeutic regimes but any therapy for an alcohol or drug problem has to take account of both the context of its own birth and the cultural context in which the relevant persons and substances alike take their shape. Similarly, moral condemnation has ostensibly given way to public health models in the prevention sphere, but there may be little point simply launching campaigns against alcohol or drugs in the name of some biomedical model of 'health', say, if in the context where the campaign is to be launched, there is no prior perception of social and moral threat which creates the space for the construction of a 'problem' and for biomedical or therapeutic intervention. Without some notion of a substance being a social, moral or political threat, there can be no secure or persuasive pharmacology of harm. Almedon and Abraham's chapter in this volume, which discusses the case of *tchat*-chewing among urban women in Ethiopia, makes this point well.

The general anthropological points that have been made about alcohol can also be made about drugs. (For a survey of some of the anthropological work on drugs, see Bennett and Cook 1990). Anthropological studies have often dealt with alcohol and drugs separately, abiding by an historical division operative in the cultures from which they themselves come. Studies of drugs and drug-taking became serious business in the 1970s, rather later than for alcohol, and many drugs studies resemble, in their basic approach, alcohol studies with a time lag. In the 1970s, in the heyday of anti-establishment movements, the very illegality of drugs invited the curiosity of social scientists and users alike. It seems important to stress, therefore, that at a conceptual level, we are still, for drugs as for alcohol, dealing with an ineluctably cultural matter. This is so whether we talk about the perception of the substance and its use as a problem or not, or we talk about the reality of the substance for users or abstainers, dealers or police, patients, doctors and pharmacologists; or we talk about its modes of sale and consumption, and the behaviours it induces. The various forms of deviance, destruction, rebellion and opposition associated with drugs are often a function of their illegality, and behaviours associated with substances in these circumstances cannot be generalised. For instance, a substance such as *tchat* may, for some, be a sordid 'drug of abuse' (see Inciardi and McBride 1991, writing in the US); for others, however, it is a substance which, when chewed by women, assures their moral virtue (see Almedon and Abraham on Ethiopia in this volume). A substance such as cannabis which can evoke a self-conscious, laid-back, peace-on-earth counter-culture in many parts of the West, means tough manliness and the daily rigours of hard work elsewhere (see Partridge 1977 on the use of cannabis among male work gangs in South America). Similarly, cocaine has very specific meanings, including strong associations with the violence of the underworld, in many western countries. In many parts of Peru, however, tourists stuffing coca leaves into their mouths as if they were their own cocaine shocks local people; in local everyday life, coca has a very different, daily, healthful and invigorating significance (see Allen 1988). When it comes to heroin, often said to be an evil substance capable of trapping the unwary, it seems that a good deal of learning is involved in the acquisition of 'addiction' and that (as the returning American troops from Vietnam demonstrated) it may be relatively easy, when moving from one culture to another, to stop taking it (Robins et al. 1974). And so on. The importance of cultural context looms large in all such studies. There has inevitably been some resistance to such findings from those, in the US and elsewhere, who see social danger inherent in the substances themselves, or risk solely inherent in certain individuals (on this point, see Bennett and Cook 1990:238).

When we talk disapprovingly about 'drugs', we are talking in priority about perceived threats to the social and moral order, threats which have been medicalised, and on which a whole scientistic edifice has been built. Some features of this edifice are now being put in question. However, it is still very difficult to touch on the fundamental points, and to relativise the realities, both medical and moral, of the substances involved, without appearing to be ignorant, woolly-headed or simply out to destroy the very fabric of society. At the same time, it is known that the illegality and moral deviance of drugs remain a potent source of their attraction, that their illegality is an important source of toxicity, that their status generates and sustains a world of violent, organised crime, and imposes or transposes the 'problem' more and more widely around the globe. On this last point, coca can serve as an example again. It has its own meanings in the modes and forms in which it is consumed in many other parts of the world (most notably in South America) but it has nevertheless become, in the official discourse of the more powerful countries, 'cocaine' and a 'narcotic', dangerous and worthy of waging war against. What might appear to some to be essentially the same substance has at least two quite distinct definitions or realities in the two different contexts. Between the reality, on the one hand, of those who consume the substance daily for their social well-being and the world of those who see it as a terrible danger and scourge on the other, it is nevertheless clear where the power of definition lies. The more powerful countries or administrations, those with greater resources of persuasion, know that 'really' what we have here is a dangerous substance. It is their definition that wins out. In other words, the power lies with those countries who have created, for themselves, a problem – a problem which, in their war against drugs, they have busily exported.

Anthropologists who have examined the meetings of the different worlds involved have argued that the countries which wage a seemingly never-ending war on drugs might more fruitfully examine the different contexts into which their war, and their problem, have extended (on coca and cocaine in various parts of South America, for example, see A. Henman 1990). These other cultural contexts, it is suggested, can often offer lessons in 'user-friendly' cultural controls on the consumption of the substances which the dominant countries find so difficult.

Points such as these are useful in any rethinking of 'the drug problem'. They do not, however, constitute an uncritical or simplistic argument for legalisation. Many of the issues posed by legalisation have now been well aired (see, for instance, Inciardi (ed.) 1991). For those who argue in favour of the legalisation of drugs, it is generally accepted that, as for alcohol, legalisation would not mean an absence of regulation (e.g. Nadelmann 1991) and it would not mean the simple or immediate absence of a 'problem'. New meanings, new realities would have to be created for the substances concerned. The cultural reconstruction of both persons and substances that would be involved is a long-term process. Legalisation would be only one factor, but a singularly important one, in this process.

Gender, Drink and Drugs

Legalisation instead of prohibition would bring changes in the contexts, in the relationships both conceptual and social, in which substances find their meanings, their allure and their danger, their price and their effects. One of the main points of this volume is that the meaning or social reality of a substance is always to be found in the cultural context in which it is placed. In summary, a substance has no reality external to perceptions of it, or to the context of its use. There is no culturally innocent substance from which either craving or behaviour stem. We cannot somehow sweep away either the cultural diversity of its use or some simple 'abuse' to get at the reality, in its pristine form, beneath. The substance is always the cultural values invested in it, and this applies whether the values be those of the police, the pharmacologist or the user, for example.

Similar points apply to gender. The categories 'man' and 'woman' always find their meaning within the system in which they exist. The terms *sex* (biological differences) and *gender* (cultural differences) were once common as a distinction in social science to emphasise that biological or physiological differences told us nothing about the cultural meanings of those differences, about their possible social significance or interpretation. However the sex/gender distinction, whilst politically and heuristically useful, is also conceptually redundant. Sex differences do not exist external to cultural perceptions of them, and these perceptions, whether 'biological' or otherwise, are gendered. Any perceived anomaly merely underlines this point.

Although we can now take a step beyond the sex/gender distinction, it is important not to lose sight of the point of making the distinction in the first place. The distinction served to emphasise that our own everyday, common-sense understandings of the differences between men and women were not given in nature or biology. Populations around the world tend to naturalise their understandings of the world in some way, but the most common way of doing this in the self-consciously 'Western' world has been to anchor ideas in biology. For instance, one well-established way of understanding differences between men and women in Europe, North America and beyond has been in terms of a rationality/irrationality dichotomy. Men are reasonable, women are prey to their emotions; men are practical, women zany; men are materially minded, women spiritual; and so on. These dichotomies, congruent with a whole host of dualities systematised by positivism and romanticism, are part of a complex of thought which came into being with force and coherence in the eighteenth and nineteenth centuries. With the help of the new national education systems, they began systematically to organise sex differences in the nineteenth century, and were part and parcel of developing industrialisation, urbanisation, and changing family structures. These dichotomies are not given in nature, therefore. They are not differences inherent in the biological differences involved. They are, however, an important way in which the biology itself is understood. Women are often said to be constrained by biology but that biology is itself understood in terms of the same social constraints that it is meant to generate (Hastrup 1978; Martin 1989). Women have, through conceptual structures of the kind I have mentioned, been deemed to be variously hysterical and prey to their nerves (see Cayleff 1988; also Littlewood in this volume). Modern psychology has tended to perpetuate the naturalisation of recensions of such differences, and the social roles that women have taken on have been congruent with, and made moral sense of, in these same terms. The rational public world has tended to be left to men and women ideally take on the emotional, caring roles of mother and home-maker.

Through the prescription of drugs such as tranquillisers, medical doctors have often colluded in structures of which medical education traditionally provides little comprehension beyond a taken-for-granted, it's-all-in-women's-nature perception. It is no coincidence that tranquillisers have been prescribed overwhelmingly to women (see Littlewood's chapter in this volume). Tranquillisers have allowed women 'to cope'. They have enabled them to be good wives and mothers. These drugs seemed to offer women the possibility of overcoming an apparently innate emotionality, nerviness and irritability. They have allowed them to remain within structures at once conceptual and social in which the centre of definition is elsewhere. (For those women who have tried to put such structures in question, the prescription of drugs in this way has inevitably seemed oppressive and irresponsible: see, for example, Ettore 1989). The quasi-medicalisation of other gender issues – including anorexia nervosa, for example – has similarly meant that the socio-historical context of gender imperatives, of which these phenomena are very much a part, are easily lost sight of in a diagnosis of illness or disease – and we are very soon back to nature again.

It has been a common observation in the 'drugs' literature that, in many western countries, women tend to be the main consumers of *licit* drugs, and men of *illicit* drugs. Pharmaceutical companies have been able to exploit the compliance of women, making money from apparently helping the nervously irritable housewife to cope (for some of the advertising involved, see C. Henman 1990; also Littlewood in this volume). This division of female/male, licit/illicit consumption requires further comment. Firstly, the same conceptual structures within which women are nervy and emotional are those within which it is the man's physiology which has become the model of the healthy body (see Cayleff 1988; Martin 1989). The processes of women's bodies have become syndromes and illnesses. For these and related social reasons, women easily seem to be ill more often than men, and appear more often in the doctor's surgery (a point which Littlewood takes up in his chapter here). Secondly, the licit nature of certain substances, sanctioned and distributed by a well-respected member of society (the medical doctor), is congruent with women's concern for social propriety, part of the natural sensitivity attributed to them (see McDonald in the volume). Thirdly, the women who *are* involved in the outside manly world of crime and illicit drugs often simply disappear from the statistical picture in which the licit/illicit, women/men dualities can seem to find empirical confirmation. The police in Britain, for example, often negotiate the women out of the picture in order to nail the men (see Young in this volume). As Young's chapter makes clear, an understanding of drug use in a context of national prohibition should include an understanding of the cultural assumptions of the police.

There is now a good deal of literature on drinking cultures in Europe, and one of the interesting points to emerge is that, in southern Europe, unlike in the north, men commonly drink together without drunkenness or problems perceived to be linked to the drink (see, for example, Driessen 1983, Gefou-Madianou (ed.) 1992, Herzfeld 1985, Loizos and Papataxiarchis (eds) 1991). Within Europe, differences in modes of drinking congruent with gender constructs are most noticeable between north and south. In the north of Europe, gender differences are organised such that women's attributed sensitivity also gives them responsibility for social propriety; in the south of Europe, it is men who have responsibility for social order, and it is men who suffer dishonour when proprieties are breached. It is in the north of Europe that we find both the heaviest drinking and the most drinking 'problems'; in the south, men drink together but apparently without the problems of the north. Their manliness does not seem to rely on alcohol (and vice versa) in the same way, and the men's own honour is differently invested. There are many qualifications we might want to introduce into these bald statements, but it seems that whereas a man in the north of Europe can find manliness and heavy drinking synonymous, a man in the south of Europe can more readily find manliness synonymous, on the contrary, with the propriety of constraint. Some of these points are taken up in McDonald's chapter in this volume.

The countries of southern Europe have come only relatively recently to issues of substance use and abuse, and the gender axis of drugs there still awaits careful investigation. In the north of Europe, however, women's responsibility for propriety means that the female 'addict' – like the female 'alcoholic' – has particularly low status. Women have to be models of self-control (Gomberg 1976, 1987; Ettore 1989). They are condemned if they drink or indulge in illicit drugs themselves, and damned if their husbands do, too. Women as the moral force of society have been prominent in campaigns in the past against drink and drugs alike. They have been active themselves in these campaigns, and they became important targets from the nineteenth century onwards (see Gomberg 1987; Kalant (ed.) 1980; Levine 1980). At that time, they were not simply becoming important moral agents but were destined to be the nation's mothers, and healthy children were essential to ensure a strong imperial race. This was the beginning of the formal banning of children from pubs (Berridge 1990:1010) and of the social inadmissibility in pubs and bars of nice women. For women to take pleasure in either alcohol or illicit drugs themselves can still exclude them from their established roles of carer and moral judge. Such women are not proper women, are not nice women. In the nineteenth century, nice women campaigned against rum and took opium-laced tonics; their great-granddaughters have been able to find their femininity in campaigning against alcohol and opium alike, and in dutifully taking tranquillisers.

The gender differences consonant with various substances differ historically and cross-culturally to the point that there need be no marked difference at all in domains in which we might expect it. For example, among the Luo in Africa, both men and women smoke and it is not a moral diminution of either to do so (Kaplan et al. 1990). In other situations, a perceived Western influence, including the influence of the Church, has associated moral laxity and smoking and has often encouraged a restriction of smoking to men (Waldron et al. 1988). This has sometimes been further encouraged by the fact that it is the men locally who have traditional access to scarce goods and imports. Where it has become women's lot to have access to novelty, however, then imported drinks and cigarettes can come within their symbolic reach.

McDonald's chapter in this volume suggests that, in France, women's smoking and drinking has been positively tied up, by some, with constructions of a regional, Breton identity. Women as the repositories of 'tradition' is not an uncommon construction but it can make very different demands. Toren's chapter on Fiji and Dragadze's chapter on Soviet Georgia both suggest how expressions of a traditional identity require precisely that women do *not* drink. In both situations, gender and ethnic imagery are wound together as moral order in opposition to disorder. In the Georgian case, disorder is located in the Russians, and Russian women pitied for the hard task they have of asserting order there. In the Fijian case, women are ideally required to represent the Fijian way of life in opposition to a 'European' way conflated with alcohol and general disorder. The boundaries of social dysfunction are both gendered and ethnically marked in each case. For the Georgians it is Russians and especially Russian men, not themselves, who have alcohol problems; for the Fijians, it is by definition among men following the 'European way' that problems reside. At the same time, in Europe, women have been explicitly exhorted to abstain from alcohol in the name of national or imperial purity (see above, p.22). Thom's chapter makes this point in the case of England, outlining how Victorians proclaimed women to be at special risk from alcohol, perceptions which were a function of the political preoccupations of the time; and Purcell's chapter on Ancient Rome reminds us that such modes of imperial self-definition are not new. The implication of women in this way in the social and political self-definitions effected by men was long ago noted in anthropology more generally (Ardener 1972), and it was this insight which served to put gender firmly on the methodological agenda.

All the chapters in this volume challenge simplistic notions of 'stress' or 'alienation' as the cause of alcohol or drug consumption. Macdonald's chapter on Scotland and Huby's chapter on the Southern Sudan do so quite explicitly and, along with the chapter by McDonald on western France, they pay attention instead to the values and imperatives composing local drinking cultures, and to local perceptions of normal and problem drinking. The fine ethnographic details of Macdonald's work, outlining the daily realities in which drink is embedded, serves to take apart many common assumptions about drinking in the Scottish Highlands, simple alienation theories included. Gender is important throughout all these chapters, both in the compulsion to consume or not to consume, and in the definition of a problem. Huby's material on the Bari of the Southern Sudan underlines the importance of kinship in these matters, and goes on to suggest some of the means by which locally perceived problems are contained or resolved by the Bari themselves. Thom's chapter on England and Dragadze's chapter on Soviet Georgia also suggest that neither women's drinking (Thom) nor their abstinence from drink (Dragadze) can be simplistically equated with female oppression.

Anthropological treatment of alcohol and drugs issues in the recent past has generated concerns that problems were beginning to be ignored or underplayed (see especially Room 1984). In the chapters of this volume, however, the 'problem' becomes very much a part of the ethnography. Where the notion of illness is relevant in the construction of a problem, then the social path to sickness is also important. McDonald's chapter on France shows how and why it is the women who draw the boundaries of social dysfunction and who are the first to invoke medical definitions. Harvey's chapter on Peru also deals with questions of sickness, but from a rather different angle. She points to some tensions between local definitions of the 'bad' (*vicioso*) and the 'sick' (*enfermo*), and to the way in which these definitions can be socially manipulated. Both men and women are involved in this manipulation, and husbands and wives accuse each other of alcohol abuse or improper drinking, of being *vicioso*. Those who persistently misjudge the social relations of drinking, or who are socially powerless, more readily become *enfermos*. Women willing to assume an indigenous identity get as drunk as the men. Richer women do not get drunk in the same way, and they both use themselves, and are used by their menfolk, to create class distinction and a non-village *mestizo* identity. Outsiders who try to take a contrary path, and to define themselves into insider status by drinking, are nevertheless likely to obey different drinking proprieties and easily find themselves classified as *viciosos*.

The ethnographic details in the chapters of this volume offer important elements of contexts in which person and substance alike take their shape. The varied correlations, and the mutual constitution, of gender and substance emerge in each chapter. The volume as a whole is intended as a contribution to both anthropology and the literature on drink and drugs. Within anthropology, two specialist areas have grown up which are covered by this volume: *gender studies* and *medical anthropology*. Both of these areas have, however, been transformed to a degree that they can now seek their own dissolution within a more general anthropology. I do not mean by this that neither area should continue to demand attention. Rather, I mean that the attention they demand has changed. Gender is gradually ceasing to be a topic apart from other domains of anthropological interest, and ceasing to be one generally taught by women while the men deal with the manly domains of politics and economics, for example (for more eloquent comment on this division of labour, see Caplan 1988). Instead, gender is now appearing in all domains of anthropology, and the full range of anthropology is, as a result, being rethought. At the same time, men are less afraid to tackle gender and are having to take gender issues seriously.

Medical anthropology has also presented some important realignments, with a two-stage process discernible here too. First of all, medical anthropology has similarly moved away from biologism. A cultural understanding has been inserted in various ways. In the 1970s, for instance, a dichotomy between *illness* (the patient's perceptions) and *disease* (the medical doctor's perception) became common currency. Cultural perceptions were thus introduced, but in terms of a dichotomy which easily tended to affirm that doctors had 'real' knowledge and their patients an ephemeral culture. A self-consciously 'critical medical anthropology' added greater contextualisation thereafter, with much of the language of context influenced by Marxism, and new attention was paid to the social paths to, and the definitions and imperatives of, sickness (see, for example, Frankenberg 1980; Young 1982). The work of Foucault encouraged fresh insights into knowledge and power, and the epistemology of medicine came under scrutiny, and the body's moral and political anatomies with it. (For some of these developments, see Johnson and Sargent (eds) 1990.) By the end of the 1980s, medical systems could readily be seen as cultural systems, and this was possible without always trailing an older notion of 'culture' which left 'something else' (biology or physiology, and so on) hanging around in the determinant or definitive wings. Medical anthropology was no longer an inherently distinct area, defined by a dependence on biomedicine, but part of anthropology more generally. From once being the handmaiden of medicine and biology, anthropology was able to hold these same areas up for inspection. This could be said to be a second stage then, similar to that outlined for gender issues: with the move of medical anthropology towards an incorporation of the newer insights of anthropology more generally, the general anthropologist has not, in turn, been afraid to tackle 'medical' issues, seeing them as ineluctably cultural like anything else.

It is hoped that this volume will further encourage these trends and – whether in anthropology or beyond it, and for theoretician and practitioner alike – help definitively to incorporate gender and medical issues the one into the other.

Notes

1. On the question of 'disease' here, see Fingarette (1983), Kissin (1983), Parssinen and Kerner (1980), Room (1983, 1985).

2. The best-known article on the development of the idea of 'addiction' is Levine (1978); see also B. Johnson (1973).

References

Allen, C.J. (1988), *The Hold Life Has. Coca and Cultural Identity in an Andean Community.* Washington and London: Smithsonian Institution Press.

Ardener, E. (1972), 'Belief and the Problem of Women' in J. La Fontaine (ed.) *The Interpretation of Ritual.* London: Tavistock.

Armstrong, D. (1983), *Political anatomy of the body: medical knowledge in Britain in the twentieth century.* Cambridge: Cambridge University Press.

Barker, F. (ed.) (1985), *Europe and its others.* Colchester: University of Essex.

Bennett, L.A. and Cook, P.W. (1990), 'Drug Studies' in T.M. Johnson and C.F. Sargent (eds) 1990.

Berridge, V. (1979), 'Morality and medical science: concepts of narcotic addiction in Britain, 1810–1976', *Annals of Science,* no. 36:67.

Berridge, V. (1984), 'Drugs and Social Policy: the establishment of drug control in Britain 1900–1930', *British Journal of Addiction,* vol. 79:pp.17–29.

Berridge, V. (1989), 'Historical Issues' in S. MacGregor (ed.) 1989.

Berridge, V. (1990), 'The Society for the Study of Addiction, 1884–1988', Special Issue of *British Journal of Addiction,* vol. 85, no. 8, August 1990.

Berridge, V. and Edwards, G. (1981), *Opium and the People. Opiate Use in Nineteenth-Century England.* London: Allen Lane.

Burr, A. (1984a), *I am not my body: A study of the International Hare Krishna Sect.* Delhi: Vikas Publishing House.

Burr, A. (1984b), 'The Ideologies of Despair – A symbolic interpretation of punks' and skinheads' usage of barbiturates', *Social Science and Medicine,* vol. 9:pp.929–938.

Burr, A. (1987), '"Chasing the Dragon": Heroin misuse, delinquency and crime in the context of South London culture', *British Journal of Criminology,* October 1987, pp.1–27.

Caplan, P. (1988), 'Engendering Knowledge. The Politics of ethnography', *Anthropology Today,* vol. 4, no.5:pp.8–12; vol. 4, no.6:pp.14–17.

Cayleff, S. (1988), '"Prisoners of their own feebleness": Women, Nerves and Western Medicine – a Historical overview', *Social Science and Medicine*, vol. 26, no.12:pp.1199–1208.

Christie, N. and Bruun, K. (1969), 'Alcohol Problems: The Conceptual Framework' in M. Keller and T. Coffey (eds) *Proceedings of the 28th International Congress on Alcohol and Alcoholism*, New Jersey: Hillhouse Press.

Cochrane, R. (1984), 'Social Aspects of Illegal Drug Use' in D. Sanger and D. Blackmann (eds) *Aspects of Psychopharmacology*. London: Methuen.

Conrad, P. and Schneider, J.W. (1980), *Deviance and medicalization: from badness to sickness*. St Louis: Mosby.

Douglas, M. (ed.) (1987), *Constructive Drinking. Perspectives on Drink From Anthropology*. Cambridge: Cambridge University Press.

Driessen, H. (1983), 'Male sociability and Rituals of Masculinity in Rural Andalusia', *Anthropological Quarterly*, vol. 56, no.3, pp.125–133.

Edwards, G. (1978), Editorial, *British Journal of Addiction*, vol. 73:pp.1–2.

Edwards, G., Arif, A., and Jaffe, J. (eds) (1983), *Drug Use and Misuse. Cultural Perspectives*. London: Croom Helm.

Edwards, G. (1984), 'Drinking in longitudinal perspective: career and natural history', *British Journal of Addiction*, vol. 79:pp.175–83.

Edwards, G. (1990), 'Withdrawal symptoms and alcohol dependence: fruitful mysteries', *British Journal of Addiction*, vol. 85:pp.447–61.

Edwards, G. and Grant, M. (eds) (1977), *Alcoholism: new knowledge and new responses*. London: Croom Helm.

Ettore, B. (1989), 'Women, substance abuse and self-help' in S. MacGreggor (ed.) 1989.

Fingarette, H. (1983), 'Philosophical and Legal Aspects of the Disease Concept of Alcoholism', *Research Advances in Alcohol and Drug Problems*, vol. 7:pp.1–45.

Frankenberg, R. (1980), 'Medical Anthropology and Development: A Theoretical Perspective', *Social Science and Medicine*, vol. 14b, no.4:pp.197–207.

Gefou-Madianou, D. (ed.) (1992), *Alcohol, Gender and Culture*. London and New York: Routledge.

Gomberg, E. (1976), 'Alcoholism in Women', in 'Social Aspects of Alcoholism', *The Biology of Alcoholism*, vol. 4:pp.117–166.

Gomberg, E. (1987), 'Historical and political perspectives: women and drug use' in T. Heller, M. Gott and C. Jeffery (eds) *Drug Use and Misuse: a reader.* Chichester: J. Wiley.

Gusfield, J.R. (1963), *Symbolic Crusade.* Urbana, Illinois: University of Illinois Press.

Gusfield, J.R. (1987), 'Passage to play: rituals of drinking time in American society' in M. Douglas (ed.) 1987.

Hall, S. and Jefferson, T. (eds) (1976), *Resistance through Rituals. Youth subcultures in post-war Britain.* University of Birmingham: The Centre for Contemporary Cultural Studies.

Hastrup, K. (1978), 'The Semantics of Biology: Virginity' in S. Ardener (ed.) *Defining females: the nature of women in society.* London: Croom Helm.

Heath, D. (1975), 'A critical review of ethnographic studies of alcohol use' in R. Gibbins et al. (eds) *Research Advances in Alcohol and Drug Problems: Volume 2.* New York: John Wiley and Sons.

Heath, D. (1987), 'A decade of development in the anthropological study of alcohol use: 1970–1980' in M. Douglas (ed.) 1987.

Heather, N. and Robertson, I. (1989), *Problem Drinking.* Oxford University Press (2nd edition; 1st edition published 1985).

Henman, A. (1990), 'Coca, an alternative to cocaine?' *Critique of anthropology* vol. 10, no.1:pp.65–80.

Henman, C. (1990), *Culture, Health and Illness.* London: Wright (2nd edition; 1st edition published 1984).

Herzfeld, M. (1985), *The Poetics of Manhood: Contest and Identity in a Cretan Mountain Village.* Princeton: Princeton University Press.

Inciardi, J.A. (ed.) (1991), *The Drug Legalization Debate.* London: Sage.

Inciardi, J.A. and McBride, D.C. (1991), 'The Case *Against* Legalization' in J.A. Inciardi (ed.) 1991.

Johnson, B. (1973), 'The Alcoholism Movement in America: a study in Cultural Innovation'. Unpublished Ph.D. thesis (Sociology), University of Illinois at Urbana-Champaign.

Johnson, T.M. and Sargent, C.F. (eds) (1990), *Medical Anthropology. Contemporary Theory and Methods.* London and New York: Praeger.

Jones, G. (1986), *Social Hygiene in Twentieth-Century Britain.* London: Croom Helm.

Kalant, O. (ed.) (1980), *Alcohol and Drug Problems in Women.* (Special Issue of *Research Advances in Alcohol and Drug Problems,* vol. 5.) New York: Plenum Press.

Kaplan, M., Carriker, L. and Waldron, I. (1990), 'Gender differences in tobacco use in Kenya', *Social Science and Medicine*, vol. 30, no.3:pp.305–310.

Kissin, B. (1983), 'The Disease Concept of Alcoholism', *Research Advances in Alcohol and Drug Problems*, vol. 7:pp.93–126.

Leland, J.H. (1976), *Firewater Myths: North American Indian Drinking and Alcohol Addiction*. (Rutgers Center of Alcohol Studies Monograph no.11.) New Jersey: New Brunswick.

Levine, H. (1978), 'The Discovery of Addiction', *Journal of Studies on Alcohol*, vol. 39, no.1.

Levine, H. (1980), 'Temperance and women in 19th-Century United States' in O. Kalant (ed.) 1980.

Levine, H. (1984), 'What is an alcohol-related problem?' *Journal of Drug Issues*, vol. 4, no.7:pp.45–60.

Lindstrom, L. (ed.) (1987), *Drugs in Western Pacific Societies: Relations of Substance*. ASAO Monograph no.11. Lanham: University Press of America.

Lock, M. and Gordon, D. (eds) (1988), *Biomedicine examined*. Dordrecht: Kluwer Academic Publishers.

Loizos, P. and Papataxiarchis, E. (eds) (1991), *Contested Identities. Gender and Kinship in Modern Greece*. Princeton: Princeton University Press.

Lowe, G. (1984), 'Alcohol and Alcoholism' in D. Sanger and D. Blackmann (eds) *Aspects of Psychopharmacology*. London: Methuen.

MacAndrew, C. and Edgerton, R. (1969), *Drunken Comportment*. Chicago: Aldine Publishing Co.

MacGregor, S. (ed.) (1989), *Drugs and British Society. Responses to a social problem in the eighties*. London & New York: Routledge.

Mandelbaum, D. (1965), 'Alcohol and Culture', *Current Anthropology*, vol. 6, no.3.

Marshall, Mac (ed.) (1979), *Beliefs, Behaviours and Alcoholic Beverages: A Cross-Cultural Survey*. Ann Arbor: University of Michigan Press.

Martin, E. (1989), *The woman in the body: a cultural analysis of reproduction*. Milton Keynes: Open University Press.

Nadelmann, E.A. (1991), 'The Case for Legalization' in J.A. Inciardi (ed.) (1991).

Nye, R. (1984), *Crime, madness and politics in modern France: the medical concept of national decline*. Princeton: Princeton University Press.

Parssinen, T. and Kerner, K. (1980), 'Development of the Disease Model of Drug Addiction in Britain, 1870–1926', *Medical History*, vol.24:pp.275–96.

Partridge, W. (1977), 'Transformation and redundancy in ritual: a case from Columbia' in B. Du Toit (ed.) *Drugs, Rituals and Altered States of Consciousness*. Rotterdam: Balkema.

Porter, R. (1985), 'The drinking man's disease: the pre-history of alcoholism in Georgian Britain', *British Journal of Addiction*, vol. 80:pp.385–396.

Riches, D. (ed.) (1986), *The Anthropology of Violence*. Oxford: Blackwell.

Robins, L., Davis, D. and Goodwin, D. (1974), 'Drug use by US Army enlisted men in Vietnam: a follow-up on their return home', *American Journal of Epidemiology*, vol. 99:pp.235–409.

Room, R. (1983), 'Sociological Aspects of the Disease Concept of Alcoholism' in *Research Advances in Alcohol and Drug Problems*, 1983, vol. 7.

Room, R. (1984), 'Alcohol and ethnography', *Current Anthropology*, vol.25, no.2:pp.169–91.

Room, R. (1985), 'Dependence and Society', *British Journal of Addiction*, 80:pp.133–39.

Room, R. and Collins, G. (eds) (1983), *Alcohol and Disinhibition: nature and meaning of the link*. NIAAA Research Monograph no.12, Washington D.C.: US Government Printing Office, DHHS Publication no. (ADM) 83–1246.

Scheper-Hughes, N. and Lock, M. (1986), 'The Mindful Body', *Medical Anthropology Quarterly*, vol. 1, no.1:pp.6–41.

Searle, G. (1976), *Eugenics and Politics in Britain 1900–1914*. Leyden: Noordhoff.

Spear, H.B. (1969), 'The growth of heroin addiction in the United Kingdom', *British Journal of Addiction*, vol. 64:p.245.

Stimson, G. and Oppenheimer, E. (1982), *Heroin Addiction. Treatment and Control in Britain*. London: Tavistock.

Stivers, R. (1976), *A Hair of the Dog: Irish Drinking and American Stereotypes*. Pennsylvania State University Press.

Waldron, I., Bratelli, G., Carriker, L., Sung, W.-C., Vogeli, C., Waldman, E. (1988), 'Gender differences in tobacco use in Africa, Asia, the Pacific and Latin America', *Social Science and Medicine*, vol. 27, no.11:pp.1269–75.

Woolgar, S. (1988), *Science: the very idea*. Chichester: Ellis Horwood.

Young, A. (1982), 'The Anthropologies of Illness and Sickness', *Annual Review of Anthropology*, vol. 11:pp.257–85.

Young, M. (1979), 'The Symbolic Language of Cannabis', *DYN*, vol. 5 (Journal of the Anthropological Society of the University of Durham).

1

Women and Alcohol: The Emergence of a Risk Group

Betsy Thom

Women – A 'High-Risk' Group?

At different historical moments, and in cultural contexts as diverse as the Roman Empire and Victorian England, women's alcohol use has emerged, disappeared and re-emerged as a focus of public concern. The past two decades have witnessed a new wave of anxiety over women's drinking and in a 1990 WHO publication entitled *Alcohol-related problems in high risk groups*, each of the six European countries contributing to the publication considered women, as a group, at high risk of developing alcohol-related problems (Plant 1990).

The rationale for the shift in women's status over the last twenty years from non-problematic and low-risk to problematic and high-risk is unclear. Statistically-minded countries tend to report much lower rates of alcohol consumption and alcohol-related problems among women when compared with men (Plant 1990; Plant 1990a; Roman 1988) and although women's alcohol consumption seems to have risen since the 1950s, the validity of categorising women as 'high-risk' on the basis of consumption figures and rates of alcohol-related harm has often been challenged (e.g. Ahlstrom 1983; Fillmore 1984; Vogt 1984). Theories that changes in the drinking habits of women were leading to a convergence between male and female consumption patterns and a rise in alcohol-related problems found little support in a recent international review which concluded that: 'On the contrary, major gender differences appear to be evident and to be persisting in a large number of varied national and cultural contexts. Evidence from countries in which several surveys have been conducted at different times does not suggest that the overall pattern of alcohol use amongst women has changed very greatly during the past twenty years' (Plant 1990a:7).

Recent research in the medical field has indicated that women may be physiologically more at risk than men of developing alcohol-related problems and there has long been recognition that drinking during pregnancy may harm the foetus. But the evidence for physiological harm is still often unclear and was certainly not available to those who debated the issue of women's drinking in Victorian times (see Camberwell Council on Alcoholism 1980; Roman 1988). Even in the case of foetal damage, where there has been greater research effort, the results are not always conclusive (Plant 1985).

When we weigh up the evidence on consumption and harm, it is clear that neither reports of how much alcohol women are consuming nor the possibility that women are more vulnerable than men to the effects of alcohol are sufficient to explain why, at a particular point in time, women's alcohol use ceases to be a private matter and becomes defined as a social problem. This chapter suggests that explanations for the prominence bestowed on women's drinking in various epochs are to be found in contemporary political and social circumstances and in ideas concerning gender and women's position in society, rather than in any 'neutral' or 'scientific' evidence of women's misuse of alcohol[1]. The focus here is on the factors which resulted in the emergence of women as a risk group in modern Britain, and more specifically in England. Some comparison with the late Victorian era (approximately 1870 to 1920) is instructive, and some points about that period are included here. This comparison highlights the way in which the modern definition of women's drinking as a social problem has emerged from a very different social and ideological context from that which gave rise to concern with women's drinking in the nineteenth century.

The Nineteenth Century – A Eugenic Concern

In England, debate over women's drinking was prominent in scientific journals, popular literature and Temperance tracts during the second half of the nineteenth century and into the early years of the twentieth. It was linked with the major concerns of that era – a declining rate of population growth, high infant mortality and an unhealthy working class, all of which were believed to threaten both the quality of the national 'stock' and the supremacy of the English abroad.

In the search for explanations and solutions, women became the focal point for many of the proposed measures to counteract the increasing 'degeneracy of the race'. Women's drinking habits, along with a whole range of female behaviours and working-class life styles, became the object of reforming zeal among the emerging groups of health professionals, charitable societies and ladies' organisations. The promotion of temperance took its place in a long list of reforms targeted on women – including infant feeding, hygiene, physical education, cookery, the provision of clean milk and involvement in paid employment (Davin 1978). Members of the Society for the Study of Inebriety, founded in 1884, were prominent in bringing alcohol to the fore in discussions of national efficiency, providing evidence of the degenerative effects of alcohol to the 1904 Interdepartmental Committee on Physical Deterioration and, in accordance with prevailing ideologies, focusing attention on the relationship between female inebriety, child welfare and racial degeneration (Berridge 1990).

Papers written at the turn of the century claimed 'strong evidence to show that alcoholism is spreading at an alarming rate among females' (Kelynack 1902). Typically, no figures were offered in support of the contention; rather, observations of changing patterns of social behaviour were provided as evidence:

> Girls and women of the labouring class now openly throng our public houses and drinking saloons. The 'ladies bar' is becoming a recognised resort...it is quite customary for women to meet in the afternoons for beer and gossip. Confectioners' shops, restaurants and various so-called refreshment houses offer ready means whereby women of the well-to-do class may obtain almost unlimited supplies of alcohol... (Kelynack 1902:197).

Young girls were alleged to be indulging in drinking and smoking (see *White Ribbon* 1905) and there was a continuing outcry over the employment of young women as barmaids and the subsequent decline of many into alcoholism (Scharlieb 1907). Women were regarded as being particularly at risk of succumbing to temptation and of drinking immoderately both because they suffered from 'an inherent vulnerability of the nervous tissues' which lowered their resistance to alcohol, and because alcohol provided a support in 'these days of incessant activity' when girls and women were 'subjected to the strain of competitive examinations, the excitement of society life or the worries of domestic duties' (Kelynack 1902:199–200).

There were close links between members of the Society for the Study of Inebriety, of the Temperance Movement, of the Eugenic Movement and of the infant welfare movement. Many of the doctors, medical officers of health, health visitors and philanthropic gentry who presided over the voluntary societies belonged to more than one group within the different movements. Dr Peiris, for instance, whose work included a publication on *Racial Poisons and How to Combat Them,* was also the author of *Alcohol and Child Welfare* (1928) and a member of both the Society for the Study of Inebriety and the Eugenic Society. Dr T.N.Kelynack, editor of *Child Welfare Annual* (1916) and a leading figure in the Society for the Study of Inebriety, couched his arguments in familiar eugenic terms when he stated that 'among the agencies making for physical decay, mental retrogression and national enfeeblement, the use of alcohol by women stands prominent' (Kelynack 1902:196).

Women professionals were no exception in laying responsibility for racial degeneration on women. Mary Scharlieb, an eminent eugenicist doctor and writer, president of the Society for the Study of Inebriety (1912–1916) and a consultant gynaecologist, also stressed the role of the individual drinking mother as nationally harmful. Mrs Scharlieb was not lacking in humanitarian sentiments about women's drinking, being well aware that environmental or social factors played an important part in women's health and feeling that much of women's alcoholism was due to 'misery drinking' because of the poverty and joylessness of their lives. Nevertheless, like most of her medical colleagues and the infant welfare movement of her time, Mrs Scharlieb believed that 'it depends on the mothers of the nation what the future men and women of that nation shall be' and she supported solutions aimed at changing individual behaviour, notably education, as the most promising way to address the problem (Scharlieb 1907).

The Women's Temperance Movement (although concentrating largely on the evils of male drinking) shared much the same view of women alcoholics as the medical profession. Writing in the late 1870s, Mary Bayly, a gospel temperance advocate, expressed the view that 'Women quickly pass beyond the range of moderate drinking. They have less power than men to resist temptation, and if the home life of our country is to be saved, temptation, to a great extent, must be removed out of the way' (Bayly 1878 cited in Kitze 1986:7). The British Women's Temperance Association (BWTA), while concerned about women alcoholics and involved in the provision of inebriate homes, clubs and activities for women, did not take on board an obviously 'feminist' approach nor espouse women's suffrage issues as did the American counterpart, The Women's Christian Temperance Union (Kitze 1986). Despite the many links and cross-memberships between the British Women's Temperance Association and other organisations more closely allied to contemporary feminist issues (e.g. the Independent Labour Party, which supported both female suffrage and temperance), the BWTA limited its campaigning to temperance issues and did not challenge prevailing conceptions of either the nature of womankind or of her place in society (Banks 1981)[2].

In short, the emergence of concern over women's drinking in Victorian England was a secondary, if powerful, element in the politics of imperialism and in the creation of a new ideology of motherhood, a trend which minimised the contribution of environmental or social factors and maximised the role of women's attitudes and behaviour in the creation of social problems. By the beginning of the 1920s, with changing social circumstances and a fall in the rate of alcohol consumption by men and women alike, the question of women's drinking ceased to have any political significance and faded from public consciousness.

The Rediscovery of Female Alcoholism – A Feminist Concern

By the late 1950s, when a new wave of concern over alcohol misuse arose, the focus was firmly on male drinking and in particular on the group of men whose drinking was clearly defined as 'alcoholic'. Women were much less visible in the treatment services and featured little in discussions of treatment approaches or in research studies[3]. It was not until the mid-1970s that the 'female alcoholic' was rediscovered in the UK – some years later than the revival of interest in the USA where research and discussion had been growing steadily for almost a decade (see the bibliography in Committee on Labor and Public Welfare 1976).

Many factors contributed to the renewal of interest in women's drinking and to the reformulation of the problem which was to take place over subsequent years, but there is no doubt that the women's movement was important. Earlier feminist and suffrage movements had not been centrally concerned with issues of women's health or experiences of health care. By contrast, the new feminism of the 1960s challenged existing orthodoxies on women's health status and the quality of health care they received. It provided a critique of medical practices and medical relationships with women, and placed women's health issues in a political and economic context. The new movement was also activist, campaigning for women's right to take control over their bodies and over the processes of medical care, and supporting the development of alternative approaches to health care and the formation of new forms of health care organisation (Boston Women's Health Book Collective 1973; Ruzek 1978; Doyal with Pennell 1979). It was the women's movement which provided the ideological motivation and the theoretical foundations for explanations of women's use and misuse of alcohol, and for the development of a critique of social responses to the female alcoholic.

By the mid-1970s changes had also taken place in the alcohol field which paved the way for defining as problematic the drinking habits of people whose alcohol use had previously gone unnoticed and who did not fit the stereotype of the typical 'alcoholic' – male, often vagrant and criminal, suffering from extreme alcoholism. The reluctance with which official sources in the 1950s had greeted the World Health Organisation's contention that alcoholism was a growing problem in western industrialised countries, including Britain, had given way by 1970 to the recognition of alcohol use as a major health issue which could affect large numbers of ordinary citizens (Baggott 1990).

Against the background of a new vigour of feminism and of an acceptance of alcoholism as a major health issue, a number of specific developments in the alcohol field were also important in bringing questions of women's alcohol use to the fore[4]. The first of these was the emergence of an 'interest constituency', drawn from among the new recruits to the growing field of alcohol research and service provision, a group of mainly female workers influenced indirectly, if not directly, by feminist ideology. The second factor was the development of a rationale which provided the theoretical and 'scientific' basis of analyses of women's drinking and which was necessary to gain recognition for, and legitimation of, the new concern. Finally, changes in the concept of the problem, from 'alcoholism' to 'problem drinking', linked to developments in research and service provision, were influential factors in the emergence of women's drinking as a concern meriting international attention.

The Emergence of An 'Interest Constituency'

The impetus for action came not from government initiatives or medical leaders but from people working at 'grass roots' in the services, many of them women, and many from backgrounds in psychology and social work rather than medicine. A key role was played by female researchers and service providers allied to the

Camberwell Council on Alcoholism, in London, which had been set up in the early 1960s in an attempt to promote a community approach to dealing with alcohol problems.

Around 1973, the number of requests for information on women alcoholics received in the Camberwell Council's office increased notably, and Council members realised that there were considerable gaps in existing knowledge about women's alcohol consumption and their needs for help (Camberwell Council on Alcoholism Annual Report 1973–4). Discussions with local agencies revealed that there had been recent changes in the number of women being referred to the services and that service providers were concerned that so little was understood about how best to meet the needs of women alcoholics. As a result, a series of seminars for local lay and professional people was arranged, covering a wide range of topics and addressed by a variety of speakers including a local police constable and a consultant psychiatrist. Most of the seminars concluded with a discussion on women's role in society (Camberwell Council on Alcoholism Seminar Minutes 1973). The success of these seminars led to the establishment of an action group with a brief to collect information, promote the study of women's alcoholism, and arrange further seminars and events. The group met, almost every week, for four years from 1974 to 1978, the members numbering some 30 people with a regular core of twelve.

The action group quickly gained recognition as an effective and prestigious aspect of the work of the Camberwell Council on Alcoholism. Representatives of the group were regularly invited to address conferences and to lead seminars at national and international levels. Information supplied by the group formed the pivot of newspaper features and radio programmes, and a slot for women was secured in the programme of the Advanced School on Alcoholism run by the Alcohol Education Centre (Camberwell Council on Alcoholism Annual Report 1974–5). Less academic methods, drama and folk songs, were also used to arouse awareness of the problem of women's alcoholism. By 1978, the work of the group had expanded to encompass international projects, including attempts to set up an international information exchange network on women and alcohol (Camberwell Council on Alcoholism Annual report 1977–8; Camberwell Council on Alcoholism 1977 Circular Letter). At this point the group began to question both its ability to continue the work on such a scale and the appropriateness of remaining under the auspices of a local council on alcoholism. The idea for a new national organisation – DAWN (Drugs, Alcohol,

Women, Nationally) – to take over the work of the Camberwell Group was born during a train journey on the way to a conference. The outcome was the formation of a steering committee in 1979 and the first DAWN Symposium in November 1980 (DAWN 1980). The Camberwell Council Women's Group brought on-going projects to completion and wound up its initiative with the publication of the book *Women and Alcohol* (Camberwell Council on Alcoholism 1980).

Throughout the seven years of its existence, the Camberwell Group had retained an informal structure relying on a network of friends and committed colleagues to forward the work in their own time. Little help was forthcoming from the institutions employing the women, although for the most part it seems, 'they did not block the work – it was just seen as our hobby'. The Group failed to attract substantial, long-term funding, possibly because of its reluctance to jeopardise its autonomy by becoming integrated into a more structured and powerful organisation (Camberwell Council on Alcoholism, Litman 1977). Although it failed to establish itself as mainstream, nevertheless, by the time it disbanded, the Camberwell Women's Group had created a new awareness of women's drinking; through contacts with workers in other parts of the country, it had established a basis of interest among service providers and research workers which ensured a continuing commitment to working with women alcoholics.

The Rationale for Action

Early efforts to bring the question of women's alcoholism to the notice of colleagues and the public at large were undoubtedly as much campaigns of conviction as the presentation of 'facts'. Knowledge culled from feminist thought, from the work on homeless women and from American research on women and alcohol gradually evolved into a rationale which then became a 'set piece' as the Camberwell Group gave talks and wrote articles. The rationale for action was based on the argument that women with alcohol problems were both quantitatively and qualitatively under-served. As in the case of male drinkers, the concern at the time was very firmly with the 'alcoholic woman', both with the visible woman who came for help and with the assumed pool of secret or 'lace curtain' drinkers (Litman 1975; Litman and Wilson 1978).

The arguments rested on two main observations. Firstly, people working within the services had reported an increase in the number of women presenting themselves for help. A report from one voluntary organisation which provided hostel accommodation for the homeless and for alcoholics stated that thirteen years previously there had been one female for every seven to eight male alcoholics approaching their services, whereas by 1976 the figures indicated one female to three males presenting themselves for help (Helping Hand 1976). Alcoholics Anonymous was reported to be experiencing a large increase in female membership in the ten years prior to 1976 from a ratio of two women to seven men, to a ratio of one to one (Wilson 1976). Some local councils on alcoholism similarly reported rising numbers of female clients (Sclare 1975). Figures for alcohol-related harms – liver cirrhosis, arrests for drunkenness and admittance to psychiatric hospitals – were also shown to be increasing among women. This led to the conclusion that: 'Female alcohol rates in Great Britain are increasing *per se* and seem to be increasing at a faster rate than male alcoholism' (Litman and Wilson 1978).

The second observation was that existing facilities were unable to meet the needs of women coming forward for help, possibly because the services had been developed with male alcoholics in mind. Women, it was argued, had specific and different needs for help, some of these arising from their 'traditional gender roles' and relationships to men (e.g. low self-esteem, self-loathing, sexual problems and abuse in childhood and adulthood). Service-providers, most of whom held traditional views and values about women's roles, were often reluctant to face change in their methods of working and there were few women workers in the services, particularly in policy-making positions (Helping Hand 1976; Litman 1975; Otto and Litman 1976; Litman and Wilson 1978).

The truth or otherwise of this 'rhetoric of woe', as it has been called elsewhere (Roizen and Weisner 1979 quoted in Fillmore 1984), was immaterial. What was important was the building of a credible argument for claims for support and funding. Those writing at the time acknowledged that interpreting the increase in women coming for help was problematic. Sclare (1975:4), for example, pointed out that the rise in incidence rates could have been accounted for by social changes which made women's alcoholism more visible: 'Are more lonely, shame-ridden women drinkers now coming to attention in the new climate of female emancipation? or is there a true increase in the incidence of alcoholism in women?' The critique of the quality of service provision largely rested on an acceptance of underlying feminist principles which linked women's alcoholism with the position of women in society in general, and in particular with the dependence of female identity on male-defined role expectations (Litman 1975). The problem of women's alcoholism was seen to require services which would 'help women to value themselves in whatever way they chose to, not in traditional ways', a treatment approach which was 'underpinned by feminist ideology' (Richmond interview; see note 4).

It was this feminist interpretation of female alcoholism, rather than an increase in women alcoholics or evidence of increasing alcoholism and harm among women since the 1950s, which was truly new in the field.

Legitimating the Concern

Gaining legitimation for the 'new' problem of women's alcoholism was not easy. For many people it was a matter of indifference; for others it was still too sensitive a topic. A member of the Camberwell Women's Group told me how she had found herself talking at meetings only to people who were already aware, or to supportive friends, while at conferences the sessions on prostitution were more popular.

Committed women working within the services had a difficult task to convince colleagues that women clients required special consideration and that changes were necessary in the structure of services as well as in treatment approaches if they were to provide appropriate help for female drinkers. In the case of ARP (Alcoholics Recovery Project), one of the first services to raise the question of separate facilities for women, the suggestion was considered outrageous at first because 'nobody had ever been singled out to be treated differently'. Opposition to the proposal was possibly due as much to the apparent feminist perspective underlying the suggestion as to the perceived deviation from normal practice: 'There was quite a lot of opposition within the organisation to separate services... I think everyone did accept that there needed to be separate groups but not necessarily separate facilities' (Graham interview). Male staff, in particular, appeared to be suspicious and to feel threatened by the move towards separate provision for women. When the issue first arose at a staff conference in the summer of 1979, it seems to have led to 'some classic debates where colleagues would say, "what do you mean there are differences, women are just men with no penises"' (Richmond interview). Even after the Women's Alcohol Centre had opened – as late as 1984 –

with a female staff, including one worker who 'came in apologising for not being a feminist', they still had to combat the attitude that 'this is a lesbian house and the buzz that went around ARP that strange things went on' (MacIntyre interview). Strategies to legitimate the proposals for women's services included 'talking about it endlessly' and writing numerous reports for staff meetings so that eventually 'the impetus to go for a women's centre became almost logical because it had been talked about so much' (Richmond interview).

By now, the time was right politically. The establishment of the Greater London Council Women's Committee provided a sympathetic power base from which ARP eventually secured funding for a women's centre.

The need for legitimation posed a particularly important dilemma in relation to the psychiatric profession. On the one hand, the support of psychiatrists was vital because it provided credibility and 'respectability' to the women researchers and service providers who campaigned for change. According to one account, when addressing an audience in the early days it was helpful to have a supportive psychiatrist on the platform nodding agreement in the background. Audiences, including professionals such as social workers, invariably looked to the psychiatrist to legitimate what the speaker was saying. At the same time, the critique of prevailing treatment approaches posed a threat to orthodox psychiatry and its management of women patients by suggesting that they were not handling the problem properly. It seemed important, therefore, to present women's alcoholism as a new problem, rather than an old problem with a new interpretation, in order to avoid alienating those with vested interest in the *status quo* or who might feel threatened by the demands of a new approach to treating alcoholic women.

The Changing Face of Alcoholism: From the Female Alcoholic to Women's Drinking

If the epidemiological and 'scientific' evidence was a somewhat shaky reason for the initial prominence bestowed on women's alcoholism, broader developments and changes within the alcohol field soon provided a firmer theoretical base from which to argue the case for special consideration for women.

Most importantly, changes taking place in conceptions of the nature of the problem resulted in a shift away from the notion of 'alcoholism' – which implied a problem affecting only an unfortunate minority – towards the notion of 'problem drinking', which implied a much less extreme form of the problem and applied to many more people (Heather and Robertson 1985). This conceptual shift was strongly influenced by the 'consumption-harm' theories which had been generated by Ledermann's work in the 1950s (Ledermann 1956) and which held that fluctuations in the total quantity of alcohol consumed by a population were a reflection of the individual drinking habits of the population as a whole. Moreover, changes in average consumption were deemed to lead to predictable changes in the same direction in the scale of alcohol-related harms (AEC 1977; Bruun *et al.* 1975). Thus, by the late 1970s, it was no longer possible to support the view that alcoholics were a group apart from other people; drinking was to be seen as a continuum and people drank problematically far below levels which had previously been considered as alcoholic.

Somewhat later, professional guidelines for the 'safe' levels of consumption also changed. In 1979 the report *Alcohol and Alcoholism* from the Royal College of Psychiatrists had suggested four pints of beer a day (or equivalent, i.e. approximately 50–56 units per week) as 'reasonable guidelines for the upper limit of drinking' and had made no distinction between men and women. By 1986, in a new report entitled *Alcohol: Our Favourite Drug*, the Royal College considered that drinking 50-plus units was definitely harmful for men, while for women the figure was now set at 35 units per week. A 'safe' limit for women was set at 14 units a week.

Concurrently with shifting definitions of the problem, the 1970s and 1980s witnessed the awakening of a 'new public health' approach to alcohol problems with emphases on community care, on individual responsibility and life style, and on the importance of prevention (Berridge 1989). The creation of public and professional awareness was fostered by the establishment of new organisations whose primary aim was public education and professional training[5]. Alcohol problems, as with health matters in general, became 'everybody's business' (DHSS 1976) and everyone who drank was at risk of developing problematic drinking at some time in their life-cycle.

Acceptance of consumption-harm theory, of the fact that female alcohol consumption had risen since the 1950s, and of the lower 'safe' levels of drinking applied to women, meant that greater numbers of women could be considered to be 'at risk'[6]. The expanding alcohol research industry fed additional fuel to the notion that women ran a greater risk than men of developing alcohol-related problems by reporting that physiological differences between the sexes made women more vulnerable to the harmful effects of alcohol. Differences in the rate of alcohol metabolism, differences in the development of alcohol-related liver disease, and the establishment of some relationship between drinking and the menstrual cycle were three of the 'areas of vulnerability' to receive most attention (see the studies reviewed in Roman 1988; also Camberwell Council on Alcoholism 1980). As in former periods of anxiety over female drinking, women's reproductive role again received particular attention. Interest in the effects of alcohol on the foetus was rekindled by research from the USA by Jones and Smith who, in a publication appearing in the British medical press, coined the phrase 'foetal alcohol syndrome' (Jones and Smith 1973)[7].

These changes in the alcohol field as a whole seemed to provide a legitimate basis for concern to stretch beyond the small number of alcoholic women coming for help in the 1970s to women's alcohol consumption *per se*. Whole new groups of women became potential clients of the helping services, and by the 1980s the services were beginning to reach out to women still in employment, with intact relationships, less physically and psychologically damaged, and more middle-class. Special efforts were also being made to address the needs of lesbian women, ethnic minority women and women with children (DAWN 1981). The overall number of services paying specific attention to 'women's needs' increased, although the expansion was largely confined to London and the south-east region of England. In London, in 1974, there were 21 agencies providing some form of help for women but many of these were non-specialist or had a main focus other than alcohol (Camberwell Council on Alcoholism 1974). By 1984, a DAWN Report could find 60 specialist agencies and 10 non-specialist agencies in London providing help for women with alcohol problems.

Not only was there greater availability of services, and easier access to services, but efforts were also made to recruit women by special advertising, by informing potential referral sources such as general practitioners and social services, and by adapting services to suit different groups of women users. In the case of the Women's Alcohol Centre, a service facility exclusively for women, the development worker spent six months visiting everyone and everywhere she thought relevant – including prisons, lodging houses, general practitioners, and social services – so that the Centre was known and referrals could be discussed before the opening. As a result, the counselling sessions and groups 'took off' immediately and the successful use of media publicity meant that within six months the Centre was working over capacity (Richmond interview).

Talks and workshops on women and alcohol brought new recruits to the ranks of enthusiastic workers keen to increase services for women, sometimes in the face of an apparent lack of demand for existing provision. The Alcoholics Recovery Project, which provided hostel accommodation, started holding beds open for women in their post-detoxification house because 'the only way to make sure we got women was to be able to guarantee beds for them even if it meant that they stayed vacant – which was quite controversial' (Graham interview). Similarly, in 1978, three of the residential houses run by the group known as 'Aquarius' in Birmingham had difficulty recruiting females to fill available spaces. Workers, having attended workshops on women and alcohol, were 'very keen on the issue of the woman alcoholic' and were worried that they might lose beds reserved for women. With the support of the director of Aquarius, the Camberwell Women's Group was approached for advice and help on recruiting women to the services (Camberwell Council on Alcoholism, Otto letter 1978).

Thus, although it was argued that adaptations in the services and the promotion of services for women were necessary responses to an unmet pool of need in the community, service expansion could also be seen as a result of the creation of demand by the efforts of committed workers to sell the services they offered and safeguard their interest in women and alcohol (Gusfield 1982).

Policy Responses to Women's Drinking

The basis for concern about women's drinking in the Victorian era differed markedly from that of the 1970s. In the earlier period, with responsibility for 'racial degeneracy' ascribed to individual patterns of behaviour and life style rather than environmental or social causes, women's drinking was linked to major issues of national well-being and women were allocated a central role in securing a healthy population. Achieving this required an improvement in women's performance in domestic and child-rearing roles, and a strong ideology of womanhood and motherhood emerged in support of these aims (Davin 1978). Movements concerned with women's suffrage and emancipation showed little interest in the question of women's drinking, and do not appear to have influenced discussion in this sphere.

In the 1970s, by contrast, the issue of women's drinking emerged from a feminist perspective on women's health which was explicitly concerned with the well-being of women rather than with the good of the nation, and which located harmful drinking primarily within a social and economic context. The need for women experiencing drinking problems to alter their behaviour patterns was accepted as part of an appropriate response to the problem as was the need to support women in their roles as mothers, wives or partners. But there was also an important drive towards providing a response which would challenge and alter existing social structures and ideologies and enable women to change their social situations rather than merely adapt to them (DAWN 1980). This dual aim can present something of a dilemma when it comes to policy responses since helping women to cope with their expected roles and responsibilities does not necessarily further the aim of challenging prevailing forms of gender relationships; it may, on the contrary, reinforce traditional roles (Moser 1989)[8].

Turn-of-the-century campaigners had faced no such dilemma. Educational efforts aimed at women concentrated on improving their skills as housewives and mothers and on inculcating the dominant ideology of motherhood. Temperance teaching formed part of a more general educational approach, and temperance leaders were frequently to be found among the supporters and initiators of educational projects (Davin . 1978). Treatment and rehabilitation aims for women alcoholics stressed control measures designed to reform women and return them to their expected roles as mothers and as the nation's breeders and housekeepers. The majority of inmates consigned to the State inebriate reformatories between 1899 and 1914 (i.e. the whole period of those institutions' existence) were women, and failure to reform was regarded as an individual problem rather than as being due to inappropriate or inadequate institutional provision (Hunt et al. 1987). Thus measures to address the problem of women's drinking generally supported rather than threatened prevailing notions of women's place in society.

Both in spite of, and in congruence with, the dominance of feminist theory in bringing women's drinking to the fore in the 1970s and 1980s, the greater part of the educational and service response to the problem was still felt to be 'on the level of attempting to relieve symptoms and no more'. Primary care workers were seen, from a feminist point of view, to be acting more often as vehicles for social control rather than social change, helping women 'to deal with the symptoms and their frustration rather than helping them to realise their potential to change the situation' (DAWN 1980). Policy continued to support women's traditional roles, and the implementation of measures to realise a more radical treatment approach to women's alcoholism were slow to develop. This was partly because they were both more threatening and more difficult to legitimate.

Concern over women's drinking appears to emerge most forcefully from social and political circumstances which include changes in, or attempts to change, women's social status. This was the case at the turn of the century when questions of women's rights to property, to employment and to political participation seemed, to those who opposed reform, to threaten the foundations of society. The well-worn phrase 'alcoholism is the ransom of emancipation' might also denote the link that is drawn today between changes in women's life styles and changes in their use of alcohol. Women's drinking seems to enter political discourse when it symbolises the threat of changing gender relationships.

At the national level in contemporary Britain, official interest in women's alcohol use has grown only in dribs and drabs. The survey by Breeze (1985), set up to study 'a general sample of women to establish their patterns of drinking behaviour and their beliefs about alcohol', marked, perhaps, official acknowledgement in England that women's alcohol consumption required special consideration. It is notable, however, that concern about women's alcoholism did not enter discussions at national level until the focus began to switch to consumption and it was clear that women's use of alcohol had risen since the 1950s. The increasing attention similarly paid to alcohol consumption patterns among population groups in other European countries, and the growing acceptance of women as a special group, undoubtedly had a part to play in the appearance of women as a 'high-risk' group at international level. The topic also seems to have gathered a self-generating momentum, as the rationale for discussion by one participant to the 1990 WHO publication on 'high-risk' groups suggests. Having noted that it was 'in some ways ironic and inappropriate for women in the Netherlands to have been identified as being vulnerable to alcohol', he continues 'however, since alcohol use and misuse by women is a subject that attracts widespread international attention, it will also be discussed here' (Plant 1990:86).

As Wiener (1981) notes, the appearance of an issue on the international agenda tends to enhance the legitimacy of the field in the national arena and, in the case of the Camberwell Women's Group, might be seen as the fruition of local efforts to gain recognition for women alcoholics. At the same time, in the process of upward communication it is not at all certain to what extent the issues and objectives selected now as policy concerns still reflect the objectives or the ideas which motivated the original activists, or appropriately address the concerns of those currently working with women 'problem drinkers'. The incorporation of women's issues into the national or international agenda may provide a safeguard against women returning to invisibility; it may also act – as has often been pointed out – as a vehicle of social control by generating policy measures which support politically acceptable solutions, and by avoiding discussion of more threatening issues.

The activities of the Camberwell Council on Alcoholism women's group and those who followed them, and the 'rhetoric of woe' which they developed to gain consideration for women, undoubtedly played an important part in the greater prominence now given to women's drinking. There is, too, a greater concern to provide suitable treatment services and to direct appropriate preventive messages towards women. But it is still doubtful to what extent current therapeutic approaches can, and do, address needs which arise from either fundamental gender constructs or from women's social position in relation to men. It seems unlikely that the scientistically erected status of 'high-risk' group will result in policies which respond to the association between alcohol problems and gender-related needs.

Notes

1. This paper is part of a study supported by a grant from the British Economic and Social Research Council. An early version of this chapter was given at the National Conference on Women and Substance Misuse, 20–21 March 1991, at the Institute of Psychiatry, London.
2. When Frances Willard, the feminist president of the Women's Christian Temperance Union (WCTU) visited the British Women's Temperance Association (NWTA) in 1892, she expressed her surprise that the latter had not given support to issues of women's suffrage and women's emancipation (Banks 1981). Efforts to involve the NWTA in suffrage campaigns were largely unsuccessful. Kitze (1986) suggests, however, that the BWTU did widen its scope to include feminist issues and that involvement in the BWTU allowed

women to develop the skills and self-confidence needed to become active in other spheres of public life.

3. Exceptions which considered women separately from men were: Woodside (1961), Glatt (1961a and 1961b), Sclare (1970), Rathod and Thomson (1971), Edwards et al. (1973). However, gender-related differences in the causes of alcohol misuse or in the needs of people presenting for treatment were rarely considered even in the few studies which analysed data by sex or which concentrated on women.

4. As well as using published sources, my discussion of these developments draws on interviews with Judy Graham, Elspeth Kyle, Ann MacIntyre, Shirley Otto and Fiona Richmond who were involved in research and service provision in the 1970s and 1980s. Data was also obtained from material produced by the Camberwell Council on Alcoholism Women's Group (London), deposited in the Wellcome Institute for the History of Medicine, Contemporary Medical Archives Centre, London. Some of this is listed in the references below.

5. e.g.: 1972 The Alcohol Education Centre; 1976 Glass (Greater London Alcohol Advisory Service); 1984 Alcohol Concern.

6. A survey by Wilson (*Drinking in England and Wales*, London: HMSO, 1980) reported 11% of women to be abstainers in 1978; Breeze (1985), from fieldwork carried out in 1982, reported 8% of women to be total abstainers and the same figure can be found in the survey by Goddard and Ikin (1988). These last two authors commented that, since 1978, the proportion of women who reported having an alcoholic drink had risen from 58% to 61% but that the increase in consumption was largely attributable to an increase in the category of light drinkers. Park (1990), among others, contends that rising alcohol consumption by women does not necessarily mean that women will consume in a manner similar to men. Alcohol, Park argues, is part of a system of meaning; it is symbolically associated with the status of adulthood and its use in both the private and public sphere is linked to transitions in women's position in the system of social exchange of which alcohol is a part. She suggests that 'strategies to moderate drinking need to take into account alcohol's role as a mediator in the ritual process of making sense of the world'.

7. Women activists made use of the information on physiological vulnerability to advance their claim for special consideration for women but they were less happy with the enthusiasm (and funding) which greeted the work on the foetal alcohol syndrome fearing that it would be used as 'yet another stick to beat women with' (Otto interview).

8. Moser (1989) makes a distinction between planning to meet practical gender needs and planning to meet strategic gender needs. 'Practical' gender needs are formulated from the concrete conditions women experience; they are a response to an immediate perceived necessity and are aimed at coping and carrying out expected roles and duties. They do not challenge prevailing forms of gender relationships. 'Strategic' gender needs are those which arise from women's position in relation to men, in particular their social position of subordination and dependence. Responses to women's alcohol problems have largely concentrated on meeting practical gender needs.

References

Ahlstrom, S. (1983), *Women and alcohol control policy: a review of findings and some suggestions for research policy*. Paper presented at the Alcohol Epidemiology Section Meetings, International Council on Alcohol and Addictions, Padua, Italy, Social Research Institute of Alcohol Studies, Helsinki. Report No. 168.

Alcohol Education Centre, (1977), *The Ledermann Curve*. Report of a Symposium 6–7 January, London.

Baggott, R. (1990), *Alcohol, politics and social policy*. Avebury.

Banks, O. (1981), *Faces of feminism. A study of feminism as a social movement*. Oxford: Martin Robertson.

Bayly, M. (1878), *Who should clear the way*. London.

Berridge, V. (1989), 'History and addiction control: the case of alcohol' in *Controlling legal addictions*. D. Robinson, A. Maynard, and R. Chester, (eds). London: Macmillan.

Berridge, V. (1990), 'The Society for the Study of Addiction 1884–1988'. *British Journal of Addiction*: Special Issue, 85, No. 8.

Boston Women's Health Book Collective, (1973), *Our bodies ourselves*. New York: Simon and Schuster.

Breeze, E. (1985), *Women and drinking*. London: HMSO.

Bruun, K., .Lumio, M., Makela, K. et al. (1975), *Alcohol control policies in public health perspective*. Helsinki: Finnish Foundation for Alcohol Studies.

Camberwell Council on Alcoholism Annual Report 1973–74 SA/CCA/96.

Camberwell Council on Alcoholism Annual Report 1974–75 SA/CCA/96.

Camberwell Council on Alcoholism Annual Report 1977–78 SA/CCA/96.

Camberwell Council on Alcoholism Seminar Minutes 1973, 9 Nov., 16 Nov., 23 Nov., 7 Dec., Wellcome Institute SA/CCA/95.

Camberwell Council on Alcoholism (1974), *Women alcoholics.* Papers by S. Otto, and G. Litman, SA/CCA/95.

Camberwell Council on Alcoholism (1977), Circular letter, June, from C. Wilson. SA/CCA/96.

Camberwell Council on Alcoholism (1977), Memo from G. Litman, SA/CCA/96.

Camberwell Council on Alcoholism (1978), Letter from S. Otto, SA/CCA/96.

Camberwell Council on Alcoholism (1980), *Women and alcohol.* London: Tavistock Publications.

Committee on Labor and Public Welfare (1976), United States Senate, 94th Congress Second Session, *Examination of the special problems and unmet needs of women who abuse alcohol.* Washington: United States Government Printing Office.

Davin, A. (1978), 'Imperialism and motherhood', *History Workshop*, vol. 5–6, pp.19–65.

DAWN (1980), *Report from the first symposium.* London: DAWN.

DAWN (1981), *Report from the first annual conference*, 13 November 1981. London: DAWN.

DAWN (1984), *Survey of facilities for women using drugs (including alcohol) in London.* London: DAWN.

Department of Health and Social Security (1976), *Prevention and health: everybyody's business.* London: HMSO.

Doyal, L. with Pennell, P. (1979), *The political economy of health.* London: Pluto Press.

Edwards, H., Hensman, C., Peto, J. (1973), 'A comparison of female and male motivation for drinking', *International Journal of the Addictions,* 8(4), pp.577–587.

Fillmore, K.M. (1984), *Issues in the changing drinking patterns among women in the last century.* Discussion paper presented at the NIAAA Women and Alcohol conference, Seattle, Washington, May 1984.

Glatt, M.M. (1961a), 'Drinking habits of English (middle-class) alcoholics', *Acta Psychiatrica Scandinavica* 37, pp.88–113.

Glatt, M.M. (1961b), 'Treatment results in an English mental hospital alcoholic unit', *Acta Psychiatrica Scandinavia* 37(1), pp.143–168.

Goddard, E. and Ikin, C. (1985), *Drinking in England and Wales in 1987.* London: HMSO.

Gusfield, J.R. (1982), 'Deviance in the welfare state: the alcoholism profession and entitlements of stigma', *Research in Social Problems and Public Policy*, 2, pp.1–20.

Heather, N. and Robertson, I. (1985), *Problem drinking. The new approach*. Harmondsworth: Penguin.

Helping Hand Organisation (1976), *Report on the Female Alcoholic*. London: HHO.

Hunt, G., Mellor, J. and Turner, J. (1987), 'Wretched, hatless and miserably clad: women and the inebriate reformatories from 1900–1913'. Paper presented at ICAA Alcohol Epidemiology Section, Aix-en-Provence, 7–12 June.

Jones, K.L. and Smith, D.W. (1973), 'Recognition of the foetal alcohol syndrome in early infancy', *Lancet*, 2, pp.999–1001.

Kelynack, T.N. (1902), 'Alcohol and the alcoholic environment in its relation to women and children', *The Medical Temperance Review*, 5, pp.195–205.

Kitze, J.L. (1986), *Enter every open door. The British Women's Temperance Association, 1876–1900*. Dissertation for the Diploma in Historical Studies, University of Cambridge.

Ledermann, S. (1956), *Alcool, alcoolisme, alcoolisation*. Paris: Presses Universitaires de France.

Litman, G. (1975) 'Women and alcohol: facts and myths', *New Behaviour*, 24 July, pp.126–129.

Litman, G., and Wilson, C. (1978), *A review of services for women alcoholics in the UK*. Paper presented at the 24th International Institute on the Prevention and Treatment of Alcoholism, 25 June, Zurich.

Moser, C.O.N. (1989), 'Gender planning in the third world: meeting practical and strategic gender needs', *World Development*, 17, No. 11, pp.1799–1825.

Otto, S. and Litman, G. (1976), *Women and alcohol*. Occasional Papers no. 1. National Council on Alcoholism, London (revised from papers first published 1974 by Camberwell Council on Alcoholism).

Park, J. (1990), 'Only "those" women: women and the control of alcohol in New Zealand', *Contemporary Drug Problems*, 17, pp.221–250.

Peiris, W.S.J. (1928), *Alcohol and child welfare*. National Health Series No. 1, Moratuwa.

Pemberton, D.S. (1967), 'A comparison of the outcome of treatment in female and male alcoholics', *British Journal of Psychiatry*, 113, pp.367–373.

Plant, Martin (1990), *Alcohol related problems in high risk groups.* Geneva: WHO Publications.

Plant, Moira (1985), *Women, drinking and pregnancy.* London: Tavistock Publications.

Plant, Moira (1990a), *Women and alcohol: a review of international literature on the use of alcohol by females.* Geneva: WHO Publications.

Rathod, N.H. and Thompson I.G. (1971), 'Women alcoholics: a clinical study', *Quarterly Journal of Studies in Alcohol*, 32, no. 1, pp.45–52.

Roman, P.M. (1988), *Women and alcohol use: a review of the research literature.* US Department of Health and Human Services, Rockville, Maryland.

Royal College of Psychiatrists (1979), *Alcohol and alcoholism.* London: Tavistock.

Royal College of Psychiatrists (1986), *Alcohol: our favourite drug.* London: Tavistock.

Ruzek, S.B. (1978), *Women's health movement: Feminist alternatives to medical control.* Praeger, USA.

Scharlieb, M. (1907), 'Alcoholism in relation to women and children' in T.N. Kelynack (ed.) *The drink problem in its medico-sociological aspects.* London: Methuen and Co.

Sclare, A.B. (1970), 'The female alcoholic', *British Journal of Addiction,* 65, no. 2, pp.99–107.

Sclare, A.B. (1975), *The woman alcoholic.* Paper presented at the Annual General Meeting, Medical Council on Alcoholism.

Vogt, I. (1984), 'Defining alcohol problems as a repressive mechanism: its formative phase in imperial Germany and its strength today', *The International Journal of the Addictions*, 19, no. 5, pp.551–569.

White Ribbon, (the official organ of the National British Women's Temperance Association) Jan. 1905, 34.

Wiener, C. (1981), *The politics of alcoholism: building an arena around a social problem.* New Brunswick, New Jersey: Transaction Books.

Wilson, C. (1976), 'Women and alcohol'. Paper presented to USAFE course on alcoholism, 8 June. Wellcome SA/CCA/96.

Woodside, M. (1961), 'Women drinkers admitted to Holloway Prison during February 1960: a pilot survey', *British Journal of Criminology*, 1, pp.221–225.

2

The Police, Gender and the Culture of Drug Use and Addiction

Malcolm Young

Introduction

The police in England and Wales maintain and operate a fiercely masculine culture. Symbols of male gender status and hierarchy hold the foreground and largely exclude any female or feminine nuance from everyday discourse[1]. Everyday police language is sprinkled with metaphors of tough masculinity, and the highly prized activity of crime-fighting is redolent of metaphorical campaigns, action plans, and targeted battles against a criminal enemy. Images of warfare predominate, while the 'softer' community-affairs activities – although paid lip-service in public – are privately negated and denigrated in a variety of ways not easily visible to the outsider. Not the least of these is the identification of such work with the culturally 'feminine' or with caring agencies.

In effect, any police claim to an equitably structured involvement in *both* crime *and* community affairs does not accord with the traditional 'macho' modes of thought which internally sustain the integrity of the system against a threatening outside. These modes of thought continue to reinforce a solidly-based 'habitus' of practice (Bourdieu 1977) directed against a narrow range of street-visible and relatively petty crimes (Young 1991).

Much of the activity surrounding drug-taking and drug abuse has a non-crime history in police classificatory terms. It has often been related to illness and weakness and linked to culturally 'feminine' qualities based on women's supposedly inherent irrationality and emotionalism. It should therefore come as no surprise to find that the police have consistently been uncomfortable when dealing with the ambiguous effects of drug abuse and addiction, for the connotations of illness and personal failure have meant that it has not always been easy to cast such dealings into the required framework of combative warfare directed against a common (male) enemy.

I have written elsewhere (Young 1979, 1984 and 1989) on the structural and symbolic invisibility of women and female activity in the police world. Women are still largely excluded from the profession or are marginal in the basic drama of 'cops and robbers' on which much police work is set out and arranged. Here the idea of 'crime' has a huge symbolic load and structures many aspects of police culture, yet it is largely related in practice to a narrow range of anti-social behaviour concerning certain acts of misappropriation of property and some acts of violence to others.

Drug-taking has largely been excluded from this high status area, and although a token police response to its presence as a 'folk devil' of the times has occurred (see Cohen 1973), the world of abuse and addiction is commensurate with other low-status activities and other areas designated by a broadly female connotation. This bias in the application of gender-related values has caused some real difficulties for the police in recent times, as they struggle to decide whether they are to retain their traditional role as a force (masculine), or take on more of a service (feminine) role in community policing.

The Place of Drug-Taking and Addiction

Although a Dangerous Drugs Act was passed in 1920 in the UK, partly in response to events stemming from the First World War, abuse of drugs was then considered to be minimal (Spear 1969) and it was not until the social revolution of the 'Swinging '60s' that legislation began to proliferate[2]. Through much of the intervening period, the incidence of 'addiction' was considered to be largely a therapeutic matter, of concern to professionals from the medical world, as the following table from Spear (1969:247) indicates:

Gender-specific aspects are clearly indicated across the 30 years covered by these official statistics. From 1936 to 1966, the number of women addicts remains relatively constant. Even the inclusion of the predominantly female category of 'Nurses' in the 1955 figures made no significant difference to the continual decline in the 'professional' addict category. What *is* striking in the statistics, however, is the increase in addiction from 1963: a seven-fold increase in male addiction is recorded thereafter. This is graphically demonstrated in Figures 1 and 2 below, which reveal further aspects of female addiction.

Year	Number of Addicts	Sex		Origin			Professional Addicts
		M	F	Thera-peutic.	N/T.	UK	
1936	616	313	300		No data		Approx. 120
1937	620	300	320		No data		147
1938	519	246	273		No data		140
1945	367	144	223		No data		80
1955	335	159	176		No data		86*
1958†	442	197	245	349	68	25	74
1959	454	196	258	344	98	12	68
1960	437	195	242	309	122	6	63
1961	470	223	247	293	159	18	61
1962	532	262	270	312	212	8	57
1963	635	339	296	355	270	10	56
1964	753	409	344	368	372	13	58
1965	927	558	369	344	580	3	45
1966	1349	886	463	351	982	16	54
1967	1729	1262	467	313	1385	31	56
1968	2782	2161	621	306	2420	56	43

* Includes nurses in 'professional addicts' for the first time.
† From 1958, the figures relate to those known to have been taking drugs in the year in question.

Table 1

Figure 1. Yearly Total of Addicts by Gender 1936–62

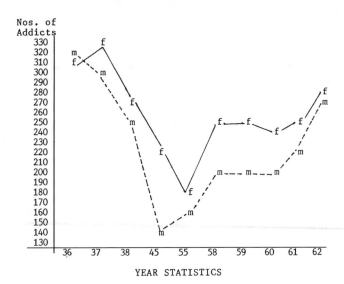

Nos. of Addicts

YEAR STATISTICS

Figure 2. Yearly Total of Addicts by Gender 1963–68

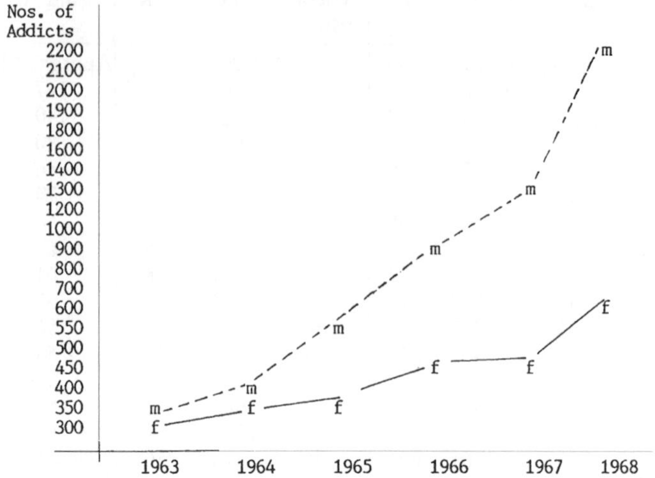

For almost thirty years, from 1936 to 1962, female addiction was officially recorded as being above that of males (Figure 1). From 1963, however, male addiction suddenly moves at a pace, and although female addiction also increased during these six years (Figure 2), its expansion was on a less dramatic scale. Why did this happen? Had men just discovered drug use, while women continued largely to ignore the phenomenon? Why was addiction a predominantly female activity until 1963, with the official figures for female addiction always above the male figure? Part of the answer seems to lie in a change of symbolic importance that drug use underwent in the 1960s, when it was taken up as a tenet of male culture and, in becoming a public affair for the 'street-wise', became linked to that side of social behaviour generally accorded masculine connotations. Furthermore, until the Notification of Addicts Regulations of 1968 placed the responsibility for identifying addicts on the medical profession, much of the statistical data came from the police – and their source material was likely to be clearly gender-specific, as we shall see.

During the 1960s, many of the provincial police forces set up Drug Squads for the first time (Young 1977). These units followed established traditions of police work by homing in on easily identifiable members of their traditional enemy in the 'dangerous classes' (Foucault 1980) – who were now beginning to dabble in amphetamines, cannabis and other drugs. Most squads then only carried a token policewoman in their ranks, and this is still the position today. The direction of police activity remains heavily male-orientated, and firmly geared to a public contest between male heroes and male villains.

Table 4 illustrates some monthly 'Drug Search Figures' from my last force, and demonstrates the continuity in this masculine activity. These figures suggest a strong relationship of public/private and male/female dichotomies, and reveal a world of symbolic boundaries where structural predominance is given to male officers pursuing male villains who operate in the public domain. This might be said to be a world where women are placed firmly in the invisible world of hearth and home; for in this arena, the dangerous classes follow a similar private/public gender orientation in their practices.

As the figures suggest, men are seven times more likely to be searched than women while in the street, yet only twice as likely to be searched in the category designated 'on premises'. The inference is that, although drug-squad work is largely about a male world, women *are* expected to be found on premises (i.e. in houses) and searches of women *do* occur there – probably involving the token female policewoman on the Squad. Once in the street, however, the women seem to take on a structural invisibility and vanish from the records.

**Table 2. Drug Searches by Gender Jan.–Oct. 1987
– West Mercia Police**

| Total nos. searched | On Premises | In the Street |

MALE/FEMALE SEARCHES – SHOWING POSITIVE RESULTS

Drug Abuse – Police and Legal Classifications

Drug-taking is often described as a 'victimless crime' and is seen as a private, self-administered activity. Unlike other traditional crimes of theft or violence, it often has no easily identified 'injured person' to set against a culprit or villain; it is not easy to set within a simple polarity on which to frame a 'cops and robbers' opposition (Young 1979a).

As a result, the addict or the user continue to hold an ambivalent place in any police hierarchy of action and response, and the semantics of 'harm' posed by the drug-user tend to mirror those of other semi-invisible crimes. For example, the blind spot with which the police have operated in relation to corporate crime (Box 1983), or to fiddling at work (Mars 1983), is often paralleled by their lukewarm response to other areas such as acts of domestic violence; for this is also socially invisible and often under-reported. Like drug-abuse, domestic violence is perceived as a social malaise – a malady, evoking the concept of illness. Its potential for 'harm' generally occurs in the private domain, often remaining hidden behind the walls of the 'Englishman's castle', and therefore beyond the immediacy and visibility of the public place in which the police operate most comfortably.

The result is that even though the police may claim a primary concern for 'the protection of life', this is narrowly defined and less rigorously applied in certain areas. An easily detected domestic murder generally has less status than one involving an investigative murder hunt, and although the public street fight has a legal basis for police action dating back to the 1861 Offences Against the Persons Act, with a ranked order of wounding, assaults and battery all surrounded by a range of metaphors of warfare which easily identify it as male work, other more injurious acts share no similar structures of significance. And belief in what is always referred to as 'real police work' is consistently based on definitions which apportion relevance and status to social arenas holding significant historical validity. Once the concept of 'harm' is removed to the private domain, or is controlled by civil law (such as in the negligent wounding or injury caused by omission in the factory or workplace), it is unusual for the police to become involved.

Although there is an increasing literature on domestic violence, and some moves to enhance police response to the 'domestic' have recently taken place, its semi-invisibility, its occurrence away from the 'public place' as commonly defined, and the ambiguities structuring many domestic relationships, all result in a continued reluctance by the police to intervene. When the symbolic boundaries necessary for the creation of an easily classifiable crime-response become blurred and uncertainty prevails, then these crimes tend to join drug-use as ambivalent areas of social harm, and become muted in action.

The value or status given to such marginal and ambiguous areas as drug-taking can therefore be set against other highly prized areas for police intervention, and a whole series of symbolic oppositions is evoked in definition and action. We might crudely summarise some of these as follows:

Public	Private
Visible	Invisible
Warfare	Illness/social malaise
Public place	Private or closed location
Victim/complainant	Victimless/personal weakness
Crime	Offences; non-crimes or civil dispute
Male	Female

In the cultural morality still upheld by the police, higher status is accorded to the categories on the left of the dichotomies as presented here. For almost all the 150 years of police history, actions against unlawful drug possession or the unlawful supply and manufacture of drugs have tended to be categorised as actions relating to *offences* (i.e. with low status) rather than the far more significant *crimes*. The difference between these two categories is considerable but is rarely made clear (see Young 1991); the mysteries of an institution concerned with power and control thus remain fittingly opaque.

Crimes are *always* given higher status in police practice. Greater resources are allocated to them and their detection is regularly used as a primary indication of police effectiveness. Those members of the institution who deal with crimes – the detectives – are attributed special status, while uniformed officers, who deal mainly with the more insignificant offences, always hold a secondary place in the order of things, regardless of assertions to the contrary by those in the police hierarchies. Offences are always of lesser significance to the institutional structure. All breaches of traffic regulations are offences, as are minor breaches of the peace, including drunkenness. Indecent exposure, indecent language and indecent publications are offences, not crimes. Prostitution and betting and gaming irregularities are classifiable offences and not crimes, while selling tobacco to juveniles parallels speeding and illegal parking – in that all are defined as offences.

Crimes, on the other hand, have a ranked order of importance based on possible sentence, ranging from murder down to petty theft. A Home Office 'Standard List of Crimes' is published as 'offences recorded and detected, which are to be counted as crimes', in what are known generally as 'The Counting Rules'. These Rules generate the highly significant, annual Crime Statistics, which are as much a symbolic statement about police management and organisational activity as they are an assessment of the incidence of criminality.

Illegal acts of drug use have been allocated to the lesser category of 'offence' for much of police history. Even in the Swinging '60s when a social revolution generated new and somewhat threatening behaviour which challenged and confused the ruling Establishment, the illegalities in the plethora of legislation rushed through in a multiplicity of Acts of Parliament[2] were always designated as offences and never included in the Counting Rules as crimes. Only in the mid-1980s, when drug-taking was once again used by the executive as a symbol of disorder, were the Counting Rules amended to elevate some drugs offences into crimes. Now the illegal supply and production of *some* drugs was to be classified as a crime, along with 'possession with intent to supply'. Possession *without* intent to supply, however, remains an offence, so that quantity becomes the criterion of a crime, and a small amount of some drugs for personal consumption will remain an offence of possession. The symbolic nature of this division should not be overlooked.

Gender in Drug Use

Whether the substance ingested be gin, whisky, beer or cider, cannabis, amphetamine, opiate or hallucinogen, tobacco or tranquilliser, the police response depends on cultural values specific to time and social space. There are written histories and a long literature on the pursuit and prohibition of all manner of substances used in an effort to change a mood, seek a spiritual nirvana, or to achieve an altered mental cognition or social situation; and each use or abuse has a varied background of exclusivity, reward, punishment, abhorrence, adulation or pursuit. Many of the plants, chemicals or substances used, furthermore, have male or female qualities attributed, or their cultural use or proscription is gender-specific. Sometimes the language surrounding the symbolic nature of the use or style of the drug identifies its gender denomination, and can give clues to its social value, potency and status.

Substances attributed male qualities are often pursued for use by the police themselves. The Policy Studies report on the Metropolitan Police (Smith and Gray 1983), for instance, commented on the masculine cult of heavy beer-drinking which surrounds much of the work of detectives in the CID (see also Hobbs 1988). This 'macho' use of alcohol links up with other symbols of masculinity, such as the metaphors of warfare which are ubiquitous in police culture, and it echoes a wider social context in which a structural invisibility of female alcohol use (and drunkenness) and a public declamation of male drinking prowess have long been normal. These trends can be illustrated by extracts from the Annual Reports of two police forces in which I have served. Table 3 summarises figures for drunkenness taken from the 1983 Northumbria Police Annual Report (p.66). Table 4 gives the 1986 figures from the West Mercia Report (p.89).

Table 3. Drunkenness 1983 – Northumbria Police Area.
Age Groups and gender breakdown

Total Proceedings	12–17	18–30	31–40	41+	Total convicted
m f	m f	m f	m f	m f	m f
4599 377	305 23	2652 213	592 77	1050 64	4414 362

Table 4. Drunkenness 1986 –West Mercia Police

Age	Male	Female
Under 18 yrs	40 (63)	4 (5)
18–21 yrs	200 (192)	10 (11)
Over 21 yrs	325 (472)	22 (48)
TOTALS	565 (727)	36 (64)

1985 figures shown in parentheses

These figures, from one rural and one metropolitan police area, give some insight into the police response to drinking and drunkenness, and give some indication of how the abuse of drink is still considered to be a masculine occupation, especially in the public arena where the majority of these police statistics will have originated. Gender is obviously important here in determining both the activity and the response it evokes. And these implicit gender assumptions are consistent with other cultural assumptions which ascribe some aspects of drug use to women and some to men[3].

As suggested by the statistical histories of addiction (Table 1, Figures 1–2), gender appears to be a significant factor in the record and is worthy of further exploration. Dependency or addiction is not an illegal state in Britain and is neither an offence nor a crime, although it has little status to sustain a place in any hierarchy of approved social behaviour. It is commonly deemed to be an illness, like insanity, and the powerful in society have tended to link it to other areas of madness or folly, or to other categories characterised by implications of idleness or irrationality, outside or beyond any recognisable human achievement. Those so proscribed have been relegated to areas of denigration, isolation or exclusion, further implying a need for purification (Foucault 1967).

This understanding of 'addiction' and its relevance to gender is illustrated by its classificatory history in the USA, where the allegedly inherent irrationality or folly of women was regularly quoted in relation to this 'condition', as it was called in the literature. Prior to 1914 addiction was not classified as a crime in the USA but was regarded as an illness supported by medical prescription, and 'most of the [recipients] were women diagnosed by their physicians as weak and fragile' (Rosenbaum 1981:3). Around this time it was estimated that women addicts outnumbered men by a ratio of two to one. This again mirrors the early figures for addiction in Britain given in Table 1.

Once opiate addiction was legislated against, however, in the Harrison Act of 1914, the incidence of female addiction dropped away dramatically and the activity took on a male identity, becoming commensurate with male criminality. This symbolic role continued, so that in 1968 the US returns for male addicts were 5 to 1 over female notifications. By 1978, however, the ratio had dropped to 3 to 1. A new, public female identity began to be created during the feminist revolution of the time. In effect, the expectations of gender in relation to this behaviour had been overturned; an earlier belief that addiction was equated with female madness had been displaced by drug-taking as a male-orientated activity, in what Rosenbaum (1981:3) describes as 'a frenzied street culture of criminality'.

This social change reflects the vision of a correct order and place which the predominantly male and masculine classifiers of society – such as the police and the medical and legal professions – accept and then reinforce. It supports the beliefs and modes of thought which they themselves prefer to operate by. The American classification of addiction as a female/private activity and then later as a male/public and criminally deviant behaviour is similar to the British experience, but pre-dates the UK situation by some forty years.

Today the street culture of addiction is heavy with a symbolism of gender. Much of this is definitionally masculine. The language, for example, is evocative of a cold, technological style, which often reveals its own intimations of warfare and battle, and again places it firmly in a culture of masculinity. The mechanistic 'fixing', jacking up with a set of works, getting a hit, blasting, making a score, crashing out, or 'shooting up with a spike' are all tinged with reflections of a male and sometimes sado-masochistic world. In such a cultural milieu, street-dealing in smack, crack, horse or 'snow' contains few of the allegedly feminine attributes of 'love, peace and communal caring' which the symbolically feminine world of cannabis-use brought into the cultural world of the Swinging '60s (see note 3).

Using a needle, as Rosenbaum (1981) contends, is an important symbolic break between the world of the soft, caring, hippie world of the counter-cultural drug-user and the junkie; and as a result of its strongly male identity, it is now something that women are predisposed to leave to men:

> Most inexperienced (women) users are shot up by someone else in the beginning... It is paradoxical that women who had independently initiated their use of heroin, would subsequently become dependent on a man to inject the drug...this pattern has symbolic import; the dependency of woman's addiction makes it somewhat less an addiction than if she were shooting up herself (1981:37).

It is worth-while drawing attention here to the symbolic content of Rosenbaum's language (on which she makes no comment), and in which the 'women users are *shot up* by (men)'. This power of men to 'shoot up women' is another reflection of the metaphoric warfare which men continue to wage; while the willingness of women to accept yet another area in which they become dependent on men recreates the idea of female vulnerability and gender hierarchy, and another domain in which women accept as socially normal a situation in which they lack control over their own lives and bodies.

Overdoses

Drug overdoses are alleged to account for over 90 per cent of all deliberate self-injuries in Britain (for further comments, see also Littlewood in this volume). Many of the overdoses involve sedatives or tranquillisers prescribed to those considered to be irrational, over-emotional or tinged with the nervous folly still often believed to be a deeply held prerogative of women.

It has been estimated that in the years between 1959 and 1974, over 27,000 people died from poisoning by self-administered barbiturates in England and Wales, while in 1978 there were some 76,339,000 prescriptions issued for psychotropic drugs in England alone. Over 1,000,000 people were estimated to take Valium on prescription and eight per cent of the adult population were alleged to be on treatment with some form of psychotropic drug (SSRC Report 1982:7).

This 1982 report on 'Research Priorities in Addiction' warned: 'The social consequences of having over a million people partly or totally sedated by such drugs has not been adequately considered.' In the same fifteen-year period of 1959–74 covered by this report, only 12,000–14,000 people were prosecuted to conviction in England and Wales for offences relating to the possession, supply or cultivation of drugs controlled by the various Acts of Parliament. These figures suggest a restricted police response to the alleged social problem of drugs; and further indicate how narrow their field of action is in relation to the 'harm' that the variety of drug taking can elicit. Most of the overdosing, the suicides and the addiction to tranquillisers remain low-key and low-status work for the police as they set out to pursue their traditional aim of 'protecting life'; this dependence and its resulting social harm are lawful and medical, and evoke caring or activities primarily seen as women's business, thereby taking on lowered status in police eyes.

Figure 3 (taken from O'Brien 1985:129) shows a rise in hospital admissions for overdoses between 1957 and 1973 in England and Wales, from 15,900 to 107,170 cases. These support figures from small-scale studies on overdosing and its relationship to gender; these studies confirm 'that it is young people, particularly females, who are predominantly responsible for the increase in the rates of self-poisoning' (ibid).

Figure 3. Adverse Effects of Chemical Substances: Hospital Admissions by Age and Sex: 1957–1973

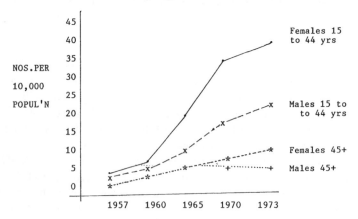

Figure 4, covering the same period, further illustrates the gendered nature of this self-poisoning, and again confirms that it is the young 15 – 25-year-old women who are most prone to this behaviour:

Figure 4. Hospital Admission Rates for Adverse Effects of Chemical Substances by Age and Sex

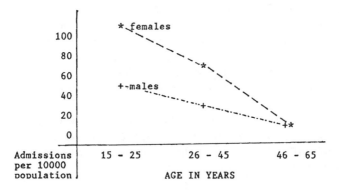

Certainly the police have little or no part to play in these areas, except perhaps to record an overdose call on some incident log or – in the more extreme cases – to produce a history of events for the coroner's inquest and assure themselves there is no need to set up a murder enquiry. There is rarely the potential for any crime detection in these cases.

Such graphical representations of female involvement in self-administered drug-taking offer positive evidence of an otherwise relatively invisible and unacknowledged social activity. In the main, the overdose (often classified later at the coroner's inquest as 'accidental') occurs in the female domestic space, in the house, the hostel or the bed-sit. Male suicide attempts are more likely to be in the public place, using the car exhaust, or by leaping from a building, bridge or cliff top. In an assessment of over 300 suicide verdicts I looked at in the West Mercia Police area, the recorded male/female ratios were nearly 5 to 1, while out of the 78 female suicides over the two-year period of the analysis, 50 were attributed to overdose, some with related causes such as alcohol ingestion. Most of these were located in the domestic environment, allowing them to be further defined as a socio-domestic aberration or as the extension of an illness – which is then a clinical or non-police matter, except at the inquest.

Although this whole overdose question might be considered large-scale and harmful, especially for young people, most community policing schemes have little or nothing to say on the matter. Their preventive campaigns are largely directed to the traditional areas of crime (e.g. the neighbourhood watch scheme to prevent burglary), while their attempts to curtail substance abuse generally relate to the continued control of illegal, street-visible drug-taking or 'excessive' alcohol ingestion; and even these are only rarely the object of innovatory schemes, of large establishments of manpower or of extensive funding.

Again, this clearly indicates the parameters of police action, and repeats simple structural dichotomies of male/female, public/private. The effects of such beliefs can be followed further in the small-scale study of a group of young people attending local doctors' surgeries carried out by Sally O'Brien (1985) and tabulated below (Table 5). In this sample she found: 'the overdose group was divided into those for whom it was a first attempt (OD 1) and those who had taken a previous overdose (OD 2). At least one previous overdose had been taken by 61% of the women. There were over twice as many women who had taken an overdose as men' (1985:22).

Table 5

	OD 1	OD 2	Total
Males	22	34	56
Females	55	84	139

As with the national situation, this small-scale analysis indicates that females taking overdoses outnumber their male counterparts to a significant degree. However, when O'Brien (ibid:32) went on to look at the incidence of criminal records in the same group (a criminal record varying 'from a prison sentence to a fine'), she found that women vanished from the equation and that the situation reverted to the dominant gender pattern, with men far outnumbering women. Table 6 below shows women virtually eliminated from this statistical tabulation of recorded criminality, although their relative invisibility is only partly due to the women's own perceptions of crime as men's work.

Table 6

People with a criminal record (shown in % of total male and female population)			
	GPR (n = 152)	OD 1 (n = 76)	OD2 (n = 176)
Male:	17	38	64
Female:	1	6	18

O'Brien's study seems to reaffirm a widely held cultural assumption that it is men who commit crime, while it is women who take overdoses. In a similar small-scale survey carried out in Cheltenham (Plant 1975), a group of 200 drug-takers was researched. Again the predominance of male over female users indicates an obvious gender bias. When these drug-users were then considered in relation to their recorded criminality and thus to their contact and search by the police (on which most of these statistical records inevitably depend), the skew is further towards a male bias: 'All of the 200 drug takers had used illegal drugs and, theoretically, could have been prosecuted for this. In fact, only 29 had ever been convicted of a drug offence – possession, cultivation, or trafficking of proscribed drugs. 27 of these 29 were non-students, 28 were multi-users and *twenty-eight (of the 29) were males'* (my emphasis) (Plant 1975:144).

Table 7

Drugs Used by the Study Group			
Drug type	Male users	Female users	Total	%
Cannabis	153	47	200	100
L.S.D.	119	36	155	77.5
Amphetamines	89	19	108	54.0
Opium	55	10	65	32.5
Mescalin	50	8	58	29.0
Barbiturates	48	8	56	28.0
Mandrax	48	5	53	26.5
Cough Linctus	41	6	48	24.0
Cocaine	26	5	31	15.5
Heroin	21	3	24	12.0
Inhalers	18	4	22	11.0
Methedrine	20	1	21	10.5
Morphine	14	1	15	7.5
Nutmeg	7	2	9	4.5
Tranquillisers	7	1	8	4.0
D.M.T.	7	1	8	4.0
Methadone	6	1	7	3.5
Banana skins	3	1	4	2.0
Others/various	38	0	38	19.0

Women once again seem to have been negotiated out of the public drama of the criminal justice system, and Table 7 (taken from Plant's study) offers more indications of the symbolically masculine nature of illegal, street-wise drug use.

Women as Exchange – 'Doing the Business'

The police continue to negotiate and manipulate a 'real' world of wheeler-dealing 'rogues, vagabonds and villains' in a fiercely traditional manner; and to some extent this still favoured and somewhat archaic language gives an indication of the conservatism that structures the practices of the institution. It is little wonder that the police perception of a world of crime and criminals has no real public place for women as yet; nor is it surprising to find that the police have become institutionally expert at the business of manipulating a version of social reality which operates symbolically gendered prestige structures that suit their own dogma and orthodoxy. In the daily bartering and bargaining pursued with their antagonists, the police – as an institution of power – need to be alive to the slightest nuance or chance as they strive to maximise their potential and maintain control over their known adversaries in the dangerous classes.

In this world of negotiated justice, women are regularly used as a commodity for what is fondly known by the detectives as 'doing the business' (Hobbs 1988). The statistical tables and figures above indicate a gender skew at more than one level. In my thirty years with the police, I have seen continual use made of women as they are 'negotiated out of the business' by the male protagonists. I have played the game myself and have been crucially aware that a suitable deal to assist the detection rates might, for example, be set against an agreement for early bail that also involved some easing of the evidence against a female accomplice. This is a normal part of the drama of the criminal justice world and I have written at length (see Young 1991) about the language forged in this situation; and also about the difficulties facing any outsider who tries to spot what is going on as deals are being struck.

The whole mode of social action undertaken in these skirmishes, between the forces of law and their street-wise enemies, maintains an in-group and largely elitist knowledge which is couched in an insider's language filled with masculine symbols and metaphors. It excludes those who have no part in the social drama, removing women to the sidelines to be used as pawns in the business of manipulating the theatre of the judicial duel. Removing women from the scenario in a deal means that they drop out of the statistically public domain and return to the structural invisibility which the world of policing prefers, and seems set up to recreate on every possible occasion. One brief example may illustrate this insider exclusivity and show the way women are made to vanish from the centre stage of this male domain. An extract from my field notes in 1987 runs as follows:

> I have a Detective Inspector on my division who epitomises this macho world of crime-fighting and thrives on the whole business. He bursts into my room, a big grin on his face to tell me of the latest on an antiques job we've had on the sub-division:

> "...good news boss, we've had a bell on our man's lay-by from a sarbut, so the boys have gone for a ticket to bogie his drum. No doubt the sarbut and the lay-by will turn out to be one and the same and she'll have to be left out when the boys come to do the business..."

In effect his message told me: 'Good news, we've had a telephone call from an informant (a sarbut or sarbot)[4] about the girl-friend (lay-by) of our suspect (our man), so the detectives have gone for a warrant (a ticket) to search (bogie or bogey) his premises (his drum). No doubt the informant (the sarbut) and his girl-friend (the lay-by) are one and the same person and she will have to be negotiated out and allowed to disappear from the events when the detectives come to interview him and make any deals (do the business)'.

This language of the insider and of dealing is tied directly into the historical structures of masculinity which ensure that this world of law enforcement remains strongly gender-specific. Shortly after this event, at a police social do, I discussed this same language of obscurity which the police seem to use to defend their systems, and linked it to the practice of using gender hierarchy and male prestige as a means of removing women from the centre stage of many criminal events[5]. My colleagues eagerly added to my field notes, from which the following is taken:

> there is talk about 'putting someone out on rubber bands and going for Georges'...

> I explain the concept of how we negotiate women out of events, making them vanish from the statistical record. S (a detective sergeant) in a matter of fact way says 'of course we do; we do it all the time...it's almost a daily event to deal with the men and leave the women out of it'

> Two others run through a range of rhyming slang. Both are southerners; one has just transferred to the Midlands from Hampshire, and pantomimes a deal between a villain and a 'jack' in colloquial police jargon which we all recognise, even though it has a cockney rhyming slang derivation:

'... put the judy down as having come along for veras and we'll agree she wasn't to know the jam was hot...'[6]

Conclusion

This brief exploration of police culture, with its understanding of, and response to, drug-taking, addiction and gender, produces few surprises. Just as in the street-game of 'find the lady', or the 'three-card trick', where illusion is used to make the Queen (or lady) appear and disappear to suit the need, so in the world of policing and drug use women are directed to appear only when a cultural belief in their presence makes it suitable; and they tend to vanish whenever drug-taking has a public persona or is given masculine symbolic relevance.

The implications of this perception can be followed through in practice once the status of drug- or alcohol-related behaviour is understood to follow a structural polarity of relevance which allocates it either to the private/domestic/feminine world, or situates it in a public/street/masculine domain. Ideas of criminality or illness are crucial in determining the police response to any classification, and after a long history of being largely considered as a female malady, addiction seems to have crossed a gender boundary in two locations and on two separate occasions in the past, to become a male activity in both the USA and the UK. Taking an overdose, however, remains firmly lodged as an aberrant female activity, linked to ideas and symbolism rooted in the realms of 'domestic/personal failure' or feminine ineptitude. However, when the statistical record of those taking overdoses, for example, is assessed for criminality – officially and historically, a street-visible public event – the female once again vanishes from the scene and the male moves back to take centre stage. There is more than women's own perception of criminality or of drug use involved here. An understanding of gender and drug use cannot ignore cultural assumptions held by the police.

Notes

1. See for example, Volume 4 of the Policy Studies Institute report on the Metropolitan Police, *The Police and the People in London*, Smith D.J. and Gray J. (1983) where aspects of the culture of masculinity in the institution of the police are explored in depth; and also Reiner's *The Politics of the Police* (1985).

2. After the creation of a Dangerous Drugs Act in 1920 and again in 1951 (both of which were generated to some extent by the changes brought about by the preceding world wars), the great period for drugs legislation occurred in the 1960s during the time of the 'counter-culture' movements. The Drugs (Prevention of Misuse) Act of 1964 set out to control amphetamine use, while the Dangerous Drugs Act of 1964 and a set of Dangerous Drugs Regulations in 1965 acknowledged an official increase in addiction indicated in Tables 1 and 2 in the text. Hallucinogens were added to the Misuse of Drugs Act in 1966 and this was followed by another Dangerous Drugs Act in 1967. Every year during this period saw new drugs (including Mandrax and Psilocybin) added to the Schedules of control, and in 1968 the Supply and Notification of Addicts Regulations set out to identify and further categorise those who were allegedly addicted or dependent on what have come to be known as 'hard drugs'. In 1971 the whole mess of legislation was consolidated into The Misuse of Drugs Act.

3. I have written elsewhere (Young 1979b) on the symbolic aspects of cannabis-use by the 'counter-culture' of the 1960s and suggested how specifically identified and socially enhanced feminine qualities were used as an integral part of its value as a root or foundation metaphor (see Turner 1969 and 1974) for underground beliefs. Indeed, the anxiety caused by the 1960s counter-cultural use of cannabis might well be a reflection of more than just a simple fear of illegal drug use, and it is a matter of ethnographic interest that users have suggested to me that its persistent prosecution by the executive owes something to aspects of gender reversal incorporated in cannabis use. The female element in the drug – which was always emphasised by the counter-culture – is active and aggressive, while the male user (see Table 7) is largely required to be, passive and receiving.

4. Although the term 'sarbut' (meaning informant) was in daily use, none of the detectives could spell it, for it was from an unwritten language. The spelling I have used approximates the pronunciation, and like 'bogie' or 'bogey' is open to amendment. One folk etymology is that 'sarbut' may well have origins in both 'sabot' and 'sabotage', for the informant who grasses on his associates really 'puts the wooden clog (sabot) in and wrecks the deal'.

5. As I drafted this part of the original version of this paper in late 1987, I listened to a news item on a big cocaine haul. Two men had been arrested by Customs and were to appear in court the next morning. A woman was reported to 'have been released on bail'. My

immediate reaction was that someone had done a deal to leave her out of it.

6. Out on rubber bands = released on bail to return to the police station at a set date in the future, often employed to 'allow further enquiries to be made'.

Georges = Rafters (afters) = a lock-in = staying behind after hours in a pub to drink (rhyming slang, relying on a play on words based on 'George Raft', an actor who played many screen villains).

Jack = detective

Judy = a woman

Vera = (rhyming slang) Vera Lynn = gin

Hot = stolen

Jam = car (rhyming slang = jamjar).

References

Bourdieu, P. (1977), *Outline of a Theory of Practice*. Cambridge: Cambridge University Press.

Box, S. (1983), *Power, Crime and Mystification*. London: Tavistock.

Cohen, S. (1973), *Folk Devils and Moral Panics*. St. Albans: Paladin.

Foucault, M. (1967), *Madness and Civilisation*. London: Tavistock.

Foucault, M. (1980), *Power/Knowledge: Selected Interviews and Other Writings*, ed. Gordon, C. Brighton: The Harvester Press.

Hobbs, D. (1988), *Doing the Business; the Working Class and Detectives in the East End of London*. Oxford: Oxford University Press.

Mars, G. (1983), *Cheats at Work: an anthropology of Workplace Crime*. London: Unwin Paperbacks.

O'Brien, S. (1985), *The Negative Scream: a study of Young People who took an Overdose*. London: Routledge and Kegan Paul.

Plant, M.A., (1975), *Drug Takers in an English Town*. London: Tavistock.

Reiner, R. (1985), *The Politics of the Police*. Brighton: Wheatsheaf Books, The Harvester Press.

Rosenbaum, M. (1981), *Women on Heroin*. New Brunswick, New Jersey: Rutgers Univ. Press.

Smith, D.J. and Gray, J. (1983), *The Police and the People in London*. London: The Policy Studies Institute.

Social Science Research Council (1982), *Research priorities in Addiction*. (A report commissioned by the SSRC exploratory panel on Addiction Research.)

Spear, H.B. (1969), 'The Growth of Heroin Addiction in the U.K.', *The British Journal of Addiction*, vol. 64, pp.245–55, Pergamon.

Turner, V. (1969), *The Ritual Process: Structure and Anti-Structure*. London: Routledge and Kegan Paul.

Turner, V. (1974), *Dramas, Fields and Metaphors: Symbolic Action in Human Society*. Cornell University Press, Ithaca.

Young, M. (1977), 'An examination of the developing perception in a local community of non-medical drug use, as a marginal, anti-structural behaviour'. Unpublished B.A. thesis, University of Durham.

Young, M. (1979), 'Ladies of the Blue Light: an anthropology of policewomen'. Unpublished seminar paper, University of Durham.

Young, M. (1979a), 'Pigs 'n Prigs: a Mode of Thought, Experience and Practice', *Working Papers in Social Anthropology,* no. 3, University of Durham.

Young, M. (1979b), 'The Symbolic Language of Cannabis' in *DYN*, vol. 5 (Journal of the Anthropology Society of the University of Durham).

Young, M. (1984), 'Police Wives: a reflection of Police Concepts of Order and Control' in *The Incorporated Wife* (ed.) Ardener S. and Callan H. London: Croom Helm.

Young, M. (1991), *Inside Job: Policing and Police Culture in Britain*. Oxford University Press.

Young, M. (1992), 'Dress and Modes of Address: Structural Forms for Policewomen' in R. Barnes and J.B. Eicher (eds) *Dress and Gender*. Oxford: Berg.

3

Symptoms, Struggles and Functions: What Does the Overdose Represent?

Roland Littlewood

'Life is more vivid in a snake than a butterfly.'
D.H. Lawrence

In all societies, distress and illness are experienced through some system which encodes indigenous notions of social order. Illness is, as Allan Young (1976) puts it, 'an event that challenges meaning in this world [and] medical beliefs and practices organise the event into an episode which gives form and meaning'. It has become a commonplace to say that the world in which most contemporary North Americans and Europeans live is one that is distinctively 'medicalised' – a world in which many types of distress and conflict are represented, indeed constituted, through professional medicine. The legitimation of our world, it is argued, no longer lies in religion but in the contemporary sciences which offer us core notions of individual identity, autonomy and causality. In its everyday context as it relates to personal experience, science is most salient for us in some form of biomedicine.

The obligation to order illness is no less when it is manifest primarily through unusual and frightening behaviour. Scott (1973) points out that the person whose actions are seen as unpredictable not only becomes an object of fear: she becomes endowed with a potentiality for a perverse sort of power, for 'the power of an illness reality is derived from its ability to evoke deeply felt social responses as well as intense personal affects' (Good and Good 1981), a power that lies in the unstated assumption that it is something outside oneself which is ultimately responsible.

Professional intervention in sickness incorporates the individual designated as a 'patient' into an overarching system of explanation, a common structural pattern which manifests itself in the bodily economy of every human being and in which accountability is transferred to an agency beyond the patient's control. Becoming 'sick' is part of a process leading to communal recognition of an abnormal state with a consequent readjustment of customary patterns of actions and expectations, and then to changed roles and altered responsibilities.

Expectations of the sick person conventionally include exemption from discharging some social obligations and from responsibility for the condition itself, together with a shared recognition that it is undesirable and involves an obligation to seek help and co-operate with treatment (Parsons 1951). Withdrawal from everyday social responsibilities is made socially acceptable through some means of exculpation, usually through a mechanism of biophysical determinism, one which is not uncommon for: 'When faced with a diagnosis for which he has equally convincing reasons to believe that either his client is sick or he is not sick, the physician finds that the professional and legal risks are less if he accepts the hypothesis of sickness' (Young 1976).

To question this biomedical schema itself would involve questioning some of our most fundamental 'Western' assumptions about human nature and agency. Because of its linking of personal experience with the social order, its standardised expectations of removing personal responsibility and initiating an institutionalised response, and its rooting in our ultimate social values through science, biomedicines offer a powerful unquestionable and, legitimate inversion of everyday behaviour.

Sacred Diseases

In what we might broadly term 'Western' society, the facts of female physiology have been transformed into 'a cultural rationale which assigns women to nature and the domestic sphere, and thus ensures their general inferiority to men' (La Fontaine 1981:347). The essential aspects of this female role are reflected in the ideals which are still held out to women: concentration on marriage, home and children as the primary focus of concern with reliance on a male provider for sustenance and status.

Women's lack of power is attributed to their greater emotionality and their inability to cope with wider social responsibilities. Dependency and passivity are expected of a woman. Her representation in clinical psychology and in doctor-directed drug advertising alike is that of a person with a childish incapacity to govern herself, with a need for male protection and direction (Broverman et al. 1970; Chapman 1979). Contemporary Western women are permitted greater freedom than men to 'express feelings' and to recognise emotional problems (Phillips and Segal 1969), enabling the woman to define her difficulties within a medical framework and bring them to the attention of her doctor (Horwitz 1977). The extent to which women adopt a characteristically 'female' domestic role within the household seems to correlate with the number of symptoms they report (Hibbard and Pople 1983). It is particularly through childbearing that every woman in the West becomes a potential patient; as a British gynaecology textbook put it not that long ago: 'Femininity tends to be passive and receptive, masculinity to be more active, restless, anxious for repeated demonstrations of potency' (James 1963).

Nature and woman stood for each other in early modern science. Francis Bacon argued that science would lead Man to 'Nature with all her children and bind her to your service and make her your slave', to a 'truly masculine birth of time' (Easlea 1980:129, 247). Jordanova (1989) suggests that medicine and science remain characterised by the action of men on women; it is assumed that women are more 'natural', passive, empty, awaiting male ('cultural') exposure, organisation and fertilisation. In the heraldry of the Royal College of Psychiatrists, as sported on the ties of its members and on the carpets of its building in London's Belgrave Square, this tradition is continued as the Butterflies of Psyche awaiting the Serpents of Aesculapius[1]. Ingleby (1982) notes that there is a close historical relationship between the psychiatric notion of 'woman' and that of 'patient', and both Chesler (1974) and Jordanova (1989) call attention to the similarity between neurotic symptom patterns and normative expectations of female behaviour. Indeed, neurotic men feel they are especially stigmatised through having 'women's problems' (Miles 1988).

We can schematically summarise in complementary pairs what Maurice Lipsedge and I have termed the Butterfly/Serpent (B/S) relationship:

$$\frac{Culture}{Nature} = \frac{Male}{Female} = \frac{Active}{Passive} = \frac{Cognition}{Affect} = \frac{Doctor}{Patient} = \frac{Public}{Private} =$$

$$\frac{Production}{Consumption} = \frac{Desire}{Need}$$

Butterfly and Serpent are in an opposed but complementary relationship; action by one engenders the opposed complement of the other. They are defined by each other. It is the relationship between the paired elements that remains constant here; and not a question of finding an identity between the superordinate or subordinate elements. Clearly, not all doctors are men (indeed, medicine has a greater proportion of women than other graduate professions) but the woman doctor's interactions with her patient replicate those of the male/female relationship: a male patient may flirt with his nurse but hardly with his doctor (Littlewood 1990). Our schema follows the binary sets of Lévi-Strauss' structuralist anthropology (for further comment on their usefulness, see Littlewood 1980). The structural model of Lévi-Strauss was elaborated largely to elucidate myth, 'a sacred tale about past events which is used to justify social action in the present' (Leach 1983:8), and I have returned to it here because we seem to be dealing with something cognate to myth in this sense. Raymond (1982) demonstrates a formal similarity between the current relations of doctor *vis-à-vis* patient and those of the priest in the Christian West with the laity, while Turner (1984) proposes the term 'sacred disease' for those 'neuroses' which continue to represent male control over women's bodies: 'both the sociology of religion and medical sociology [are] inevitably cultural responses to the problem of theodicy' (pp.83–4). Sin becomes sickness. A truism perhaps, but where do we locate the similarities?

The doctor/patient and husband/wife complementarities are neither primary nor autonomous. Notions of paternity or of the family 'are not the building blocks of society but products of its overall organisation' (La Fontaine 1981). Societies may be said to expropriate their own social world from the material of an environment which they transform, but the nature/culture opposition, although common, is far from universal; and neither 'nature' nor 'Nature' is a neutral field. The notion that contrast is inherent in all systems of symbolic classification is not of course limited to French structuralism although it is there that it found its fullest flowering. To decide when a 'complementarity' becomes an 'opposition', a 'tension' or a 'conflict' depends on our weighting of the social causalities outside the equation itself. Similarly for 'dominance' (Lawrence's expressly phallocentric 'vividness': see my epigraph); whether 'the charisma of dominance comes from a particular power – that of ultimately defining the world in which non-dominants live – to reveal it will require more than the examination of crude, arbitrary cruelties or exploitations' (Ardener 1989: 187, 186). I am less concerned here with the 'problem of consent' than with how, once we consent, we can nevertheless retain some freedom of manoeuvre.

A Nineteenth-Century Representation

In the nineteenth century, hysteria was a well-recognised pattern, mainly found in women. The middle-class woman was taught that aggression, independence, assertion and curiosity were male traits, inappropriate for women. Women's nature was emotional, power-less, passive and nurturant, and they were not expected to achieve in the public domain. Hysteria offered a solution to the onerous task of running a household, and of adjusting husband/wife or father/daughter relations, and it was one which did not challenge these core values.

The hysteric could opt out of her traditional duties and be relieved of responsibilities; as 'sick' she enjoyed sympathy and privileges whilst others assumed her tasks as a self-sacrificing wife, mother or daughter. The scope which this allowed for considerable, if ultimately limited, power in the household is superbly described by Proust in his characterisation of Aunt Léonie. Proust himself, like Darwin and Nightingale, was personally familiar with how the same role could offer the non-dominant individual extensive and sophisticated scope for autonomy and influence.

The development from simple conversion symptoms to a recognised discrete position as 'a hysteric' seems to provide a parody of some core social values: women's expected dependency and restricted social role, an exaggeration of the socially extruded female. The hysteric was characteristically female, the hysterical woman being perceived as the very embodiment of perverse femininity, an inversion of dominant male behaviour (Smith-Rosenberg 1972). Hysteria was a conventionally available alter-native behaviour pattern for certain women, which permitted them to express some dissatisfaction. Many of Freud's patients with hysterical symptoms were women who had been forced to sacrifice their public lives in nursing a sick relative. Employing this model, they might themselves take to their bed because of pain, paralysis or weakness, and remain there for months or years. What Freud was to term the 'secondary gain' conferred by the hysterical role allowed a limited adjustment of wife/husband power relations in the family: 'Ill health will be her one weapon for maintaining her position. It will procure for her the care she longs for... It will compel him to treat her with solicitude if she recovers; otherwise a relapse will threaten' (Freud 1946). The hysteric was engaged in a battle then, a battle fought with weapons from the armoury of men, double-voiced, a parody of male dominance but a strategic parody with certain very specific advantages. And yet, the general schema of power remained undisturbed. Turner (1984) argues that hysteria provided the Victorian bourgeoisie with a 'solution' for the perceived sexuality of their unmarried women in a period of delayed marriage.

The status of the 'hysteric' before Freud did not involve acceptance of individual responsibility for the illness. Male physicians, and men in general, employed biological arguments to rationalise this exaggeration of a traditional gender role as one immutably rooted in anatomy and pathophysiology (Smith-Rosenberg 1972). Female problems were deemed to be problems of biology, and hysteria was only their logical extension. As Freud's friend the gynaecologist Otto Weininger put it: 'Man possesses sexual organs; her sexual organs possess woman'; this was to be expected if, according to Moebius (*On the Physiological Imbecility of Women*), the woman was an intermediate form between the child and the adult. Thus the nineteenth-century view of women, or at least of bourgeois women, was of frail and decorative creatures whose temperamental excesses were the result of a peculiar functioning of their sexual organs and whose very physical nature limited their activities to family roles. The fact that these hysterical women tended to be particularly sexually attractive for men (Ellenberger 1970) was regarded by psychoanalysts as a clue to the pattern only in that a sexual (rather than a gender) aetiology was still implicated: repression rather than oppression.

The dominant male/passive female opposition which embodied the hysterical reaction was mirrored in the therapy: the rational physician actively relieving his passive patient from the grip of her nature. The pattern of symptoms of Charcot's patients has been described as 'a folie à deux...a culture-bound syndrome emerging from the interaction between the professor and his clientele', to be replaced later by a less dramatic pattern of diffuse somatic complaints (Eisenberg 1977). Such a counterposed female identity is particularly reinforced in collective and passive settings such as nurses' training schools, convents and boarding-schools, and these are the contemporary settings in which doctors still occasionally detect hysteria (Littlewood 1990): 'a picture of women in the words of men' (Chodoff and Lyons 1958).

A Contemporary Representation

To describe the social matrix of a pattern which has now virtually disappeared in Europe is not difficult. To examine one in which we ourselves are still embedded is less easy. A contemporary pattern which offers us some analogies with the relationship between doctor and patient in hysteria is 'parasuicide' with medical drugs. As in hysteria, the normative situation of active male (husband, doctor) and passive female (wife, patient) is reproduced, and reflected in the drama of the casualty department. The unease and anger which parasuicide evokes in the medical profession reflect its perverse transformation of the clinical paradigm.

In England and Wales more than one hundred thousand people are admitted to hospital each year after taking an overdose, and another forty thousand are treated in casualty departments. Eighty per cent of them are women. Why the idiom of drugs? Women are already closely identified with 'psychotropic' medication. It has been argued that physicians expect female patients to require a higher proportion of mood-altering drugs than 'less expressive' male patients (Cooperstock 1971). A study of people taking minor tranquillisers in Britain found that 67 per cent of them were women (Dunbar et al. 1989), a rate consistent with that of other industrialised nations.

That we are not dealing simply with a 'real' gender disparity in psychological distress – in which women require more medication simply because they are more depressed or anxious – is suggested by the symbolism of medical advertising. Women outnumber men by 15:1 in advertisements for minor tranquillisers and anti-depressants (Stimson 1975). A typical advertisement depicts the woman with a bowed head holding a dishcloth and standing beside a pile of dirty dishes represented larger than life size; the medical consumer is told that the drug 'restores perspective' for her by 'correcting the disturbed brain chemistry'. Employed women are rare in drug advertisements and women are usually shown as dependent house-wives and child-rearers: the world acts on them, they do not act on the world. Seidenberg (1974) and Chapman (1979) too found that psychotropic drug advertisements show women as the patients; they are represented as discontented with their role in life, dissatisfied with marriage, with washing dishes or with attending meetings of the parent-teacher association. The treating doctor is never depicted as a woman and all his patients appear as helpless and anxious.

While advertisements for psychotropic drugs tend to picture women as patients, those for other medications show men (Prather and Fidell 1975). Within the psychotropic drug category alone, women are represented with diffuse emotional symptoms, and men with discrete episodes of anxiety due to specific pressures from work or from associated physical ('real') disease. The men have problems located not in their nature but in their social position.

Overdoses in Britain are by far the most common form of parasuicide. They are particularly common among young women of Asian and White origin, less so among British Afro-Caribbeans (Merrill and Owens 1988). Of a group of patients who attended hospital following a non-fatal act of 'deliberate self-harm', ninety-five per cent had taken a drug overdose: half of the episodes involved interpersonal conflicts as the overt precipitating factor (Morgan et al. 1975). Only a minority described obvious plans to prepare for death or to avoid discovery, or subsequently regretted not having killed themselves. Doctors rate 'suicidal intent' and risk to life as low, especially as overdoses are usually taken with somebody close by (Hawton et al. 1982): sixty per cent carried out the act in the presence of or near other people. The medical debate on overdoses has concentrated on the 'genuineness' of the wish to die, with a terminological shift from 'attempted suicide' to 'parasuicide'. While the reasons given by the individual herself for taking an overdose may be described as symptomatic or expressive (explaining the overdose as the result of depression or personal predicament), they are frequently seen to be instrumental or pragmatic – that is, they are explicitly interpreted in terms of the desired consequences of the act, usually increased support or understanding (Bancroft et al. 1979). Overdoses have been interpreted as a standardised transaction between the woman and her intimate group (Kreitman et al. 1970); that they are culturally available patterns of adjusting one's situation is supported by the finding that they are concentrated in socially linked clusters of individuals and may follow other widely-reported episodes, real or fictional (Platt 1987). 'The individual within the "attempted suicide subculture" can perform an act which carries a preformed meaning: all [she] requires to do is invoke it' (Kreitman et al. 1970:465).

By contrast, O'Brien (1986) criticises the popular medical notion that overdoses are a trivial 'cry for help' and argues that, like anorexia nervosa, they can serve as a way of asserting control over a chaotic life. A study of fifty adolescent overdosers suggested that they themselves viewed their act as a means of gaining relief from a stressful situation or as a way of showing other people how desperate they felt; the staff who assessed their motives regarded them as symptomatic but noted that adolescents took overdoses 'in order to' punish other people or change their behaviour (Hawton et al. 1982). Typically, a teenage girl took tablets after a disappointment, frustration or difference of opinion with an older person (usually a parent); many reported afterwards that the induction of guilt in those whom they blamed for their distress had been a predominant motive for the act (Bancroft et al. 1979).

Thus, while overdoses may be seen at one level as strategies to avoid or adjust certain specific situations, the self-perception of the principal is one of social dislocation or extrusion. Her action exaggerates this extrusion, offering a threat of refusing membership in the human community altogether – an inversion of normal life-seeking norms. As in Tikopia (Firth 1961), 'attempted suicide' is, among other things, a dangerous adventure.

The conventional resolution of the inversion involves its complement: medical intervention returns the patient into everyday relationships. Not surprisingly, the overdose meets with little professional sympathy, particularly when it is interpreted as an instrumental mechanism rather than the sign of underlying individual hopelessness or psychiatric illness. Explanations communicating despair and a desire for withdrawal, escape or death are more acceptable and evoke more sympathy or readiness to help, in both doctors and nurses, than pragmatic explanations (Ramon et al. 1975).

Doctors tend to distinguish acts as either 'suicidal' (symptomatic) or 'manipulative' (instrumental), paralleling their perception of factitious illness as 'genuine' (hysterical) or 'false' (malingering). They are more accepting of the 'wish to die' motive, while nurses seem generally more sympathetic than do doctors to instrumental motives. Perhaps because of their ambiguous position in the B/S (doctor: patient:: male: female) equation (Littlewood 1990), nurses are more likely to perceive overdoses as legitimate attempts to escape from distress (Ramon et al. 1975). Women taking overdoses are regarded by doctors as a nuisance, extraneous to the real concerns of medicine and less deserving of medical care than patients with physical illnesses. This is especially so when the self-poisoning episode appears 'histrionic' (Hawton et al. 1981). As the *British Medical Journal* (1971) has put it, doctors 'feel a sense of irritation which they find difficult to conceal'. Women who take overdoses still gain access to medical care, despite the physician's antipathy, through the threat of death and the popular conception of suicidal behaviour as a discrete event, *something that happens to one,* rather than something one intentionally brings about (Ginsberg 1971). Immediate relatives may be less sympathetic (James and Hawton 1985). At one level then, it is accepted that the patient's action is outside her direct personal control, and responsibility is thereby attributed to some agency beyond her volition. (In the language of attribution theory, an *environmental* rather than a *dispositional* explanation (Shaver 1975)[2]). Thus we have the continuing use of the popular (and passive) term 'overdose' as opposed to (active) 'self-poisoning' or 'attempted suicide'.

The official translation of the event into symptoms takes place, under socially prescribed conditions, by the physician who alone has the power to legitimate exculpating circumstances. As with nineteenth-century hysteria, the resolution of the event invokes a 'mystical pressure' (Lewis 1966) which replicates the social structure in which the action or reaction occurs; like hysteria, it displays core structural antagonisms but shows they are 'soluble' at the individual level within the existing political and symbolic framework. The drama of the scene in the casualty department replays the male doctor/female patient theme without questioning it, but it does afford a degree of negotiation for the principal who induces a mixture of responses, mainly sympathy and guilt, sometimes anger, in close relatives and friends.

Symptoms, Struggles and Functions

The popular and medical understandings of the overdose – symptom of real suffering or duplicitous attempt at adjusting life? – are mirrored in academic literature on the topic, as is also the case with anorexia nervosa or 'women's illness' in general (Orbach 1986, Showalter 1987). Are they 'real' – thus aligning the medically-orientated therapist with the radical positivist who perceives them as the expression of the oppression of women (Chesler 1974), as male concerns written on the palimpsest of women's bodies – or are they ludic strategies, dangerous double-voiced parodies of patriarchal ascription, lateral strategies of resistance? I would argue that they can usefully be interpreted as both, and more.

If overdoses are an inscription of male power on women's bodies, they are (like anorexia nervosa) at one level inscribed by women themselves, even if this self-infliction can be experienced as a gain in control. We could argue that women *do* in a sense 'control' their own bodies – through dieting, depilation, sleeping in curlers, ear-piercing, liposuction, corsets – to achieve economic relationships with men, and thus achieve control over social relationships. Chesler (1974) suggests that they are 'conditioned to lose in order to win', and evokes the appeal of helplessness which Devereux (1970) characterises as *chantage masochiste* (masochistic blackmail), recalling the popular idea of 'emotional blackmail'. Devereux suggests millennial movements among peoples colonised by Europeans carry out the same kind of self-inflicted wounds: if I am powerless to stop you insulting me I can nevertheless obtain some aspect of your power by insulting myself (Anna Freud's 'identification with the aggressor'). Grottanelli (1985) similarly describes social waves of self-mutilation and castration as types of Luddite resistance against dominant norms, proletarian martyrdom as aggressive suicide, rebellion by refusal. We might note the parallels with recent interpretations of 'holy anorexia' – self-starvation in contexts whether religious or mundane where women are expected to suffer (Bynum 1988) – or with ethological models of submission behaviour which appear to verge on the suicidal, or indeed with patterns of courtship and physical sexuality[3].

If overdoses can be interpreted as instrumental (*function for*), as opposed to the medical and structural perception of them as products or reflections of 'stress' or disease (*functions of*), where is such instrumentality (which retains its symbolic dimension) located? We can start by asking the actors. In many instances a clear pragmatic intent to alter personal relations is verbally expressed by principals; in contrast, the functionality of anorexia nervosa lies in the therapist's explanations during family therapy; in other instances it can be located in our own, more distanced, analysis. It is inappropriate to assign a uniform 'meaning' to any action, particularly one which, once established, is available for fresh interpretations, sometimes in a derived form. What is instrumental for some may be expressive for others and our categories of instrumentality and pragmatics may, in any case, be quite different from the categories of the people concerned. In general, however, such actions or reactions can only continue when they involve a common assumption that participants are 'not aware' of any immediate goal, thus allowing social invocations of the compelling 'mystical sanctions' of biomedicine or of the spirit world. Ioan Lewis (1966) has argued that 'spirit possession' and neurotic patterns have an equivalence: the idiom of possession and disease alike remove personal responsibility for action and constrain others to assistance.

It is of course problematic to attempt to distinguish pragmatic from 'unconscious' participation, even in such obviously iatrogenic reactions as those of the late nineteenth-century vogue for multiple personality (Kenny 1986). In the case of work disability symptoms ('compensation neurosis'), the symptoms are now believed to continue longer after financial settlement than was formerly thought. (It is more appropriate in most instances to talk of identification or 'fit' with models than of 'intent' but a complete description of the transformations of participant experience and reflexive self-perception by cultural typification lies beyond the scope of this chapter.) While the precipitating event would appear on my model to be some type of excessive 'stretch' between the oppositions (Bateson's 'complementary schismogenesis') this may be no more representative of the central symbolic reactions than a relative loss of self-determination. Overdoses are more common in the working class. Not only women but men, particularly when unemployed, take overdoses. In these situations, the alignment of the individual with Butterfly in the B/S opposition is not an identification with women but an opposition to Serpent structures as represented by the dominant – parents, 'society' – powers that be. Interestingly, parasuicide among working-class men decreases after a Labour election victory but increases after a Conservative win (Masterton and Platt 1989).

A related question concerns sociological views of institutions as *functioning to* preserve social homeostasis, a point emphasised by many scholars following Max Gluckman. Conflicts, in this model, are taken as adjustment reactions for a society, allowing repressed impulses and potential rebellions to burn themselves out in harmless 'rituals'. As Kapferer (1979:121) points out, 'rituals [may] function to paper over and to resolve conflicts and tensions'. This may often be the case but it is not necessarily so. Arbitrarily isolating individual institutions as 'functional' is often little more than seeing how the total field of data under the observation of the fieldworker must somehow fit together to make sense (Leach 1970:120): indeed, it is only a disguised form of description[4]. If our reactions may be glossed by the observer as parodic 'rituals of rebellion' (Gluckman 1963), this is not the participants' exegesis even if they have experienced some enhanced control over their lives (O'Brien 1986). Nineteenth-century hysterics do not seem to have been conscious of their part in what De Swaan (1981) calls 'a revolt enacted as mental disease'.

Rituals can also lead, for those analysts who still favour a functionalist model, to the expression or unmasking of other tensions. (And at the Panglossian level of functionalist catharsis we can of course argue that worse conflicts were thereby avoided.) A common experience of family therapists working with neurotic patients is that therapy leads to marital separation; but we cannot assume in such instances that the illness simply 'masked' an inevitable separation. Therapeutic explanations and techniques carry their own models and implicit goals.

To what extent can the overdose itself be regarded as the direct representation of gender 'tensions' rather than as some relatively discrete adjustment reaction? The structural-functionalist models still attractive to some analysts of overdoses have the deceptive advantage of a hierarchy of causality, of allowing us to differentiate 'core' from 'adjustment' patterns. Their explanations assume that rituals are occasioned by social tensions and that they are merely occasions when the tensions find expression, with the assumption that the precipitating cause of the discrete episode is identical with the social themes demonstrated in it. While I would argue that patterns such as overdoses (and we may also wish to include a variety of 'neuroses' – agoraphobia, shoplifting, baby-snatching, perhaps bulimia and Munchausen's Syndrome by Proxy) do articulate the B/S opposition, the initial precipitating event may be relatively unconnected with these themes (although articulating the Butterfly's inaccessibility to everyday power). It is nevertheless professionally shaped in the course of medical diagnosis, exegesis and treatment along B/S lines; as the B/S relationship is present both between Butterfly and significant others before the reaction and in the biomedical construction of it, Butterfly's response becomes more truly Butterfly-like (the opposite of the psychotherapist's transference). Even after 'resolution' of the individual episode this sensitisation continues as a potential: 'Aspects of the everyday social experience and world of the actors are made to become explanations, or causes, of the illness event with which they have been brought into contact. Whether these explanations are antecedents to the illness event in the strictly logical sense often assumed in the functionalist argument is open to question' (Kapferer 1979:121).

Nevertheless, if the reactions reflect social oppositions, and show that they are 'soluble' at the individual level without being fundamentally challenged, they can be said to reinforce these oppositions.

The overdose raises questions which echo those raised by feminist debates on anorexia nervosa (Orbach 1986). Is it a disease or an attempt to gain control? A breakdown or a restitution? A wound or a healing? While the answer is perhaps located less in the phenomenology of the pattern itself than in the frame of analysis, the argument in favour of a 'rebellion', for example, would be supported if we found a communal organisation of the drama with simultaneous participants. In American women's colleges, collective bingeing and bulimic purging might constitute a sorority (like the 'mass hysteria' observed by doctors in convents and boarding-schools), but shared overdoses are rare in Britain. We do not know enough about their local meanings to argue whether or not they might be considered to be a 'rite of passage', say, from adolescence to adulthood, or from married to single status. Women's therapy groups regard the pattern as symptomatic, not as a rite for re-enactment.

The same phenomenon is susceptible of a variety of interpretations: reflection of social structure or product of 'stress'; social catharsis; social homeostasis; cultural loophole; individual catharsis; role reversal; theatre; entertainment; ritual reaffirmation of gender relationships; genesis of sorority; rite of passage; revolutionary prototype; expression or resolution of symbolic ambiguity; not to mention the simple expression of such impulses as distress, parody, play, adventure or revenge. I would suggest that overdoses may usefully be understood still in any of these ways, or all of them. Claims to the primacy of a particular interpretation ultimately remain structurally arbitrary, grounded in the observer's own academic and political perspective.

Notes

This chapter is a revision of a section of a paper originally published in 1987: 'The Butterfly and the Serpent: Culture, Psychopathology and Biomedicine', in *Culture, Medicine and Psychiatry*, II, 289–335. I am grateful to Byron Good, the editor of *CMP*, and to the co-author of the original paper, Maurice Lipsedge, for permission to reprint part of the text. In a joint paper it is difficult to recollect who originally wrote what but I should like to pay tribute to Dr Lipsedge with whom this argument was elaborated.

1. 'Or, a Staff of Aesculapius Gules within a bordure Sable charged with four Butterflies of the Field... And the Supporters are on either side a Serpent or Langued Gules'.

2. I would argue for a causal-linear association between the increase in overdoses over the thirty years since the 1961 Suicide Act has decriminalised deliberate self-harm; similarly with the medicalisation

of 'shop-lifting'. By contrast 'baby-snatching', not uncommon for a brief period in the early 1970s, was countered with punitive custodial sentences. 'Medicalisation' is itself double-voiced, engaging on the one hand with personalistic and dispositional interpretations, on the other with naturalistic and environmental ones.

3. Doubtless the possibilities are to an extent 'hard-wired', as some instances of 'personality disorder' in both sexes would indicate – where unusual EEG patterns are associated with a variety of 'passive' and 'self-destructive' behaviours; or self-damaging activity in brain-damaged children. However, these are not directly causal but contribute to a phenomenological world in which the individual has recourse to culturally standardised patterns.

4. While these interpretations are closer to Durkheim's collective functionalism ('The function of a social fact ought always to be sought in relation to some social end', Durkheim 1938:19) than to Malinowski's individual need-orientated functionalism, the principal's own interpretations are of course Malinowskian. If we seem to pass with 'modernisation' from collective calendrical ritual reversals of the Gluckman sort to individual problem-orientated patterns for which we find the term *ritual* inappropriate (e.g. Loudon 1959), the sense of *function* tends to shift from the collective to the individual, from the sociological to the psychological. Our 'data' choose their discipline. Giddens (1985) has extensively criticised the development of social theory for exaggerating 'the degree to which normative obligations are "internalised" by the members of societies [who] do the best they can with the parts prepared for them'. That we appear to find a general progression from periodic ritual, via possession states and hysteria, to overdoses is not to identify some sort of linear evolution (as many cultural psychiatrists still assume). My point is that the choice made by the devalued or the oppressed is from the available weapons. Kleinman (1986) has shown how, during the Chinese Cultural Revolution, the psychological shifted to the physical, and Good and Good (1988) suggest how the Iranian Revolution reframed the psychological into the politico-moral.

An instance: I was working as a doctor in Handsworth in Birmingham during the 1986 riots. These were perceived initially by the media as 'West Indian', directed against the predominantly White police and against local South-Asian-owned shops and businesses. An Asian postal worker was burned to death when the local post office was gutted. One Birmingham psychiatrist argued in evidence to the Silverman Inquiry into the riots that they were the work of cannabis-stoned young Afro-Caribbean men. The Inquiry and re-examination of television news and police video film, together with the ethnic origins of those prosecuted, suggested however that the rioters comprised White and Afro-Caribbean men in numbers proportional to the local population. And some women. And a few young men of Asian origin. The eventual press consensus was that this was no race riot but the frustration of the unemployed in a ghetto area who had destroyed their own neighbourhood in despair (Littlewood and Lipsedge 1989:276–281). Four days after the riots ended, I was telephoned by a local (Asian) general practitioner who asked me to visit a fifteen-year-old girl from Bangladesh who had been in Britain for two years. She lived with her family, spoke English and attended the local mixed secondary school. She was, he said briefly, hysterical.

Myself? White male. Psychiatrist.

The streets were still full of debris being cleared up, charred timbers, bricks and shards of glass. Along the neighbouring road many shops had been burned down, and those that remained had their shutters still up or boards nailed across the windows in case of further looting. The police had withdrawn to a discreet distance, and people were gathering on the broken pavements to assess the damage and exchange stories. The smell of burning still hung in the air but daily life was cautiously re-establishing its pattern. I stopped to talk to a café owner I knew who had just opened up again for business. He complained about a story on the local radio describing Asians burning down their own shops to collect the insurance. Turning the corner I found the house. No damage in this street. The family warily opened the door. I introduced myself. Hasmat (as I shall call her here) was in the downstairs room lying on the floor, eyes closed, occasionally thrashing about with her arms and legs, and shouting out something nobody could understand. Her parents stood about rather helplessly, placing cushions under her head, holding her hands and trying to calm her down. Every now and then this seemed to work. She got up and quietly joined the others and denied any knowledge of what was happening, assuring them of being quite well, appearing puzzled by their concern and drinking a tonic, but refusing food saying she was not hungry. Then she would collapse back onto the floor. Her father told me she had been like this, on and off, for two days, that she was seriously ill with fits and he was glad I had come to take her to the hospital. He was distressed but also, I thought, angry. Her elder brother called me aside and said in a loud whisper that she 'was putting it on' because she had been arguing with her father for months about going out in the evening with her school-friends. Another brother stood at the side, watching his concerned family with what seemed to me ironical amusement.

Having greeted Hasmat, I asked her father what they had been able to do to help her. He reluctantly agreed that he had taken his daughter to the mosque when she had started talking strangely (the general practitioner had told me this and also that he had told the father off for such 'nonsense'); someone at the mosque had said some (Qu'aranic?) verses over her to make the spirit leave but it had not worked of course because she was really sick, as the general practitioner had explained to him. Or else the spirit had left her sick. I stopped myself wondering who the spirit might have been and asked instead whether the family had lost anything in the riots. No, the father was a foundry worker. No property. No one they knew had been hurt. The riots were nothing to do with them. I persisted. Could the riots be the cause of Hasmat's distress? He said no: how can riots, however terrible, make people have fits?

I thought he was probably right and asked the family to leave, saying I wanted to talk with Hasmat alone. Standard psychiatry. I told her she was upset by something. She gazed at me, past me. I felt uncomfortable. Somehow embarrassed. In between episodes of behaviour that recalled to me the robot in Fritz Lang's *Metropolis*, she asked me to promise to keep a secret. I agreed reluctantly. If I *was* a doctor, she said, shouldn't I now examine her? I declined hastily. What then was the secret? What had happened? She recounted how, on the morning after the rioting ended, she and her brother's wife (aged nineteen) had secretly unpadlocked the door (her father had secured it firmly from the inside when the looting spread down the neighbouring road), and had gone out to have a look, 'for fun'. Terrified (deliciously terrified, I thought) at the devastation, they had returned immediately without anyone else in the family knowing. She had seen a boy from her school and thought he might attack her. Why? Just thought he might. Back in the house she had 'felt dizzy' and was still unwell. That was all. Could I tell her father she was sick but that it was not serious and she could not go into the hospital? I called the family back and told them that Hasmat had become ill (I said 'ill') because of the awful things which had been happening but that she would soon be well without any medicine. What was the sickness then? Well, she was 'weak'. They looked nonplussed. I suggested she had something to eat and said I would call again the next day together with a Bengali community worker (a local housewife who was training part-time in counselling). That afternoon I got a telephone call from the GP who had been round to see how I had got on. Hasmat seemed much better. He congratulated me (ironically?) on my successful intervention, saying that he had reinforced my advice but that the family nevertheless felt let down because I did not seem very interested. No treatment, no hospital. He had given her some sleeping-tablets to keep everybody happy, a placebo for the whole family as he put it. Did I agree? Well, why not? The next day the father left a message for me at the hospital: his daughter was much better, thanks, and they felt they didn't want a psychiatrist or a community worker coming again. I telephoned back and said OK, could they make an appointment with my secretary for the next week? He said he would try. They didn't. The general practitioner dropped by and told me everything was back to normal, and so I forgot about the whole business. About a month later I was contacted by the West Midlands Poisons Unit for details of my patient, who had just taken an overdose of tranquillisers.

The full details of the family dynamics, of its political context, and its 'ultimate' resolution (on the whole happy, I think) are beyond the scope of this chapter. I merely want to note here the ambiguities of power, and the choices and identifications which are available in different models, each with their own personal experiences and external ideologies, including of course my own as a White male biomedic, embedded in and controlling (in some part) the process – and as the not entirely distanced White male writer of this paper. The events seem to condense down in a single representation what we define as distinct perceptions and processes, the religious, the medical, the psychological, the sexual and the political. And yet there is a unity.

References

Ardener, E. (1989), 'The Problem of Dominance' in Ardener, *The Voice of Prophecy and other Essays*, ed. M Chapman. Oxford: Blackwell (paper originally published in 1981).

Bancroft, J., Hawton, K., Simpins, S., Kingston, B., Cumming, C. and Whitwell, D. (1979), 'The Reasons People Give for Taking Overdoses', *British Journal of Medical Psychology*, 52, pp.353–365.

British Medical Journal (1971), (Editorial) 'Suicide Attempts', II:483.

Broverman, I.D., Broverman, D.M., Clarkson, F.E., Rosenkrantz, P.S. and Vogel, S.R. (1970), 'Sex Role Stereotypes and Clinical Judgements of Mental Health', *Journal of Consulting and Clinical Psychology*, 34:1–7.

Bynum, C.W. (1988), 'Holy Anorexia in Modern Portugal', *Culture, Medicine and Psychiatry*, 12:239–248.

Chapman, S. (1979), 'Advertising and Psychotropic Drugs: The Place of Myth in Ideological Reproduction', *Social Science and Medicine,* 13:751–764.

Chesler, P. (1974), *Women and Madness*. London: Allen Lane.

Chodoff, P. and Lyons, H. (1955), 'Hysteria, the Hysterical Personality and Hysterical Conversion', *American Journal of Psychiatry*, 114:734–740.

Cooperstock, R. (1971), 'Sex Differences in the Use of Mood-Modifying Drugs: An Explanatory Model', *Journal of Health and Social Behaviour*, 12:238–244.

De Swaan, A. (1981), 'The Politics of Agoraphobia', *Theory and Society*, 10:359–385.

Devereux, G. (1970), *Essais d'Ethnopsychiatrie Générale*. Paris: Gallimard.

Dunbar, G.C., Perera, M.H. and Jenner, F.A. (1989), 'Patterns of Benzodiazepine Use in Great Britain as Measured by a General Population Survey', *British Journal of Psychiatry*, 155:836–841.

Durkheim, E. (1938), *The Rules of Sociological Method*. New York: Free Press.

Easlea, B. (1980), *Witch Hunting, Magic and the New Philosophy: An Introduction to Debates of the Scientific Revolution 1450–1750*. Sussex: Harvester Press.

Eisenberg, L. (1977), 'Disease and Illness: Distinctions between Professional and Popular Ideas of Sickness', *Culture, Medicine and Psychiatry*, 1:9–23.

Ellenberger, H. (1970), *The Discovery of the Unconscious: The History and Evolution of Dynamic Psychiatry*. London: Allen Lane.

Firth, R. (1961), 'Suicide and Risk-taking in Tikopia Society', *Psychiatry*, 2:1–17.

Freud, S. (1946), 'Fragment of an Analysis of a Case of Hysteria', *Collected Works, Vol.55–56*. London: Hogarth.

Giddens, A. (1985), *The Constitution of Society: Outline of the Theory of Structuration*. Cambridge: Cambridge University Press.

Ginsberg, G.P. (1971), 'Public Conceptions and Attitudes about Suicide', *Journal of Health and Social Behaviour*, 12:200–201.

Gluckman, M. (1963), *Order and Rebellion in Tribal Africa*. London: Cohen and West.

Good, B.J. and Good, M.-J.D. (1981), 'The Meaning of Symptoms: A Cultural Hermeneutic Model for Clinical Practitioners', in L.Eisenberg and A.Kleinman (eds.) *The Relevance of Social Science for Medicine*. Dordrecht: Reidel.

Good, M.-J.D. and Good, B. (1988) 'Ritual, the State and the Transformation of Emotional Discourse in Iranian Society', *Culture, Medicine and Psychiatry*, 12:43–63.

Grottanelli, C. (1985), 'Archaic Forms of Rebellion and Their Religious Background' in B.Lincoln (ed.), *Religion, Rebellion and Revolution*. London: Macmillan, pp.15–45.

Hawton, K., Marsack, P. and Fagg, J. (1981), 'The Attitudes of Psychiatrists to Deliberate Self-Poisoning: Comparison with Physicians and Nurses', *British Journal of Medical Psychology*, 54:341–348.

Hawton, K., Osborne, M. and Cole, D. (1982), 'Adolescents who take Overdoses: Their Characteristics, Problems and Contacts with Helping Agencies', *British Journal of Psychiatry*, 140:118–125.

Hibbard, J.J. and Pople, C.R. (1983), 'Gender Roles, Illness Orientation and Use of Medical Services', *Social Science and Medicine*, 17:129–137.

Horwitz, A. (1977), 'The Pathways into Psychiatric Treatment: Some Differences Between Men and Women', *Journal of Health and Social Behaviour*, 18:169–178.

Ingleby, D. (1982), 'The Social Construction of Mental Illness', in P.Wright and A.Treacher (eds) *The Problem of Medical Knowledge*. Edinburgh: Edinburgh University Press.

James, C.W.B. (1963), 'Psychology and Gynaecology', in A.Cloge and A.Bourne (eds.) *British Gynaecological Practice*. London: Heinemann.

James, D. and Hawton, K. (1985), 'Overdoses: Explanations and Attitudes in Self-Poisoners and Significant Others', *British Journal of Psychiatry*, 146:481–485.

Jordanova, L. (1989), *Sexual Visions: Images of Gender in Science and Medicine Between the 18th and 19th Centuries*. Hemel Hempstead: Harvester.

Kapferer, B. (1979), 'Mind, Self and Other in Demonic Illness', *American Ethnologist*, 6:110–133.

Kenny, M.G. (1986), *The Passion of Ansel Bourne: Multiple Personality in American Culture.* Washington: Smithsonian Institution Press.

Kleinman, A. (1986), *Social Origins of Distress and Disease: Depression, Neurasthenia and Pain in Modern China.* New Haven: Yale University Press.

Kreitman, N., Smith, P. and Tan, E-S. (1970), 'Attempted Suicide as Language', *British Journal of Psychiatry*, 116:465–473.

Kreitman, N. and Screiber, M. (1979), 'Parasuicide in Young Edinburgh Women', *Psychological Medicine*, 9:469–479.

La Fontaine, J. (1981), 'The Domestication of the Savage Male', *Man (n.s.)*, 16:333–349.

Leach, E. (1970), 'The Epistemological Background to Malinowski's Empiricism' in R.Firth (ed.) *Man and Culture: An Evaluation of the Work of Bronislaw Malinowski.* London: Routledge and Kegan Paul.

Leach, E. (1983), 'Introduction', in E.Leach and D.A.Aycock (eds) *Structuralist Interpretations of Biblical Myth.* Cambridge: Cambridge University Press.

Lewis, I.M. (1966), 'Spirit Possession and Deprivation Cults', *Man (n.s.)*, 1:307–329.

Littlewood, R. (1980), 'Anthropology and Psychiatry: An Alternative Approach', *British Journal of Medical Psychology*, 53:213–225.

Littlewood, R. (1991), 'Gender, Role and Sickness: The Ritual Psychopathologies of the Nurse', in P.Holden and J.Littlewood (eds) *Nursing and Anthropology.* London: Routledge.

Littlewood, R. and Lipsedge, M. (1989), *Aliens and Alienists: Ethnic Minorities and Psychiatry*, revised edition, London: Unwin Hyman.

Loudon, J.R. (1959), 'Psychogenic Disorders and Social Conflict Among the Zulu' in M.K.Opler (ed.), *Culture and Mental Health.* New York: Macmillan.

Masterton, G. and Platt, S. (1989), 'Parasuicide and General Elections', *British Medical Journal*, 298:803–4.

Merrill, J. and Owens, J. (1988), 'Self-Poisoning among Four Immigrant Groups', *Acta Psychiatrica Scandinavica*, 77:77–80.

Miles, A. (1988), *The Neurotic Woman: The Role of Gender in Psychiatric Illness.* New York: New York University Press.

Morgan, H.G., Burns-Cox, C.J., Pocock, H. and Pottle, S. (1975), 'Deliberate Self-Harm: Clinical and Socioeconomic Characteristics of 368 Patients', *British Journal of Psychiatry*, 127:574–579.

O'Brien, S. (1986), *The Negative Scream*. London: Kegan Paul.

Orbach, S. (1978), *Fat is a Feminist Issue*. London: Paddington.

Orbach, S. (1986), *Hunger Strike*. London: Faber.

Parsons, T. (1951), 'Illness and the Role of the Physician: A Sociological Perspective', *American Journal of Orthopsychiatry*, 21:452–460.

Phillips, D.L. and Segal, B. (1969), 'Sexual Status and Psychiatric Symptoms', *American Sociological Review*, 29:678–687.

Platt, S. (1987), 'The Aftermath of Angie's Overdose: Is Soap (Opera) Damaging to your Health?' *British Medical Journal*, 294:954–957.

Prather, J. and Fidell, L. (1975) 'Sex Differences in the Content and Style of Medical Advertisements', *Social Science and Medicine*, 9:23–26.

Ramon, S., Bancroft, J.H.J. and Skrimshire, A.M. (1975), 'Attitudes to Self-Poisoning Among Physicians and Nurses in a General Hospital', *British Journal of Psychiatry*, 127:257–264.

Raymond, J.C. (1982), 'Medicine as a Patriarchal Religion', *Journal of Medicine and Philosophy*, 7:197–216.

Scott, R.D. (1973), 'The Treatment Barrier', *British Journal of Medical Psychology*, 46:45–55.

Seidenberg, R. (1974), 'Images of Health, Illness and Women in Drug Advertising', *Journal of Drug Issues*, 4:264–267.

Shaver, K.G. (1975), *An Introduction to Attribution Processes*. Cambridge, Mass.: Winthrop.

Showalter, E. (1987), *The Female Malady: Women, Madness and English Culture 1830–1980*. London: Virago.

Smith-Rosenberg, C. (1972), 'The Hysterical Woman: Sex Roles and Conflict in 19th Century America', *Social Research*, 39:652–678.

Stimson, G. (1975), 'Women in a Doctored World', *New Society*, 32:265–266.

Turner, B. (1984), *The Body and Society: Explorations in Social Theory*. Oxford: Blackwell.

Wilson, P.J. (1967), 'Status Ambiguity and Spirit Possession', *Man (n.s.)*, 2:366–378.

Young, A. (1976), 'Some Implications of Medical Beliefs and Practices for Social Anthropology', *American Anthropologist*, 78:5–24.

4

Drinking and Social Identity in the West of France

Maryon McDonald

Introduction

This chapter concentrates on one part of the world which has long gathered a reputation for merriment and festive excess. The area in question is Brittany, in the western part of France.

Seen from Great Britain, France as a whole easily appears to be one of the stars of the drinking world. Its consumption of alcohol (measured in chemistry's pure ethyl alcohol per inhabitant) has often been more than double that of the UK. Within France, however, such attention is turned to the 'West'. A large region known as *L'Ouest* ('the West'), running roughly from Normandy down to the Loire-Atlantique, and including both, has frequently occupied the top symbolic niche in the French statistical drinking tables. Some of the *départements* of this area were already topping the national table of consumption per *département* in the 1880s (Fillaut 1984:379). Within this West of France, however, it is Brittany particularly which has regularly received the symbolic accolade of the most heavily drinking, drunken and alcoholic area. This is an image which seems to have gained a firm foothold in the nineteenth century, and it has persisted since.

It is interesting to note that, at the time of its construction, this image had no support from available statistics – an important lack of 'evidence' in a nation then in the grip of statistical self-obsession. There was an increase in alcohol consumption in Brittany, as in other parts of France, during the nineteenth century (Prestwich 1988:4–5) and there was also an increase in numerical and statistical representation. However, figures established between the 1880s and the early years of this century, for example, clearly suggest that within the West of France, it was Normandy and the Mayenne who were by far the highest consumers of alcohol, and figures established for deaths from cirrhosis of the liver indicate that the urban and wine-growing areas of France, among which Brittany does not figure, were well ahead. Brittany was at the bottom of the regional table (Fillaut 1983a:chapter 2; 1984:378).

At the turn of the century, there were some scholars and medical doctors who both became aware of, and were surprised by, the apparent discrepancy between the image that was being created of Brittany and the 'evidence' of the figures, and there was protest at the region's heavy-drinking image from within Brittany itself (Lavarenne 1901; Falher et al. 1906; also Fillaut 1980:1). It would now seem naïve to treat the available statistics (or indeed, any statistics) as simple factuality, and there are many questions about them which must remain unanswered. In general, however, the questions we might ask of them, and the problems we might find in them, could be asked and found for the figures relating to other regions also. The nineteenth- and early twentieth-century image of Bretons as especially heavy drinkers seems to derive from structures of moral apperception external to what was actually going on within the region. At the same time, an image of heavy drinking was one for which a nineteenth-century visitor to Brittany could find empirical confirmation of a kind. These are points to which we shall return in a moment.

Turning from the past to the present, we find that the statistical picture has changed. Since the 1920s and 1930s, Brittany has moved up the tables, reaching the top in the 1950s. Until very recently jostled by the Nord-Pas-de-Calais region, Brittany has been top of the French tables for mortality from both cirrhosis of the liver (about one and a half times the national average) and especially 'alcoholism' (covering both the international categories of 'alcoholism' and 'alcoholic psychosis', and reaching over twice the French national average[1]). In the construction of these modern statistics, the historical image of Bretons as heavy drinkers has undoubtedly weighed heavily. Death from causes deemed to be alcohol-related in some way is far more likely to be found on a death certificate in Brittany than on one from elsewhere. It has already been calculated that, in France overall, about twice the number of deaths are certified as due to 'unknown' or non-specific causes as they are in parts of Brittany (and precisely in those parts of Brittany where 'alcoholism' is readily assumed to be a cause; see Caro and Bertrand 1981:25–6). However, we cannot account for the mortality differences wholly in these terms, and modern Brittany has had equally starred ratings in tables of alcohol consumption (see especially HCEIA 1984). Many areas of social life in parts of contemporary Brittany are indeed afloat on alcohol. The reasons for this lie, in priority, in the present – in values and ideas at the local level through which alcohol now gains its meaning – although historicist explanation is common.

One historicist explanation involves the Breton language, which about 500,000 people in Lower Brittany still speak. In the circles of the Breton language movement in Brittany, and in the writings of those who work with similar political assumptions, it is common to learn that Bretons drink so much because of the 'traumatism' of language difference: Bretons have had French imposed on them in the schools, and they may well be drinking to drown the sorrows of being French (see, for example, Bertrand and Caro 1977). This history in which Bretons have, over the last two hundred years, been 'traumatised' by an 'imposition' of French is a history constructed out of modern political preoccupations on the part of the Breton language movement, and tells us more about these preoccupations than about the past of which it pretends to speak (McDonald 1989a). We have no evidence that the language issue contributed to heavy drinking in Brittany, and the historicist framework in which it is implicated fails to explain why the non-Breton-speaking parts of Brittany, and areas outside Brittany altogether, have sometimes been well ahead in the alcohol tables. The language issue has, however, undoubtedly contributed quite directly to an *image* of Bretons as heavy drinkers.

How then did the Bretons manage to acquire, in the nineteenth century, the image of being heavy drinkers – an image which they gained before apparently warranting it? The paragraphs of the next section attempt to set out just a few of the factors involved.

'Once a Breton, Always an Alcoholic'

Eighteenth- and nineteenth-century French politics played an important role. The 1789 Revolution, and events which followed, helped to give Brittany an enduring image of difference, a more robust tradition of oddity and resistance to change than, say, Normandy. The political spotlight was cast on the large, reactionary West, but it was particularly on Brittany that it shone. This was partly due to the existence of the Breton language and to the political, moral and intellectual investments made in it by certain nobles and priests during the battles surrounding the creation of the French (and, by definition, French-speaking) Republic. This was a

Republic to which many members of the clergy and nobility were, of course, opposed. In other words, Brittany came to the fore partly because Brittany received more attention. If there were odd or troublesome things going on in the West, the weight of prejudice through much of the nineteenth century was that it was most likely in Brittany that they were happening.

The riotous Bretons already constituted a conceptually ripe category then for a place in any table of social problems. It was bound to be the Bretons who were downing alcohol in a country beginning, in the second half of the nineteenth century, to problematize certain modes of drinking. The statistical indications which might have contested this were further rendered powerless by empirical confirmation coming from the observations of travellers to Brittany, a terrain in which events were already prejudged. The 1789 Revolution and Napoleon's Celtic Academy had launched an interest in 'popular traditions' comprising all that was curious, irrational and uncivilized, and bound to disappear. Since the eighteenth century, Brittany had served as one ready site for the location of the odd and the primitive, and this picture of the area gained coherence during the nineteenth century with the promotion of schooling, and through romanticism and folklore studies. In thinking about themselves and defining their own characteristics, the dominant rationalities of Europe both sought and constructed on their boundaries their own moral contraries. The 'Celt' was one such contrary thrown by the thought and theory of majority society on to its own moral and geographical boundaries. Brittany was made Celtic in language and ethnology, and became the place to go to find the primitive savagery and irrationality which, whether in condemnation or celebration, the self-consciously rational French nation was, like other nations, actively constructing on its peripheries, at its own conceptual frontiers (McDonald 1989a). The increasing number of travellers who came to Brittany in the nineteenth century already knew what to expect.

It is now well established in anthropology that when different cultural or conceptual worlds meet, they do not match up neatly, and this lack of 'fit' regularly leads to misunderstanding (Ardener 1982; McDonald 1989a, 1989b, 1993). The rural Breton world which moved, in riot or splendour, around the categories, events and proprieties of the travellers' own world, could easily offer confirmation of the image, positive or negative, which the observers brought with them. The different drinking culture which the travellers encountered joined with other cultural mismatches to become wildness and anarchy, savagery and irrationality, disorder and excess. The travellers were urbane, educated men, most of them from Paris. In their world, normal drinking was already involving taste and proprieties of an oenological kind which we might still recognize. In rural Brittany, these men encountered a world of different proprieties, and one which to them was therefore confirmed as being devoid of rules, control, moral order and manners. They did not encounter the delicacy, taste, quality-appreciative drinking of salon conviviality; instead they encountered loud, celebratory, quantity-concentrated bouts of drinking with inebriates rolling in ditches. Reports of this abound. (For a catalogue of such reports, see Fillaut 1980, 1983a and 1983b; Audibert 1984.) Here indeed were uncouth, uncivilized bumpkins, strangers to order, control, reason and progress.

The empirical confirmation of these travellers' convictions was often concentrated and unrelenting. The scenes which these observers encountered were the festive drinking scenes of special occasions. Drinking, in this local culture, was to get drunk, and getting drunk meant behaving in a manner visibly different from the expectations of everyday life. Noise and visible rolling and prostration seem to have been important. This was the drinking of an episodic and celebratory drinking culture, the drinking of special feast days, of family occasions (including both weddings and funerals), the drinking of Sundays (usually after Mass), or the drinking of market days and fairs. It was not an everyday drinking and those whom the travellers saw may well not have drunk another drop from one special occasion to the next. The travellers and artists, however, were inevitably drawn to the special occasion, the festivities, the traditional and picturesque, the costumes and the ritual. In pursuit of traditions and curiosities, they inevitably pursued the occasions of drink and drunkenness, encountering each time a mode of drinking which did not match their own and in which they could find only surfeit and disorder. Bretons, apparently, did little more than drink to excess and roll in ditches.

It is worth bearing in mind that these observations came from, and gained conviction in, a metropolitan world which was consuming more alcohol and dying from higher rates of cirrhosis of the liver. Nevertheless, it was the Bretons who drank. The observers had seen it for themselves.

Travellers' reports both fed into, and were in turn confirmed by, legislation against public drunkenness (on which, see Barrows 1979; Fillaut 1983a, 1983b; Prestwich 1988). Legislation against *ivresse*

publique was introduced in the 1870s and 1880s. A watchful eye
was kept on Brittany and, predictably enough perhaps, it was
Finistère – the westernmost and most Breton-speaking
département of Brittany – which topped the tables straightaway
for the number of prosecutions for public disorderly behaviour
under this regime.

A further factor giving conviction to the 'drunken Breton' image,
and the danger that drinking posed to public morals, was the
attitude of the clergy – for whom, increasingly, sin, drink and
republicanism seemed to merge. Some areas of social life which,
prior to the 1789 Revolution, had been under the control of the
Church, had since been secularized. Public carousing, of which the
local clergy seemed to approve in the early years of the nineteenth
century, was increasingly outside the Church's ambit by the middle
of the century (Ogès 1953). The growing uneasiness of the clergy
was, moreover, something which local republicans exploited.
Cabarets became places where drink and political opposition to
the clergy mingled, and the bars became – and have often remained
– favourite locales for political meetings.

Certain modes of drinking became definitively problematized
from the 1870s onwards. Clerical conviction that drink was
somehow at the root of radicalism was joined in the 1870s by a
very much more general fear in France about the 'demoralization' of
the country and the 'degeneration' of the French nation (Nye 1982,
1984; Pick 1989; Prestwich 1988). Defeat by Prussia and the uprising
of the Paris Commune were two major events at this time which
both gave rise to and confirmed a structure of interpretation in
which 'alcoholism' took hold as an important explanatory idea.
Alcoholism was invoked as both symptom and cause of France's
apparent instability, vulnerability and decline. Moral reform of the
peasantry and the working classes generally was agreed to be
essential, and medicine was now to play a role (Barrows 1979; Borel
1968; Fillaut 1983a). What had once been an offence against public
morals was now medicalized as a 'disease'. Some argument ensued
between the clergy and members of the growing profession of
medicine, but as psychiatry became confidently established so
alcohol issues were firmly placed in the domain of, and defined
by, the medical doctor. 'Alcoholism' became a paradigm of mental
illness, and 'alcoholic' part of educated vocabulary. By the turn of
the century, the expression *Bretons et alcooliques toujours* (which we
might translate as 'Once a Breton, always an alcoholic') was
becoming a common depiction of Breton drinking habits.

The idea is now well established that Bretons have always been prone to heavy, uncontrolled drinking. The story is made both radical and historicist, with a supposed continuity of drinking habits stretching back from the contemporary Breton to the ancient Celt – an ethnological fiction invoked as ancestor. (On the invention of the 'Celts', see Chapman 1978; McDonald 1986b, 1989a: chapter 6.) Two major stages are involved in the construction of this story. First of all, contemporary drinking cultures are read back into the nineteenth century, with traveller's reports of the time drawn on as clear-sighted observational evidence. Then this drinking of the nineteenth century is read back into the world of the ancient Celts – this time with classical writers' reports of Celtic festiveness similarly assumed to be unproblematic proof and truth. The two stages are often collapsed, and the more so since nineteenth-century writers themselves were already looking to classical writers for further confirmation of their own observations. However, the 'Celt' was but one metaphor of the odd and barbaric summoned in the self-definition of ancient civilization's own boundaries. Cultural difference was interpreted by the classical writers rather in the way I have already described for the nineteenth-century travellers' tales of the rural Bretons. There is a structural and metaphorical similarity, therefore, in the relations between the classical world and its periphery, and those between educated France (or Britain) and its periphery; however, there is neither racial nor cultural continuity between ancient 'Celts' and modern Bretons. If any continuity exists, it is in a continuity of interpretation of one culture through the assumptions and ideas of another – resulting in various constructs of disorder and reversal on the frontiers of the interpreting culture's own self-defining normality and rationality (McDonald 1993). The continuity resides in the process of interpretation and misinterpretation. Nevertheless the image of *Bretons et alcooliques toujours* is regularly sustained, in uncritical writing and argument, by reference to some essential and enduring quality imagined to inhere in a people called Celts.

In their uncritical collapse of millennia, those who have gone back in this way from modern Brittany to ancient Celts have been able to take in, *en route*, Breton sailors of the Middle Ages. Breton sailors were actively involved in the wine trade, especially from the fourteenth to the seventeenth centuries, transporting wine between, for example, Bordeaux and England. They were allowed rations of wine for themselves and were known for their drink and drinking. For nineteenth-century observers preoccupied by contemporary ideas about 'alcoholism', Brittany seemed self-evidently a proper locus of concern. It became possible and plausible to construct a history from contemporary peasant disorder back to medieval sailors and then back to the Celts of ancient times, with observers reading their own nineteenth-century, medicalized moralities back into the past, and conflating the ethnological drinking fictions born of contemporary mismatch, or cross-cultural incongruity, at each stage. Such an edifice of historicist misinterpretation is still inhabited by many writers, administrators and psychiatrists in Brittany today.

Occupation, Locality and Gender

The idea that Bretons drink heavily – an idea which owed much to the kinds of cultural mismatch I have suggested – was gradually given substance by changes in modes of drinking within Brittany itself.

Several factors contributed to these changes, including improved communications in the latter part of the nineteenth century, rural-urban migrations, an increase in markets and fairs between the 1870s and the 1930s, a corresponding increase in wholesale and retail drinking licences and outlets, and an increase in production and consumption in France generally, which made alcoholic drink already relatively cheap to buy by the end of the nineteenth century. All these changes both encouraged and were consonant with a general and growing appropriation, by the countryside, of both the drinks and aspects of the drinking modes of the towns. Military service and then the First World War brought a recognizable version of urban masculinity as an image of the ideal man, and part of this image involved the consumption of alcoholic drink, especially wine. Wine was increasingly assimilated, at local and national levels, to ideas of manliness, Frenchness and hardy good health (Barthes 1972). This was so to the point that at one stage 'alcohol' and any associated evils came, in national debate, to imply only the industrial alcohols increasingly produced in the north of France. Wine, on the other hand, was what a true and healthy Frenchman drank. Soldiers in the First World War were positively encouraged to drink a ration of it, and temperance movements in France have never taken the profoundly 'unFrench' step of recommending abstinence from wine (Prestwich 1988).

Several modes of drinking now co-exist in Brittany, with features of older modes of drinking persisting alongside newer modes, or with the older structure taking on new content. Wine, for example, has replaced cider in many homes but may be served in the same old bowls, cups or tumblers, full to the brim. There is now immoderate festive drinking, the drinking of special occasions, the drinking of worldly men, drinking with work, drinking after work, social drinking and some integrated drinking with meals. Some of these modes coexist, and some have collapsed into each other. An immoderate, festive, episodic drinking culture has encountered a daily drinking culture and has become an immoderate, daily drinking culture. Alcohol has become an important non-linguistic medium pervading much of the daily round of many people in Brittany. This would be especially true of men in manual occupations.

My own research has been carried out in the central, mountainous area of western Finistère, in Lower Brittany. Within Brittany, this is deemed to be one of the dark areas of alcoholic concentration. In the following paragraphs, I draw out three important axes of identification: occupation, locality and gender. Of course, these are only three of many possible modes of identification, and their daily reality is far more subtle and contextual than any written text of this length could present. The point to note here is that, in the way they are lived in everyday life, these modes of identification, through which person and substance alike take their moral shape, contain within themselves important imperatives to drink.

Occupation

Agriculture, mostly on small, owner-occupied dairy farms, constitutes by far the largest single occupational category in this mountain area. Agricultural occupations can carry with them here a strong cultural compulsion to drink. There exists an ideal which could be summarised as self-sufficient sobriety and collective inebriety – although the latter may interfere with the former and the balance is often delicate. A good farm is run by a hard-working provider and head of household (generally expressed as *un bon père de famille* in French, or *ur gwaz* in Breton). Part of this involves participation in a strict system of reciprocity for mutual help in agricultural labour. A good provider will always want to see himself on the credit side, but no one gets any help who is not likely to be able to realise the same aspiration.

Cider came to this area in the late nineteenth century and by the end of the century it was available in the fields in a good year at the time of important collective works, notably hay-making and the harvests. Progressively, cider gave way to wine and the German occupation of the Second World War helped to institutionalise the idea that all *travailleurs de force*, agricultural and manual workers, required a ration of red wine (Barre 1984:235–6). Older systems of hospitality and payment have now joined with newer images of 'real men' derived from military service, and the fact that agriculture in the fields has become a predominantly male occupation. At the time of any collective work – weeding, harvesting or silage-making, for example – bottles of red wine litter the edges of the fields. Wine has to be served regularly to each worker, using the same glass for each, and filling it to the brim. Without this drink, labour would be hard to get, and tales of meanness and of a stuck-up unwillingness to drink with the lads spread fast. When viewed from other occupations, or from other systems of agriculture, the mode and amount of drinking in the fields in this part of Brittany can seem excessive, and out of place and immoral. For those from elsewhere for whom drink is synonymous with recreation, it becomes difficult to take this work seriously. This was very much the view of a visiting delegation of British farmers I once met in these parts – visitors from a world in which 'agriculture' and 'wine' alike are very different realities. In the mountains of Brittany, however, drinking and offering drinks in this way are very much a part of knowing how to run a farm.

A similar drinking culture is sometimes found transposed to other occupations, especially by those from recent agricultural backgrounds. This is so in the collective work of building, for example. Wine is commonly placed on site for the building workers daily, and also served to them at the end of each significant stage of the construction work. One local municipal councillor left no wine for builders employed to build him a smart new house. He even made statements about drink and work not mixing well. Anti-drinking discourse has been difficult to establish in France generally (see Prestwich 1988), and can imply unFrenchness or snobbery or simple meanness. This councillor lost his seat at the next election. He ostentatiously bought rounds of drinks after the election results and boasted of his days of camaraderie in the Resistance. All this came too late, however. 'He never left any wine for the builders, you know' was a common and persistent comment about him, both during and after the election campaign.

Drinking is incorporated not only into the work but also into the homes of the agricultural milieu, as part of general hospitality. This is not quite the same as the drinking which occurs in the homes of the non-agricultural milieu. Alcoholic drink – usually red wine – has to be offered in peasant homes to any male visitor who may call, at any time of the day or night. This can pose difficulties for those in other occupations – those who supply animal feed or fuel, for example, to the farms – who do not wish to lose custom and who must therefore accept a drink at each farm where they make a delivery. They have to take care to remember that this is not drinking which allows drunkenness of a kind that might suggest recreation or foolery. Some salesmen perceive a problem here, for themselves or for the locals or for both, but most seem to praise the hospitality in the mountains.

Sometimes a group of male visitors arrive *en piste* (which is rather like an extended pub or bar crawl, but involving one home after another in this area). This is a common form of recreation indulged in at weekends or after a group visit to a calf market, for example. Money is usually left on the table of the host. This enables the visiting drinkers to remain on the credit side, and ensures, it is said, that there will be a supply of wine for the next time round. During this kind of drinking, or during festive drinking (at New Year, for instance) or drinking at the end of collective agricultural work, then a visible drunkenness among the men is normal. The event is deemed a success if tales of drunken shouting, singing, laughter and loudness can afterwards be told. If someone falls over or ends up lying on the table, then a good time must have been had by all. Every man should be ready to get drunk. Drink in these circumstances is felt to involve the levelling effects of nature, and these men together do not readily allow modes of self-distinction. There is special delight in this politically 'red' and anti-clerical area in trying to get the priest very drunk, should he be daring enough to make a festive appearance, and there were shrieks of joy when a visiting male anthropologist friend of mine dutifully swallowed a mixture of rum and red wine (having been mischievously assured that this was a 'local' speciality) and then went outside and fell in a gorse bush in the dark. It is also permissible to bring up accusations of unpaid debts or to discuss delicate matters of land rights, rents or succession. Angry or violent confrontations can occur in these circumstances, and are then blamed on the drink.

In local non-agricultural homes, social drinking in the homes tends very much more towards self-distinction and can involve affable wittiness of a kind which has been seen as the properly French and educated way to be drunk (Prestwich 1988). There is also wine with meals. It is still not common in peasant homes to serve wine with meals. When it *is* served along with a meal, it is for a special occasion and does not become part of the food, as it does where integrated drinking exists, but remains instead a festive adjunct. Misunderstandings can arise therefore when different systems confront one another, and I have seen people from the agricultural milieu become very drunk, in their own open mode of festive appreciation, when offered wine in the home of educated newcomers to the area – expensive wine which in the newcomers' world was meant to be part of a tastefully prepared dinner.

Locality

Linked to occupation, and also to gender which I shall come to in a moment, is the question of locality. An important distinction is made between those who live in this mountain area and those who live further down the slopes in the Léon plain. The plain and the mountains – rather like nations and their peripheries – divide up between them many of the metaphors and priorities of positivism and romanticism, with identities constructed from the dualities of reason and emotions, rationality and irrationality, work and fun, and so on. It is part of local self-commentary that the more one goes up geographically, the more one goes down socially. However, the same imagery is turned to virtue by those in the mountains and a relative poverty and backwardness become an unaffected naturality: 'at least we're not snobs' like those in the plain, and 'we may not be rich but we're happy'. It is strongly felt in the mountains that 'at least we know how to have a good time'. This is regularly demonstrated in the bars in the mountains when outsiders from the Léon plain are present (as they often are since, by the same token, the mountain area is the place to go to have a bumptiously good time). Such a demonstration on the part of locals tends to involve several rounds of drinking ('we would never refuse anyone a drink') and much self-conscious merriment and displays of foolery. The identity imagery, with its metaphorical differences between mountains and plain, is thereby given substance and lives on to impose its imperatives again.

The structures of identity which the mountain villages inhabit tend to cast them, in a self-confirming way, as a metaphorical and empirical world of rough-and-ready masculinity. Women have, since the 1950s, emigrated from agriculture and from the mountains especially in far greater numbers than have the men, leaving a high rate of unmarried men in this area. This high rate of male celibacy both encourages certain modes of drinking and is exacerbated by it. 'Who would marry them anyway?' I have heard it said in other areas, for 'they drink'. Occupation, locality and gender collude here such that unmarried men in agriculture in the mountain area live with unrelenting compulsions to drink.

Gender

Gender difference now carries with it here cultural requirements to drink or not to drink; at the same time, drinking or not drinking – as well as what is drunk or not drunk – constitute gender and intra-gender differences. The common image here is that men drink and women do not. Constructs of masculinity and femininity are built around this and invoked in explanation. For example, women do not drink, it may be said, because they are more sensitive and moral, with men the unsophisticated victims of natural urges. Men can choose to cast this in a different light, with the women becoming sober spoilsports, interfering in their fun: men are order, women the source of disorder. These common expressions of gender difference, in which men gather order to themselves and women disorder, can elide in other contexts with divisions of reason/emotions, rationality/ intuition, logic/sentiment, and so on, which in varying ways can also express and constitute the proprieties of the urban, salaried husband and his nice housewife. Indeed, to become part of such a household has been very much an ambition of the women in these parts (McDonald 1986a).

In many respects, the way in which men and women are talked about here – the way in which men and women are deemed to be by nature – shares much with the way in which the differences between the plain and the mountains and between nation and periphery are discussed, not in every detail but in the more general evocations of the metaphoric involved. Various versions of order and disorder, rationality and irrationality, have been common in making sense of centre/periphery relations more generally; we have seen this with both the classical writers' views of the Celts and the nineteenth-century travellers' views of the Bretons. There have been important historical discontinuities in the imagery used (McDonald 1993) but some version of order/disorder is a commonly found delineation of us/them difference. Anarchy or reversal of the known order have been common features of the 'them' so constructed. Elements of a discourse which construct centre/periphery relations also distribute qualities between the sexes. In matters of gender elsewhere, anthropologists have most commonly pursued or been confronted with male-centred constructions of the men's world and their women, wherein women are ambiguously placed in the 'wild', and deemed to be the point of entry of social disorder (Ardener 1972). Most anthropologists have, of course, been educated men or have carried their own male-centred models with them. It is now easy to find such a model in Brittany. Men in this part of Brittany are ideally at the centre of things, out in the public world of politics in the town hall and also running the farm; women's business is at home. Any intrusion of women into the world of men can be invoked to be laughed at or condemned, and the lines of difference thereby redrawn.

In many ways, however, the most effective moral drawing of such lines in this part of rural Brittany is not the work of men. It is the women who are the moral architects and guardians of social order. When it comes to matters of the home and family and related women's business, it is women who are order and the men the source of disorder. Women in their gossip order the world, and they clean, sew and tidy it, and men in their drinking and dirt turn it to disorder. Within these same constructs, therefore, men can also claim their own 'wild' (Ardener 1972, 1975), a 'wild' for which the women have no equivalent. This domain of masculinity is asserted in the mountains in *pistes*, fighting and football, hunting, soil, dirt and drinking.

In the most popular local model, the burden of social propriety is one that is borne almost entirely by the women and inflicted on the men. Men can choose to blame on women's sense of propriety the fact that they have to shave, wear clean clothes occasionally, see their relatives, and (they say) have to smoke and drink less than they would like. Women have, for their part, keenly reshaped their responsibilities to enmesh with their aspirations to be a housewife and to have the roles of wife and mother; these roles came in a form we would recognise after the Second World War, and more especially from the 1960s onwards. Ideal femininity in this area has, since this time, carried a familiar symbolism of fuss and finery, and responsibility for the niceties of sophistication and social discrimination (McDonald 1986a, 1989a).

Within these constructs of difference, it often becomes the task of the women to try to stop the men drinking, and of the men at least to affect to avoid being stopped by the women. At collective gatherings in the homes, women usually sit together arbitrating on social propriety and, while the men drink heavily, the women's enjoyment manifestly lies in watching carefully, occasionally stopping more wine being poured to their own husbands, but otherwise listening, talking and allocating reputations. It is perhaps not surprising that those who generally drink most tend to be ageing, unmarried peasants who have no woman to stop them and who cannot be so easily tidied away.

Celibate drinking culture is given further life and conviction in the mountain area at every turn. Drinking offers a means to assert masculinity, and the more so if there is no woman to draw the boundary in other ways. It is not *only* celibate men who drink heavily but it is they who are the most noticeable and they who are more likely to be accorded a bad reputation with impunity. For married men who have lost their jobs or livelihood or are unemployed, drinking with the lads offers one certain means to be a man. There is no farm or no job through which to be a man and provider, and they have more time to drink. The more they drink, however, the more drinking is likely to become a dominant avenue through which masculinity is asserted or regained. Ultimately, married or celibate, some men end up drinking alone, drinking themselves into the ambience of male camaraderie. It is when men drink alone that a 'problem' is most obviously perceived.

A man who drinks with other men is a real man, and real men's drinking is self-evident to the point that it would not normally be mentioned or commented upon (cf. Mars 1987). But drunkenness requires boundaries, evidence of non-drunkenness of some kind, if it is to have any sense at all. A real man, no matter how much he drinks, can also demonstrate sobriety. If he cannot demonstrate sobriety, then it is said of him, by women, that 'he drinks'. His manliness, his capacity to be *ur gwaz*, are in question.

The terms 'alcoholic' and 'alcoholism' (*alcoolique* and *alcoolisme* in French) are known in this area, although rarely used. When they are, they will generally be used by women and applied to men. A man who is said to drink now has, increasingly, the chance of being said to be 'ill'. 'It's an illness, they say' may just occasionally be heard should a man 'who drinks' be discussed. Women can thereby release from moral opprobrium the wife of anyone said to drink.

Most men who end up in treatment centres in the nearest towns get there through accidents or convictions for driving offences. Increasingly, however, the local doctors are being involved in a process of primary diagnosis and referral. Usually, it will be a woman – a wife most commonly but sometimes a mother – who accompanies the man to the local doctor's surgery. It will be she who talks to the doctor. Her aspirations to feminine sophistication have given her greater access to, and competence in, a world of refinement. She is deemed more able than a man to talk to the doctor, and it is a woman who is deemed more likely to know about new-fangled ideas. More than this, her special responsibility for, and sensitivity to, social propriety mean that she is all too aware of her own vulnerability to gossip and the necessity of keeping order and propriety in her own home. The public position and prestige of her husband are both determined by and reflect upon her own competence as a woman. A man's drinking can mean incapacity and perhaps economic ruin, but it is also the moral ruin of the woman that is at stake. It is generally women who decide, in priority, when the boundaries of social incapacity or dysfunction have been reached.

Some households will go to great lengths to hide alcohol purchases and empty bottles. Medicine may never intervene. Should the man appear in the doctor's surgery, however, it is generally the obvious worries of an accompanying woman plus behavioural background knowledge which form the basis of the doctor's diagnosis of 'alcoholism'. Physiology is secondary. Local doctors tend to hold fast to the idea that alcoholism is a 'disease', stressing that this removes moral responsibility from the sufferer and the sufferer's family. 'Treatment' usually involves taking the 'patient' out of the local milieu entirely for a while, into residential homes or psychiatric hospitals some miles away, where total abstinence is practised. There are a few – but still only a few – men in this area who will decline drink altogether, claiming that one drink will cause them to drink far too much because they have an 'illness'. Their social life is difficult, however, and 'relapse' or a house move are serious temptations.

In most such treatment programmes, the influence of Alcoholics Anonymous is obvious, and the disease concept fits well with a felt need to lift the moral burden not just from the drinker but from any associated woman. Amongst some psychiatrists in Brittany, however, there exists a mode of explaining alcoholism which sometimes quite explicitly resurrects blame, and places it on the women. This is an explanation which leans heavily on notions of 'matriarchy'.

When men drink and are drunk in the manner in which they are in this part of Brittany, they further generate around themselves metaphors of disorder, and this in turn means that women's responsibility for social propriety is writ large. In many respects, their position resembles, in caricature, the position of women a few decades ago in parts of working-class, urban England, especially in the North. It is Andy Capp land, but the men drink that much more and have that much less domestic sway. The women watch over their men's drinking that much more assiduously, and appoint themselves the guardians of propriety with that much more certainty of the validity of their role. They hold the domestic purse-strings, and the reins of domestic government, that much more tightly. There are many aspects of their position which resemble that of women elsewhere in agricultural areas in northern France, but contrast with aspects of gender relations in the south and in the towns (see, for example, Rogers 1975 and 1985). This has encouraged some psychiatrists to suggest that there is a pathological power of women in these parts. The ancient Celts are drawn into the picture and a 'Celtic matriarchy' has been said to be inherent and enduring in Brittany (see, for example, Carrer 1983; also Audibert 1984).

Several misinterpretations could be disentangled in such a model. They are misinterpretations involving apprehensions of categorical transgression, incongruity or mismatch of a kind I mentioned earlier when outlining the way in which the nineteenth-century image of the drunken Bretons seems to have been constructed. Firstly, the whole question of just what 'power' women have is far more complex and contextual than any simple binary division – of men's power or women's power, for instance – can suggest (see Rogers 1975 and 1985, and Harding 1975, for some important early insights here). However great the power of women may seem to be, as wives, mothers or gossips, they will often find themselves, within the same structures that accord them those powers, on the 'wrong' side of the order/disorder symbolism and thereby excluded from serious business. Although no woman would openly admit it here, physical blows can await some at home whose self-sanctioning is deemed to have failed. There is, therefore, in the simple label of 'matriarchy', no space for the more or the less subtle ways in which gender constructs are relational and, in ever changing contexts, mutually delimiting.

Secondly, the notion of matriarchy was invented largely in the nineteenth century in debates between writers and lawyers – including men such as Maine, Bachofen, Morgan and McLennan, for example – about jurisprudence and the governance of India, and about the 'origins' of human society. Matriarchy, in opposition to the contemporary patriarchy (in which participants to the debate felt themselves to be living), was drawn up as the original state of society. This original state was then 'discovered' in contemporary 'primitives', and it became wholly credible for some time to find empirical proof of this historicist scheme in contemporary exotic societies, in the form of matriarchal 'survivals' (for further details of the debates involved here, see Kuper 1988). The failure of the kinship categories of the observers' own society – categories such as wife, mother, father, for example – to render comprehensible categories of social worlds elsewhere, led to highly elaborate and widely accepted conclusions about primitive promiscuity, group marriage and matriarchy – with the last notion often used to include and explain the other aspects. Victorian modernity both defined its own proprieties and made sense of the categorical and behavioural incongruities which other cultures posed, through the construction at its frontiers of a primitive world of rampant and random sexuality. Since behaviour did not follow the categories, rules and proprieties of the Victorians, then the conceptual floodgates were open: among primitives, historical or living, everyone had sex with everyone else, and no one knew who their father was. Within the evolutionist schemes then fashionable, it seemed plausible, therefore, that social systems had evolved around the female line, as matriarchies. Such conclusions have, in these terms, long since been overthrown within anthropology, but in the nineteenth century their reality was persuasive.

Thirdly and finally, their reality was all the more persuasive because many nineteenth-century writers who thought in this way could look, once again, to classical texts for simple 'proof' of their observations. Classical writers, in defining the frontiers of their own proprieties, had found in the barbarians (including the Celts) all that their own society, ideally, was not; to alcoholic excess, therefore, were added sexual promiscuity and group marriage, for example (Woolfe 1990), all of which resurfaced as the empirical flesh of nineteenth-century human 'origins'. It might need, at any stage, only the most minor transgressions of the category boundaries of the classical observers, of the nineteenth-century writers or of the modern psychiatrists for the whole edifice of misinterpretation, with surfeit and disorder in the other, to feel real and true.

Modern psychiatrists could be said therefore to have misinterpreted gender relations in parts of Brittany, and to have drawn on ideas of nineteenth-century writers who misinterpreted the exotic societies they observed, and they in turn on the ideas of classical writers who misinterpreted the barbarians around them. At each stage, one might surmise the confrontation of different conceptual systems of which gender and kin relations were a part, and out of which understandings of 'man' and 'woman' were constructed but did not quite fit from one system to another. Many of the metaphors of opposition by which majority civilization defines itself, the metaphors by which it defines its rationality, its economy, its religion, its manners and its sexuality, can be rolled together to produce an 'ethnic minority'. Such a minority has been constructed in Brittany (McDonald 1989a), reaching back into prehistory, and constructed so persuasively that a regional 'ethno-psychiatry' group has been formally established. These psychiatrists find a continuity in the mess of categorical misinterpretation I have outlined by appeals not only to an historical ethnicity but also to essentialist understandings of gender: the natural qualities of women are generally those of the ideal femininity they espouse for their wives in their own world, and they are qualities which are deemed inherent and substantial (as are those of the 'Celt') rather than the metaphorical attributions of conceptual, lived oppositions. Ethno-psychiatrists have felt comfortable, therefore, discussing the 'pathology' of 'Breton culture' and invoking 'matriarchy' and Celtic ancestors; and one psychiatrist in charge of a local unit for alcoholics insisted to me that feminism should be kept at bay in Brittany because women had 'far too much power' already.

Whatever problems one might find in these assertions, there is nevertheless an understanding within psychiatry in Brittany that women play an important role. However, this role is not to be understood, I have argued, through historicist explanation but through the contemporary gender constructs and categorical proprieties on which it depends.

New Drinks, New Men, New Women

I have tried to suggest some central features of drinking in this area by drawing out the three linked axes of occupation, locality and gender. They are all interwoven the one in the other, which makes the compulsion to drink all the more irresistible for men working the land in the mountains.

The compulsion resides always in contextual difference, and being a man or a woman, from the plains or the mountains, and so on, are important elements here. In many respects, it matters little whether we are talking about the relational difference of persons (man/woman, for example) or of substances (beer/wine, for instance), for person and substance continually implicate and constitute each other.

There is always a danger that attempts to construct a readable, written text will make a social world appear more uniform and perhaps more static than it is. In any lived world of ideas in action, there is a continuous process of relating, structuring, evaluation and revaluation. Some aspects of change, however, become more obvious than others, and sometimes quite self-consciously so.

Intra-gender distinctions through new and different drinks and modes of drinking have been evident in this area in recent years. They have been especially evident because, through romantic or political commitment, many educated newcomers have either come to live in or have passed through this area, and their presence has added new dimensions to the modes of self-construction and self-distinction available. For example, in the domain of drinks, there is generally an increasing sophistication when one moves from cider to wine to beer, correlating with decreasing age and with a move from agriculture to occupations outside it. In other words, the older peasant drinks cider; the younger person outside agriculture opts for beer. However, educated newcomers and visitors generally prefer and pursue the now apparently 'traditional' cider, and this revaluation means that the older, local peasant can drink cider at home on lean days and then dress up and go out to drink it, economically and morally transformed, as a substance of some sophistication served in a new *crêperie* opened for tourists further up the mountain slopes.

There are some similar changes in the bars. The many bars in the mountains can be roughly divided into three types. Firstly, there are the one-room, sawdust-on-the-floor, glass-and-bottle bars where red wine is the drink, Breton the most common language of communication, and older men in working overalls the customers. Rolling and chewing tobacco are on sale plus *Gitanes Maïs*, the workman's cigarette which sticks to the lips. The second type of bar, more sophisticated, has several rooms – for different ages or interests – and a wide range of drinks is stocked, including wines, spirits and beers, both home and imported, with a corresponding range of cigarettes. Both French and Breton are spoken, and a few women may occasionally be seen drinking in these bars, although usually seated at tables away from the bar, and never alone. The third type of bar is the *boîte* or night-club/disco. These bars are the most sophisticated, few in number, always expensive and driving-distance away. Both sexes are present, the clientele young, and the language French with a high *franglais* content. No wine is on sale, only beers, spirits and cocktails, all at high prices. The next stage of sophistication after these night-clubs seems to be one that is already available: to go into the first type of bar mentioned, drink red wine and try to speak Breton. This is what many educated newcomers and visitors like to do. The result in a few instances has been a gentrification of these bars, with the locals moving on to the second, intermediate type mentioned, and moving on to their range of drinks, too.

Some related changes have occurred in the options of drinking and smoking available to women. Since women have taken on the symbolic lot of finery and social discrimination, men generally have, in the bars, options of drinking and smoking which are not open to women. The men, for example, can drink red wine, beer or imported spirits, depending on who they are with and how they wish socially or generationally to place themselves; and they can smoke the ordinary French *brunes* (the dark-tobacco cigarettes) as one of the lads in contrast to the girls, or the foreign *blondes* (light-tobacco cigarettes) which place a distance between themselves and their parental generation. Men can thus take on a masculine chic which their fathers did not know and which young women now admire and require.

The young, feminine woman, if she smokes at all, will smoke the *blondes*. There was a time when women both smoked and drank in Brittany – a sight which added to the exclamations of moral horror on the part of the nineteenth-century travellers (see Fillaut 1989 for some examples). Women in the observers' own world already occupied the space of ideal femininity which the observers quite explicitly found lacking at that time in Brittany (McDonald 1989a:245). After the First World War, when drinking and smoking became increasingly assimilated to statements of masculinity, then femininity as it came to these areas found expression, as I have suggested, in not smoking and not drinking. Fine wines and sweet liqueurs have, on special occasions, been within the symbolic reach of women, but this is not described as drinking. A woman 'who drinks' is rare but is quite quickly a moral outcast. Since she does not know how to behave nicely herself, she cannot possibly be party to gossip, responsible for the behavioural niceties of others. Women in this position have been known to report themselves to the local doctor, and to move away if they possibly can. A mother-in-law's presence will, it is known, make rehabilitation very difficult. Such women far more easily reconstruct themselves elsewhere. Staying put may mean drinking one's way, alone, into the chic that can now surround a glass in the hand.

Although women not drinking is the established norm, women born after the Second World War and especially those born since the 1960s (whose length of education has caught up with that of the local men) can show their sophistication by taking up smoking and drinking within a new evaluation of what both drinking and smoking involve. They can now, in the more sophisticated bars, take light beers and exotic cocktails and smoke imported cigarettes, in statements of cosmopolitan style. Some of these younger women say that they expect to be part of a 'couple', a notion still very new in this area. They do not readily tolerate young men who hunt, shout and drink heavily together; they are not impressed by manly dirt and drunken foolery. They do not consider it their lot to have to try to stop men drinking, and find it unseemly to have to contemplate doing that in front of other people. Ideally, they want young men to share their own interests, and to drink with them.

Some young men and young women are taking on new cultures of drinking and smoking, therefore, along with new modes of being a man or a woman. Amongst 'couples', intake of alcohol could be said to have decreased; at the same time, the boundaries of social unacceptability and dysfunction have in many ways narrowed in such circles, and 'alcoholic' comes more readily to the lips. In these circumstances, an *increase* in alcoholism accompanies a *decrease* in alcohol consumption, underlining the social nature of the definition of 'alcoholic'.

Outside the new local culture of 'couples', however, overall consumption seems to have been increasing, raising concern that here and in other parts of rural Brittany, the example of educated newcomers drinking and smoking heavily in their own image of the 'Breton peasant' and the 'Celt' alike could be contributing to increases in consumption at the local level (cf. Blanchard 1984). Educated visitors and newcomers have arrived, pursuing the virtue seen to inhere in all that is peasant and local, and there are now locals pursuing the sophistication seen to inhere in the educated. In this part of Brittany, only outsiders, or women cast as such, have so far taken to smoking the dark-tobacco *brunes* or the roll-your-own cigarettes, the property of the male and generally the older male peasant. An educated outsider or newcomer often finds sophistication in these items, as she does in the one-room bars and the red wine and cider, all of which to the local girl would normally seem uncouth. However, as outsiders and newcomers bring sophistication to these items, then their appropriation or reappropriation by local young people, both women and men, in pursuit of refinement, is possible and is happening. The material substances of alcohol and tobacco are thus finding new meanings again, new moral forms and new imperatives, in another transformation which socially reconstructs substances and persons alike.

It is in these ever-changing relational values, these cultures, that we find the compulsions determining who shall drink or smoke, and when and why, rather than in something located, external to cultural perception, within either the substances or the people themselves.

Notes

The research on which this paper is based was begun as part of a postdoctoral project financed by the Economic and Social Research Council. Early drafts of this paper were presented in research seminars at Brunel, Oxford and Cambridge Universities, and also at The London School of Economics. I am grateful to all participants for their comments.

I am also grateful to Dr Gwenaël Bonthonneau and to members of the organisation *Bretagne, Alcool, Santé* in Rennes (Brittany, France) for their discussions and their help in locating and supplying documentation.

1. Comments and figures here are based on the published tables of L'Institut National de la Statistique et des Etudes Economiques, and of L'Institut National de la Santé et de la Recherche Médicale. On the categories and calculations, see Damiani and Masse 1986.

References

Ardener, E. (1972), 'Belief and the Problem of Women' in J. La Fontaine (ed.) *The Interpretation of Ritual*. London: Tavistock.

Ardener, E. (1975), 'The Problem Revisited' in S. Ardener (ed.) *Perceiving Women*. London: Dent.

Ardener, E. (1982), 'Social anthropology, language and reality' in D. Parkin (ed.) *Semantic Anthropology*, ASA 22. London: Academic Press.

Audibert, A. (1984), *Le matriarcat breton*. Paris: P.U.F.

Barre, H. (1984), 'Manières de boire parmi les travailleurs manuels en Bretagne de 1930 à nos jours', *Actes de la Rencontre "Cultures,*

Manières de Boire et Alcoolisme". Rennes: Bretagne, Alcool, Santé.

Barrows, S. (1979), 'After the Commune: Alcohol, Temperance and Literature in the Early Third Republic' in J. Merriman (ed.) *Consciousness and Class Experience in nineteenth-century Europe.* London and N.Y.: Holmes and Meier.

Barthes, R. (1972), *Mythologies.* London.

Bertrand, Y. and Caro, G. (1977), *Alcoolisme et Bretagne.* Rennes: CIRREES.

Blanchard, L. (1984), 'Alcooliques et Bretons: toujours?' *Actes de la rencontre "Cultures, Manières de Boire et L'Alcoolisme".* Rennes: Bretagne, Alcool, Santé.

Borel, J. (1968), *Du concept de Dégénérescence à la notion d'alcoolisme dans la médicine contemporaine.* Montpellier: Causse.

Carrer, P. (1983), Le matriarcat psychologique des Bretons. Paris: Payot.

Caro, C. and Bertrand, Y. (1981), *Yec'hed Mad. A Votre Santé.* Le Guilvinec: Editions Le Signor.

Castell-Tallet, M. (1983), *'Géographie et Mortalité en Bretagne'.* Unpublished *Doctorat de Troisième Cycle* thesis (*Géographie*), Université de Bretagne Occidentale.

Chapman, M. (1978), *The Gaelic Vision in Scottish Culture.* London: Croom Helm.

Csergo, J. (1988), *Liberté, égalité, propreté. La morale de l'hygiène au XIXe siècle.* Paris: Albin Michel.

Damiani, P. and Masse, H. (1986), *L'Alcoolisme en Chiffres.* (*Haut Comité d'Etude et d'Information sur L'Alcoolisme.*) Paris: *La Documentation Française.*

Daumer, Y. (1977), 'Les Champions du Monde de l'Alcoolisme', *Le Peuple Breton,* no. 168, pp.4–7.

Falher, J. et al. (1906), 'Enquête sur l'ivresse bretonne', *Revue Morbihannaise* 1906: pp.73–86, 317–26, 345–57; 1907: pp.5–11.

Fillaut, Th. (1980), 'L'alcoolisme dans l'Ouest de la France pendant la second moitié du XIXe siècle: Approche bibliographique.' Unpublished DEA thesis, Université de Haute-Bretagne, Rennes.

Fillaut, Th. (1983a), *L'alcoolisme dans l'Ouest de la France pendant la second moitié du XIXe siècle. (Thèse pour le doctorat de 3e cycle en histoire, Université de Haute-Bretagne,* Rennes, 1981.) Paris: *la Documentation Française.*

Fillaut, Th. (1983b), 'Comportements alcooliques et alcoolisation en Bretagne au XIXe siècle', *Annales de Bretagne et des Pays de l'Ouest,* vol. 90, no. 1: pp.35–45.

Fillaut, Th. (1984), 'Manières de boire et alcoolisme dans l'Ouest de la France au XIXe siècle', *Ethnologie française*, xiv, no. 4: pp.377–86.

Fillaut, Th. (1989), 'Femmes et alcools en Bretagne (1830–1918)' in P. Carrer et al. (ed) *Conduites de Dépendances Pathologiques en Bretagne*. Rennes: Institut Culturel de la Bretagne/Skol Uhel ar Vro.

Harding, S. (1975), 'Women and words in a Spanish village' in R. Reiter (ed.) *Toward an anthropology of women*, pp.283–308. New York: Monthly Review Press.

HCEIA (1984), *Les différences régionales des consommations d'ethanol et des risques d'alcoolisation pathologique.* (*Colloque d'Esclimont*, March 1983, *Haut Comité d'Etude et d'information sur l'Alcoolisme*.) Paris: *La Documentation Française*.

Kuper, A. (1988), *The Invention of Primitive Society*. London and New York: Routledge.

Lavarenne, E. de (1901), 'Alcoolisme et Tuberculose', *Annales d'hygiène publique et de Médécine légale*, vol. 45, pp.193ff.

Ledermann, S. (1956), *Alcool, Alcoolisme, Alcoolisation: Données Scientifiques de Caractère Physiologique, Economique et Social* (*Institut National d'Etudes Démographiques, Travaux et Documents, Cahier no. 29*). Paris: P.U.F.

Leroy, R. (1900), 'L'alcoolisme dans le Finistère', *Annales d'hygiène publique et de médécine légale*, vol. 44.

McDonald, M. (1986a), 'Brittany: Politics and women in a minority world' in R. Ridd and H. Callaway (eds.) *Caught up in Conflict*. London and New York: Macmillan.

McDonald, M. (1986b), 'Celtic ethnic kinship and the problem of being English', *Current Anthropology*, vol. 27, no. 4, pp.333–47.

McDonald, M. (1989a), *'We are not French!' Language, Culture and Identity in Brittany*. London and New York: Routledge.

McDonald, M. (1989b), 'The exploitation of linguistic mismatch: towards an ethnography of customs and manners' in R. Grillo (ed.) *Social Anthropology and the Politics of Language*. London and New York: Routledge.

McDonald, M. (1993), 'The Construction of Difference: an anthropological approach to stereotypes' in S. MacDonald (ed.) *Inside European Identities*. Oxford and New York: Berg.

Mars, G. (1987), 'Longshore drinking, economic security and union politics in Newfoundland' in M. Douglas (ed.), *Constructive Drinking: Perspectives on Drink from Anthropology*. Cambridge: Cambridge University Press.

Nye, R. (1982), 'Degeneration and the medical model of cultural crisis in the French *Belle Epoque*' in S. Drescher et al. (eds) *Political Symbolism in Modern Europe*. New Brunswick and London: Transaction Books.

Nye, R. (1984), *Crime, Madness and Politics in Modern France: The Medical Concept of National Decline*. Princeton: Princeton University Press.

Ogès, L. (1953), 'L'Ivrognerie en Bretagne', *Bulletin de la Société Archéologique du Finistère*, vol. 74, pp.19–30.

Pick, D. (1989), *Faces of Degeneration: A European Disorder c.1848–c.1918*. Cambridge: Cambridge University Press.

Prestwich, P. (1988), *Drink and the Politics of Social Reform: Anti-alcoholism in France since 1870*. Palo Alto, California: The Society for the Promotion of Science and Scholarship.

Rogers, S. (1975), 'Female forms of power and the myth of male dominance', *American Ethnologist*, 2, pp.727–56.

Rogers, S. (1985), 'Gender in Southwestern France: the myth of male dominance revisited', *Anthropology*, vol. IX, nos. 1 & 2, pp.65–86.

Sadoun, R. et al. (1965), *Drinking in French Culture*. New Brunswick, New Jersey: Rutgers Center of Alcohol Studies.

Woolfe, G.D. (1990), 'Cultural change in Central France under Roman Rule'. Unpublished Ph.D thesis, University of Cambridge (Classics).

5

Whisky, Women and the Scottish Drink Problem. A View from the Highlands[1]

Sharon Macdonald

Introduction

Alcohol, especially in the form of whisky, has an important place both in Scotland's national imagery and in her 'drink problem' statistics. Women are not prominent in either. Theirs is, however, a constructive or symbolic absence: their relationship to drink and especially to the national drink – whisky – is just as much a socially defined, and in its way problematic, matter as is that of men. Whisky, as far as Scotland is concerned, is much more than a drink, or a means of getting drunk, of course. It is also a vital ingredient in various rituals, and a symbolic distillation of many images of Scottishness, especially hospitality, camaraderie, joviality and masculinity. Despite the positive associations of the national drink, however, Scotland – and especially particular areas such as Glasgow and the Islands – is widely said to have 'a drink problem' and this is reflected in statistics on alcoholism[2].

Scotland seems to have lagged behind England in cutting her 'alcohol-related' mortality rates[3]. Glasgow in particular is a black spot, and more research has been done there on alcoholism than in any comparable part of the UK[4]. The Celtic infiltration of the city, from Ireland and the Highlands of Scotland, is often thought to be part of the cultural background of alcohol abuse. On the one hand it is assumed that the Celtic immigrants bring with them a natural love for high spirits and hard spirits, and on the other that, in the city, disaffection with the way of life turns a happy relationship with drink into one of abuse and addiction.

This paper is not, however, about Glasgow directly, but focuses instead on the rural setting from which some of Glasgow's immigrants come – the Highlands and Islands. This region acts as

125

a symbolic locus for positive images of drinking and of the national drink within Scotland. In particular, I look at the Isle of Skye where I have carried out fieldwork, although material here is drawn from other parts of the Islands too[5]. Skye, perhaps more than any of the other Islands, is imbued with romantic ideas about the Highlands, and it is these ideas – the associations with history, tradition, peat, heather, Highland hospitality, and the virility of the bekilted Highlander – which play a part in the imagery of the dram.

There are other starkly different images of Highland drinking, however. One is that of alcoholism as a symptom of the decay of the Highland community. As the population dwindles, and as men cease to work and live in tune with the land and their kinsmen, then, so the argument goes, they turn to alcohol to relieve their sense of alienation. The other image, which stands opposed to the romantic vision taken up by the nation, is that provided by Calvinism. In much of the Northern Highlands, the Calvinistic Presbyterian Churches hold significant sway, and the free flow of alcohol as well as the jovial excitability of the stereotypical Highlander are at odds with the churches' teachings.

By looking at the detail of everyday and special-occasion drinking practices within a Highland community I hope to illustrate some of the complexities and contradictions which lie beyond and within the various images. My case is not, however, that the detailed practices constitute a separate reality: on the contrary they are shaped and articulated within, and sometimes in turn sustain, those images. Gender plays a key role throughout. My intention here is to try to show how drinking is regarded by people actually living in the townships of the Highlands rather than to attempt to construct a general theory about alcohol consumption and abuse in which Highlanders are but one example. In doing this my argument is, in part, against some of the simplistic 'alienation' theories which have been put forward to 'explain' why drinking – and in particular 'problem drinking' – occurs. An analysis of alcoholism – or indeed of other 'addictions' – needs to take account of the historically located and socially defined nature of the issues involved.

The 'Drink Problem'

The idea that Scotland, and more particularly the Highlands, has a drink problem is not new, though the way in which the problem has been cast and dealt with has changed significantly over time. In the seventeenth century numerous Acts were passed by Scotland's Privy

Council to try to curb 'the great and extraordinary excesses in drinking in wyne' amongst islanders, a habit which it was believed led to general barbarousness and the proclivity to steal from their Lowland neighbours (Grant 1961:303). Whisky was not at this time considered to constitute a problem, perhaps because it seems to have been regarded to some degree as a 'physic' or medicine (ibid.:304). However, during the late eighteenth and early nineteenth centuries, as duties on whisky made illicit distilling increasingly profitable, whisky came to be the drink most associated with the Highlanders and with what was seen by Lowlanders at that time as their general lawlessness. Drinking amongst Highlanders was regarded as a manifestation and aggravation of 'the Highland problem', a whole series of problems of lack of control and civilisation which included godlessness and poverty.

Whisky's elevation to the status of the national drink was effected as part of a romanticisation of the Highlands which began in the late eighteenth century, a romanticisation which involved a general appropriation of Highland symbols by Scotland as a whole (see Chapman 1978). Sir Walter Scott's choice of whisky as the drink with which to toast King George IV on his famous visit to Edinburgh in 1822 was a key event in defining whisky's new national status[6].

In this change of attitudes towards the Highlands, illicit distilling, once seen as a symptom of lawlessness and even depravity, came to be recast as a romantic adventure in which the canny locals try to outwit the forces of authority, the evil excise men. This is a favourite theme in the tales and songs of people living in the Highlands today (cf. Grant 1961:305), and many stories about the Highlands and Islands, such as Compton MacKenzie's *Whisky Galore* (1947), cast whisky as the site around which locals trick and deceive the authorities. In one song (about a village in which I worked – but no doubt repeated with variations in many other parts of the Highlands) a woman hides the illegally produced whisky in hot-water bottles in her bed and then pretends to be in labour. In another it is the old woman of the household who gets rid of the unwelcome officials by pouring the contents of a chamberpot over them. But more usually men are the main figures in these dramas and sometimes, as in much of *Whisky Galore,* the men have to hide their whisky from the women as well as from the authorities. These two, apparently contradictory, roles for women are not simply a matter of the individual story-teller's whim, however; rather, they illustrate a more deeply held general ambivalence around women's roles with regard to drink and with regard to their place within, and as representatives of, the people.

On the whole it is men – an idealised egalitarian community of men – who represent the 'Highland people' and, at another remove, the 'Scottish people'. Women are sometimes subsumed within this category: when conflict with outside authority is involved, women take their place as members of the people and they can play as strong a part as the men in defending their people's interests. But in other circumstances, where male egalitarianism is being lived out without a marked conflict with outsiders, women may become the counter-image against which 'the people' and its values are defined. Whisky, like many other symbols of the Highlands and of Scotland (e.g. the kilt and bagpipes), is imbued with very masculine imagery, and this – together with the fact that it is also very much part of everyday social life too – makes it one of the key arenas around which this process of counter-definition takes place. Scotland's drink problem, and the gender asymmetries of the problem, are to be understood within this matrix of national and gender images and their refractions in everyday life.

Although there has long been a perception of Scotland and the Highlands in particular as having a drink problem, the problem was not scientised until recent years. The collection of statistics on drinking and the development of organisations to treat alcoholism as a specialised problem have both increased rapidly since the beginning of the 1970s[7]. This scientisation does not just identify the problem; it also constructs it and this construction may well differ from other indigenous ones. In the scientised construction of problem drinking, alcohol is often associated with physical and moral degeneracy: with heart disease, cirrhosis of the liver, unemployment and domestic violence. It is also something which can be 'treated' – by doctors, social workers and counselling services. By and large, it is still construed as an individual problem, a loss of individual control, a *succumbing* to drink, and the treatments are predominantly individual-directed, though this is changing in much of Scotland now as elsewhere, with more emphasis placed by the medical and counselling services on family and group therapy. Even here, however, it is not clear that the social patterns within which drinking has its place have been fully appreciated by those advocating new modes of treatment and prevention campaigns.

Men's drinking and women's drinking are not viewed as equally problematic by Highlanders or by the Scottish population in general. The consumption of alcohol *per se* is not generally regarded as unacceptable and the great majority of adults in Scotland drink at least occasionally (Grant, Plant and Saunders

1980)[8]. Although men constitute a vastly greater proportion of the alcoholism statistics, in many ways their drinking is viewed as a lesser problem than that of those women who drink. Drunkenness has to a large extent been accepted, and even expected, of the Highland male, and indeed it has even been treated as something of a joke as it is, for example, in Compton MacKenzie's *Whisky Galore*: of course, the Highland man drinks – he is out of his element if he does not. The stereotype of the drunken male Highlander is that of an amiable, affable buffoon. A drunken woman, however, is quite a different story: she is undoubtedly unrespectable, slovenly and loose, always a despicable or pathetic rather than a humorous figure. In a survey of attitudes about drinking in Scotland over 90% of respondents agreed with the statement: 'A drunken woman is a far worse sight than a drunken man' (Dight 1976:193)[9].

The traditionally tolerant attitude towards the drunken male Highlander is part of the reason why the violence, and in particular domestic violence, which may accompany drinking is often not acknowledged. What is more, the socially defined roles and expectations which surround men's drinking make it difficult for women to deal with the sons, husbands or fathers in their families who drink. To argue against drinking and alcoholism is not simply to align oneself with a worthy moral cause. On the contrary, women can find themselves up against the forces of tradition and even nationally vaunted symbolism.

For many outsiders and incomers to the Highlands heavy drinking appears to be a symptom of social decay, of the loss of community[10]. Drink is perceived as a palliative to which locals turn in the face of crumbling social support systems. For some outsiders, so jarring is the contrast between the romanticised life which they had expected to find in the Highlands and the presence of what they term 'alcohol abuse' that they charge Highlanders with some sort of moral degeneracy, with having allowed their culture to disappear. To give an example of this view, let me quote the words of one incomer who had become extremely disaffected with what he found in the townships of the Hebrides, having expected to find something much closer to the jovial imagery of whisky advertisements: 'It's a dying community – there's nothing left here. All you've got are the dregs. Look at the alcohol abuse – I've seen it in other dying communities. It's just like the Aborigines in Australia.' What might have been cast as the sort of drinking that would be expected amongst fun-loving Highlanders has, once coupled with the notion of 'dying community', become 'alcohol abuse'.

The Bible and the Bottle[11]

The coexistence of 'drink problems' and Calvinistic religion in many areas of the Highlands is a matter about which incomers and outsiders tend to speculate endlessly, and a number of theories have been devised to account for the apparent contradiction. These theories often revolve around the notions of alienation and community.

Skye, like most of the Northern Highlands, is predominantly 'Wee Free', a pejorative term which is widely used to describe the austere Sabbatarian Calvinism preached by most of the churches[12]. Wee Frees are often assumed to be teetotal, though temperance rather than abstinence is the Churches' official position. There are, however, frequent stories in the press about ministers or elders who have been summarily dismissed after having had a little too much to drink (usually at funerals or weddings), or about Church and Lord's Day Observance Society opposition to the opening of bars or the sale of drink on the Sabbath.

For the visitor or 'incomer' to the Highlands – and even perhaps for the returning Islander – Presbyterianism provides one of the most marked experiences of 'culture shock': it seems strange and austere[13]. Drawing a sharp contrast with heavy drinking – a contrast between the Bible and the Bottle – magnifies this strangeness and implies, too, that Presbyterianism is strange and alien to local people. In this way, drinking is explained simplistically as a rejection of the austere religion that is seen as a 'blight upon the free spirit of the Gael' (Condry 1980:291). There is an assumption in this theory that the Bottle is more 'natural' to Highland culture than Calvinism and also that drinkers are taking an active stance against this alien culture – Peter Mewett actually describes them as 'anti-religious' (1982:117). However, the matter is more complex and its indigenous definition is rather different. Many heavy drinkers will turn up for church on the Sabbath and will claim themselves to be believers (though will not be 'saved'); and although heavy drinkers might regard themselves as 'sinful' this is a category within religious discourse and not opposed to it. Take Domhnall Sheumais, for example, who probably spends more man-hours drunk than anybody else that I have ever met, but who is 'a great man for the Bible', capable of reciting the whole of the book of Isaiah from memory.

The other framework for explaining the high rates of drinking in the Highlands is a variation on the general alienation model; that is, alcohol 'abuse' and religious austerity, along with depression and other forms of mental illness, are regarded as a means of escaping the harsh realities of everyday life. The Bible and the Bottle, therefore, become two faces of the same underlying problem of social dislocation or alienation. Gender is sometimes brought into these arguments: it is pointed out that just as there are many more male drinkers than female, so too are there more female communicants than male (although the imbalance is far from being so marked). The usual explanation for women's escape into religion rather than into drink is that there are social constraints upon women drinking, their access to alcohol being less easy. In this explanation then, Presbyterianism is depicted as an escape mechanism for those for whom the easier route of alcohol is not so readily available. While Presbyterianism clearly does put an emphasis on the other-worldly as opposed to this-worldly dimension of existence, the idea that it can somehow be explained simply as a means of escape – a deprivation thesis – has been generally discredited because it neither fits the empirical observations nor accounts for the complexities of the ideas involved.

None of this is to say, however, that there are not oppositions made within the Highlands between drinking and religion, or that gender plays no part in this. In many respects the position of the communicant (i.e. one who has been 'saved' and become a member of the 'Elect') within society is a 'female' one: it is a status which entails a withdrawing from certain domains of social life, particularly the male-dominated arena of the bar. Furthermore, the patterns of social life represented by communicants are in many ways equivalent to those represented by women: that is, they stand apart from the idealised masculine, egalitarian community.

Although problems such as unemployment and the shortage of wives for Highland bachelors may play a part in aggravating alcoholism and depression – though there is no evidence that they increase the number of communicants – drinking is also seen in the Highlands as a 'normal' and even 'positive' dimension of social life, and we need to look at this, too, in order to understand the cultural construction of alcohol use and abuse. We turn first, however, to the way in which 'heavy drinking' is constructed in local social life, and to its implications for women.

Heavy Drinking

Local people draw a distinction between heavy drinking and alcoholism, a distinction which is shared by a majority of other

Scots (see Dight 1976:248), but which is not generally recognised in medical or statistical accounts. The distinction rests on a notion of compulsion or need: the alcoholic *needs* drink, he cannot help himself. The heavy drinker, by contrast, could abstain if he wished, or so, at least, it is believed. I was frequently told by heavy drinkers, 'I could stop tomorrow if I wanted to' or 'I sometimes go days without a drink.' Such a distinction obviously has important policy implications for campaigns against alcoholism, for very few individuals would classify themselves as alcoholics. Indeed, the amount of alcohol consumed is generally underestimated (except for in particular circumstances such as boasting between young men) and individuals who drink a great deal may not regard themselves even as 'heavy drinkers'. In Dight's survey, only 11% of the heaviest drinking group, and only 1% of all male drinkers, saw themselves as heavy drinkers, even though by informants' own criteria of what would constitute heavy drinking at least 5% of male drinkers would be identified as heavy drinkers (1976:155)[14].

Heavy drinking, as we have said, is predominantly a male activity, although figures for Scotland as a whole suggest that the number of women drinkers is increasing (Green 1986:12; Goddard 1986). It is likely, too, that drinking among women is even more markedly underestimated than it is among men due to the added stigma associated with women's drinking. When I was told of female alcoholics during my fieldwork it was always in hushed, conspiratorial tones. That a woman's serious drinking habits should become 'public' is regarded as particularly shameful, and female heavy drinkers or alcoholics often make rather desperate attempts to hide and conceal their drinking. One woman, for example, buried her used bottles in the garden and another nearly drowned after falling into a loch while trying to throw away her empties. Crucially too, women's heavy drinking is far more likely to be confined to the home than is that of men. Although some women do go to the hotel bars, they are not as likely as men to become drunk there; nor are they as likely to be seen drunk out on the streets.

Even so, it is rather difficult to be a totally invisible or anonymous alcoholic on an island where the main town has a population under 3,000 and the island as a whole of 8,000. Even in the supermarkets – where alcohol must be purchased from special kiosks – it must soon become apparent to the cashiers when individuals make large and regular purchases. And although women may move more easily in supermarkets, being the ones generally responsible for household shopping, they must rely on a small number of places for their purchases as they are not so likely to buy alcohol from hotel bars. Male drinkers, on the other hand, will often be seen carrying the plain white carrier bag supplied by hotels which, far from being inconspicuous, has become something of a Highland institution known as 'the carry-out'.

On the whole then, the numbers of women who drink heavily, by both official figures and popular knowledge, are small. The most prevalent problem for women is less that of becoming 'addicted' themselves than of their menfolk turning to the bottle. This, of course, causes serious problems not only for the heavy drinker but also for his family. Even apart from the extreme case of any associated domestic violence, there are economic difficulties caused by a man's expenditure on drink and in many cases the difficulties of his holding down a job; and the loss of a driving licence through drunken driving can be a serious handicap in a rural area where employment is often distant and public transport poor. Men's drinking habits are one of the main causes of separation and divorce in the Highlands.

The foolishness of men who drink too much is often a subject of conversation, particularly among women, or more particularly among women whose own husbands do not drink heavily[15]. Perhaps by reiterating their disapproval, and stating it categorically as an activity opposed to the family and its values, they hope to guard against their own husbands participating too much in the male drinking fraternity.

Despite disapproval of heavy drinking from many women and also from the Church, there seems to be little effort made to express that disapproval to drinkers in public or to alter their behaviour. It is extremely common to see drunks out on the streets, and even to find them asleep in one's car or byre in the mornings[16]. As one observer has commented, in the case of the Outer Hebridean island of Lewis:

> A man who is obviously the worse for drink is not shunned, nor is it common to see an attempt made to remove him from a public situation in order to return him to sobriety. Instead it is much more usual for people to act as if nothing is out of place, to ignore the social incapacity of the drunk and behave as if the situation were 'normal' (Ennew 1980:103).

Furthermore, there rarely seems to be any attempt made to keep drink out of the way of those who easily take too much. Thus an already drunk man will be given a lift to the bar; a local shopkeeper will be plied with drink by the men delivering goods, and he will remain behind his counter unless he actually becomes so inebriated that he can no longer stand; children talk politely to a local drunk and when he pulls out his carry-out their father takes a dram too. There are some homes where nobody would take a drink with him and where he would be told to put his bottle away, though this would rarely be done forcibly. That drunks are allowed into the home and that they are usually fed is testimony to the fact that the pretence of normality does not necessarily entail a lack of *care* about the heavy drinker or alcoholic. It is just that the form that the care takes does not as a rule include any attempt to prohibit access to alcohol.

Although women may talk about the foolishness of men who drink too much, this tends to be in abstract cases or with regard to drunks who are not part of their own families. On the whole, the reaction of women to men who drink too much within their families is to attempt to ignore the behaviour. One of the most marked examples of such avoidance that I witnessed was in a family I sometimes visited for Sunday lunch. The family consisted of two bachelor sons in their early forties and their elderly parents. Both sons were locally regarded as heavy drinkers although not, as a rule, as drunks. On Sunday mornings, while their mother was at church, the sons would gather with various other unmarried men in the hay-loft to drink – beer and whisky. Sunday lunch, when the mother returned, would be played out as a perfectly normal event, the florid faces and the smell of liquor being ignored as grace was said and the roast carved. One Sunday, however, the father of the household became angry and began complaining of the sons' drinking habits and the way they were wasting their money and their lives. The mother's response to this was to begin to sing loudly in order to drown out their voices, a technique she often used when things were being said which she did not want to hear. This may, of course, have been something which she did because I was present, but in any case her response was an attempt to prevent open statement of her sons' drinking habits. In other cases too the drunken behaviour of men in families was ignored by the women, hangovers sometimes being explained as colds even in cases where it was well known that the men were drinkers.

The Social Location of Drinking

Within the home, these sons – like the majority of men not living alone – did not drink regularly. Alcoholic beverages never accompany everyday meals in the Highlands but are mostly reserved for specifically 'social' occasions when friends visit in the evenings; and this drinking is at least partly controlled by women. Bottles are never displayed openly in a cabinet or on a shelf but will be fetched from a closed cupboard, often in the kitchen, the heart of the woman's domain[17].

It is the woman who will generally serve the guests with drink and the snacks and tea which accompany it in the home. Her presence, and that of the 'strupach' (tea and food) so symbolic of domestic hospitality, defines the event as a controlled domestic one, a matter of hospitality rather than as part of the male domain in which drunkenness can occur. However, a woman cannot be fully in control of the amount of alcohol which is drunk – particularly if all the guests are male – for here an ethos of generosity and hospitality comes into conflict with any desire to maintain temperance. A husband may call to his wife to fill the glasses or to leave the bottle on the table, in which case, after doing so, she will probably leave the room, so acknowledging that the domain has passed from her control, that the event has been transformed. Male visitors may well have brought carry-outs themselves too and in this case the host feels that he must be at least equally generous with his own supplies of drink. The progressively heavy drinking which may ensue is only likely when all the visitors are men, and a woman may be able to mark the end of the male activity by returning to the room, making tea and probably commenting on how late it has become. In this way she attempts to reclaim the domestic arena and control from the male world of drinking and camaraderie.

The locations in which men mostly drink, however, are all-male arenas outside the home: hotel bars, the homes of local bachelors, caravans, hay-lofts, cars and fanks. Hotel bars are not exclusively patronised by men, though in rural areas they are predominantly so. When women do attend – especially on Friday and Saturday nights – they usually sit in all-female groups. The scene in the local bar on a Saturday evening, then, will be one in which the men are sitting on one side, perhaps the older ones at different tables from the young bloods (who are most likely to be playing darts and pool), and they will be drinking pints of beer and chasers of whisky. Domhnall Sheumais may be telling his hilarious stories or crude jokes depending on just how drunk he has become. The women will be on the other side drinking vodka and orange or whatever the most recent fashion is. Perhaps some young incomer couples will be sitting at other tables, the women probably drinking beer or lager.

Fashionable drinks like vodka and orange, and others such as Bacardi and more traditionally sherry, are not really regarded as alcoholic – as 'real' or 'hard' drink – and indeed they are often referred to as 'ladies' drinks'. These 'ladies' drinks' are acceptable in many circles in which whisky, with its very masculine imagery, would not be. A church communicant might refuse a dram but accept a sherry, Tia Maria or Martini. At first footing – the visiting which goes on for several days at the New Year – men typically carry a bottle of whisky for the men and one of sherry for the women.

I had not fully appreciated this distinction between ladies' drinks and spirits when one man, who had a tendency to drink too much, repeatedly emphasised that he did not usually drink whisky, although I had often seen him doing so at agricultural events and the like. However, his insistence was intended to show that he was not the heavy drinker that I might think. Thus, after he drove his car off a road one night, miraculously escaping serious injury, he insisted that he had not been 'drinking' – he had only had Bacardi and Coke!

Men also drink at the communal township agricultural events known as fanks – and it is always whisky that is drunk. Usually, the bottles or half-bottles are passed from man to man, though sometimes the liquor is poured into the cups from the men's flasks. Fanks are very much a male domain, being defined as such through their location on the moor, far from the domestic domain of the household, and through their agricultural role, crofting being in many ways the preserve of men. The ethos of the fank is that of male egalitarianism and camaraderie; and the drinking that goes on there is a symbolic affirmation of this. Whisky, both in the local world-view and the national imagery, is classless and masculine. Women are regarded in some respects as counter to this ethos, as can be seen in various apocryphal tales about women who try to participate at the fank. These women fail to play properly by the rules of egalitarianism and anti-bureaucratic sentiment, and in particular they often try to curb the drinking that goes on amongst the men.

The associations between drinking and national imagery are also seen in various rituals, particularly those which mark the seasonal and life-cycles. The New Year – Hogmanay – is one of the most important events in the annual calendar for most Scots, and drinking, redolent with the positive national symbolism of hospitality, community and classlessness, is very much a key activity. In the Highlands first-footing continues for several days with people going from house to house to visit neighbours, friends and relatives, mapping out their social relationships through their movements. Those visiting take drink with them – whisky for men and sherry for women (though women may drink whisky) – and the usual practice is for them to offer their hosts a drink and for the hosts to offer drink in return. The reciprocity, and the act of moving from house to house, are statements of the egalitarian and community ideologies of which drink is a part.

Similarly, at weddings and traditionally at funerals (though this is no longer the practice – the churches having put a halt to it) alcohol, and especially whisky, is drunk. Again these are rituals in which the household and the community come together and which provide occasions for defining and reifying social relationships and ideals. It is on these occasions that the social values of 'the people' as a whole are affirmed, and drink is one of the symbolic markers of this affirmation. As I have suggested, however, women – or the values that they are seen to represent – are in some circumstances conceptualised as contrary to the values which define the people. The clearest instance of this is in funeral rituals where it is only men who go to the cemetery, and only men who would in the recent past have participated in the whisky-drinking that went on there[18]. The exclusion of women was, and is, I suggest, a symbolic exclusion of the status and worldly differences with which they are particularly associated, differences which are denied by the sharing of drink, especially the sharing of whisky.

Of Men and Marriage

Bachelors typically drink more than married men. Indeed, in the Highlands the fact that a man is a bachelor is usually taken as an explanation for why he drinks and in turn the fact that he drinks too much as an explanation for the fact that he does not have a wife. The shy bachelor who needs to get a drink inside him before he can face talking to a woman is part of the Scottish stereotype, a stereotype which – as I found during my fieldwork – is readily encountered in everyday life.

There are large numbers of bachelors in the Highlands due in part to differential migration of the sexes and also the fact that a man may have to wait until his late thirties or forties to inherit a croft and will probably not consider marrying before then. One reason that more men tend to stay on the islands is that they tend to be less 'at home' on the mainland than are women for whom the shift is generally from one domestic-centred domain to another. For men, leaving the Highlands means leaving what is idealised as a classless world of their 'mates' and of their self-definition through the idiom of crofting. This does not hold true of all men, of course, but for the core of the drinking fraternity – which is in many ways the idealised representation of manhood in the Highlands – taking part in what they regard as a more status-conscious, competitive society is anathema.

If men's domain is considered relatively classless, it is also regarded as more 'natural', as part of a relatively uncultivated and undomesticated arena. Marriage effects something of a transformation for men, however: they become incorporated into the controlled world of the household and familial respectability. For some bachelors, indeed, marriage is described in much the same terms as religious conversion; one telling element of these descriptions being that upon marriage – as upon conversion – a man should give up any heavy drinking. His unmitigated participation in the world of men should come to an end – or rather, the egalitarian, communalistic aspects of his social world should mesh nicely with the more individual and hierarchical interests of the household as represented by women. In practice, however, the attractions and demands of the male world may create a conflict between the two dimensions of his life.

Within the home – women's arena – then, drinking is usually conceptualised as relatively controlled, whereas within the male social world it is dominated by notions of generosity and egalitarianism. A man may even try to express the controlled nature of his own drinking through reference to women and domesticity. Thus one man told me at the fank that his mother always put whisky in the tea in his flask – so implying her approval of his alcohol consumption. I had, however, watched her make the tea and know for sure that no alcohol had been added.

The possibility of going 'over the top' is an ever-present one for men, particularly if they do not have the tempering influence of a wife. It is unusual to hear any explanations of why a particular man should drink heavily: alcoholism is seen more or less as an occupational hazard of being male, particularly of being unmarried and male.

Women's Drinking

Women's drinking, however, needs to be explained – it is abnormal to an extent that that of men is not. Generally these explanations bear on particular family problems, drunken husbands being one such. For a long time, however, I was puzzled by a remark made of one woman who was medically deemed to have become an alcoholic: 'Well, you see', I was told, 'she and her husband had become social drinkers.' There seemed to be nothing unusual in being a social drinker to me but the woman who made the remark went on to describe the controlled drinking that went on in her own home. She told me how, when she and her husband had a drink together, they would allow their children a drink in an egg-cup because this would accustom them to responsible drinking. Being a 'social drinker' was clearly meant as a contrast to drinking within the home, or rather, drinking within a narrowly defined as opposed to broadly 'social' group of people.

Given that the imagery of women is of a more controlled consumption of alcohol we might ask why women do not take more active steps to prevent men from drinking too much. The problem, however, is that in many ways the values associated with men's drinking are presented as those of the people as a whole. Generosity and hospitality in particular are highly valued and the offering of whisky is one of the most symbolically resonant gestures of such hospitality. Sometimes men would actually signify their approval of a woman – illustrating that she was not mean-spirited – by noting that she would take a dram herself now and then[19]. Just as whisky, the national and Highland drink, is portrayed as classless and traditional, in contrast to the fashionable, sophisticated ladies' drinks, the values of men and their drinking behaviour – egalitarianism, hospitality and generosity – are those to which both men and women subscribe as a community or people.

Notes

1. This chapter was originally presented at a workshop on 'Women, Alcohol and Addictions' organised by Maryon McDonald in December 1987. I would like to thank all the participants there for their comments on the paper, and also Maryon McDonald and the late Edwin Ardener for their help when much of the material was embedded within my D.Phil. thesis. I also thank my husband Mike Beaney for helping me to investigate drinking in Scotland.

2. Statistics on 'alcoholism' are notoriously problematic for a number of reasons (cf. McDonald in this volume). In the UK they are calculated by extrapolating from figures on gross per caput alcohol consumption, mortality due to cirrhosis of the liver, and convictions for drunkenness (see for example, Davies and Walsh

1983:ch.18). More general statistics on drinking have been collected biennially as a specific part of the General Household Survey since 1978. In addition, various more focused studies have been undertaken (see OPCS bibliography on alcohol and alcoholism, 1989).

While Scotland fares worse as far as alcoholism is concerned by some of these statistics, notably those concerning cirrhosis of the liver (see note 3) and convictions for drunkenness, the data is by no means unequivocal, for in terms of per caput alcohol consumption and numbers of heavy drinkers (calculated by units of alcohol consumed) Scotland does not show significantly higher rates than the UK average. Davies and Walsh conclude that: 'Alcohol problems are consistently higher in Scotland than in England and Wales, though drinking patterns are very similar in these countries' (1983:260), so suggesting that there is no simple correlation between 'problem drinking' and the amount of alcohol actually consumed.

3. Scotland shows a higher proportion of deaths from cirrhosis of the liver than other parts of the UK (Davies and Walsh 1983:247–8; Government Statistical Service 1988). However, this may be due in part to other contributing factors such as diet (cf. Davies and Walsh 1983:247). Between 1970 and 1979, Scotland showed an increase in the number of deaths from cirrhosis of the liver of 80%, compared with an increase of 56% in the UK as a whole (ibid.:248). Over the following decade the number levelled off or decreased slightly (Registrar General Scotland 1988; Green 1986).

4. See the OPCS bibliography on alcohol and alcoholism (1989).

5. Fieldwork in Skye was carried out mainly between 1983 and 1985. I also spent time in other parts of the Highlands, however, and some of my examples here are drawn from them, though in all cases I think that the patterns they suggest apply equally to Skye. In the examples here I have changed some details in order to try to protect the identity of individuals for this is sensitive subject-matter.

6. The recently opened 'Scotch Whisky Heritage Centre' in Edinburgh, itself a significant marker of the drink's status, includes a recreated scene of Sir Walter Scott toasting the tartan-bedecked King (an image also recorded in various paintings).

7. See OPCS 1989. Scotland's Alcohol Studies Centre was established in 1979 and the Scottish Council on Alcoholism in 1972, though the original Glasgow Council on Alcoholism had been in existence since the 1960s. A network of local councils operates under the aegis of the Scottish Council on Alcoholism. I should point out that the SCA has itself become concerned not to see

alcohol problems as a disease or illness but rather 'as a progression through various levels of problem drinking where different levels of problems are experienced' (SCA information leaflet).

8. Grant, Plant and Saunders cite a survey giving figures of 5% of men and 15% of women who never drink (1980:4).

9. A similar disparity in attitudes towards male and female drinkers is found in many other surveys: see, for example, Jahoda and Crammond 1972, Aitken 1978, Aitken and Leathar 1981.

10. Cf. McDonald in this volume. This is a theme of various studies of the loss of community in other areas of the Celtic Fringe such as rural Ireland (e.g. Brody 1973).

11. This subtitle is taken from Susan Parman's discussion of drinking in Lewis (1972). She too makes a case for going beyond this opposition – and the hypocrisy or failure it implies – to a fuller account of both drinking and religion.

12. The situation is in fact more complicated than this. In most areas of the Highlands there are three different Presbyterian Churches: the Free Presbyterian Church, the Free Church and the Church of Scotland. Of these, the Free Presbyterian is the strictest (or most 'uncompromising' as they would put it themselves) and the Church of Scotland most liberal (though it is not generally as liberal as Church of Scotland congregations on the mainland). To outsiders, all church-goers are usually termed 'Wee Frees'. Within the Highlands only the Free Presbyterians, and sometimes but not always the Free Church congregations are called 'Wee Frees'. The general differences between them in terms of strictness and liberality apply equally to their attitude towards alcohol.

13. 'Incomers', along with 'white settlers', is a term used in the Highlands to describe people who have come to live in the locality from other areas, particularly the mainland. There is a common life-cycle pattern for islanders of leaving in young adulthood to work and perhaps raise a family, and then returning in later life. Most of my discussion here is not about incomers, though they may take part in some of the practices described here. On the whole, however, the heavy drinking which I describe here was viewed by incomers in the area in which I worked as characteristic of the 'locals'. Indeed, local consumption of drink was a matter of fascination and a symbolic marker of group difference for incomers.

14. Local people's own estimates of what constitutes heavy drinking were 30.2 pints of beer or 2.2 bottles of whisky per week. This is about 60 alcoholic units (Dight 1976:155). Thirty per cent of the alcohol consumed in a typical week in Scotland is drunk by only 3%

of the total population, and this group consists almost entirely of men (ibid.:44–6).

15. Judith Ennew writes that: 'Throughout Lewis and Harris one question above all was put to me by the women with whom I spoke. "Does your husband take a drink?", was the query, meaning specifically "Does he drink whisky?". And there would be a nod of agreement or a sigh of relief when I said that he did not.' (1980:101).

16. One finding in Susan Dight's survey on which she casts doubt is that a higher proportion of people in the Western Isles claim to have seen a drunk on the streets in the previous week than is the case anywhere else in Scotland (1976:230). She assumes that this must be an aberration resulting from the small sample of islanders studied. In fact a rate of 68% does not seem surprisingly high from knowledge of the locality.

17. Sometimes the alcohol is stored alongside medicines. The perception of spirits as medicinal or even health-giving is quite common, and this perception may legitimate drinking. In one strict Free Presbyterian home that I visited at New Year – when the offering of drink to visitors is expected – the woman made me a drink of whisky mixed with condensed milk and fresh cream. As she gave it to me she remarked: 'It's not really a drink – more of a tonic really.' Whisky is considered by many people to be a protection against the cold and a good treatment for colds and sore throats.

18. Increasingly women do go to the cemetery at funerals, though usually it is only close female relatives who do so. The presence of even these women is frowned upon by some in the community, however. After a death a service, attended only by men, is generally held in the home. It used to be the custom – and some say still is – that whisky was drunk there too.

19. Amongst men, the fact that I drank whisky – and drank it neat – seemed to be viewed with more amusement than disapproval. I soon learned, however, that in wider social gatherings it was right to choose a ladies' drink – indeed, these would usually be the only ones offered.

References

Aitken, P.P. (1978), *Ten-to-fourteen-year-olds and alcohol. A developmental study in the Central Region of Scotland.* Edinburgh: HMSO.

Aitken, P.P. and Leathar, D.S. (1981), *Adults' attitudes towards drinking and smoking among young people in Scotland.* Edinburgh: HMSO.

Brody, H. (1973), *Inishkillane. Change and Decline in the West of Ireland*. London: Jill Norman and Hobhouse.

Chapman, M. (1978), *The Gaelic Vision in Scottish Culture*. London: Croom Helm.

Condry, E. (1980), 'Culture and Identity in the Scottish Highlands'. Unpublished D.Phil. thesis, Oxford University.

Davies, P. and Walsh, D. (1983), *Alcohol Problems and Alcohol Control In Europe*. London: Croom Helm.

Dight, S.E. (1976), *Scottish Drinking Habits. A survey carried out for the Scottish Home and Health department*. London: HMSO.

Ennew, J. (1980), *The Western Isles Today*. Cambridge: Cambridge University Press.

Goddard, E. (1986), *Drinking and attitudes to licensing in Scotland*. London: HMSO.

Grant, I.F. (1961), *Highland Folk Ways*. London: RKP.

Grant, M., Plant, M. and Saunders, W. (1980), *Drinking and Alcohol Problems in Scotland*. Edinburgh: Scottish Health Education Unit.

Green, H. (1986), *Drinking. General Household Survey*. London: HMSO.

Jahoda, G. and Crammond, J. (1972), *Children and Alcohol. A developmental study in Glasgow*. London: HMSO.

MacKenzie, Compton (1957), *Whisky Galore*. Harmondsworth: Penguin (originally published in 1947).

Mewett, P. (1982), 'Associational categories and the social location of relationships in a Lewis crofting community', in Cohen, A.P. (ed.) *Belonging. Identity and Social Organisation in British Rural Cultures*. Manchester: Manchester University Press.

OPCS (1989), *Alcohol and Alcoholism: some works in OPCS library*. London: Office of Population Censuses and Surveys.

Parman, S. (1972), 'Sociocultural Change in a Scottish Crofting Township'. Unpublished Ph.D. thesis, Rice University, Houston, Texas.

Registrar General Scotland (1988), *Annual Report*. Edinburgh: HMSO.

6

Gender, Ethnicity and Alcohol in the Former Soviet Union

Tamara Dragadze

Introduction

Different forms of state apparatus and government institutions seem to define and promote different patterns of social 'deviance'. The former Soviet Union is an interesting case in which alcohol and deviance were linked, both officially and locally. This brief chapter refers to the period before 1989, when diversity was hardly apparent in the Soviet system. The main relevant aspects of Soviet rule were the command system of the economy together with the coercion accompanying government decrees; the absolute status of official ideology could not be questioned. This official ideology postulated a vision of the ideal Soviet citizen, man or woman, uniform throughout the Soviet Union: healthy, courageous, hard-working, respectful to communist justice. There would be no room for racism, sexism or alcoholism.

The persistent failures of a totalitarian state at implementing its values is an interesting theme in itself. The social deviance which 'alcoholism' constituted could, for some Soviet people, become one way in which, through the very act of excess, defiance against authoritarian rule could find expression. For others, such deviance could be both enacted and claimed as the result of official ideals never having been supported by a practical infrastructure which would allow them to be carried out. Tremendous disparities existed in housing, income and access to consumer goods, resulting in the marginalisation of certain groups of individuals living in deprivation. Furthermore, the poverty trap of such groups was exacerbated and the people brutalised by the indifferent or even vindictive attitude of the state authorities. Those representing the state apparatus were often angered by the embarrassing visibility of such contradictions of their own statements, for official denials of the very existence of such poverty were frequent.

The apparent emptiness of official ideals encouraged some people to resort to seeking patterns of meaning for their everyday life in their own national culture, wherever such a possibility had not been forcibly destroyed. In the Soviet Union, although Russification was almost synonymous with Sovietisation, the non-Russian peoples clung to their national identity tenaciously, creating and recreating it in the process. They therefore tended to resent laws that were applied throughout the Soviet Union, regardless of ethnic diversity.

The drive against alcoholism in 1987, launched in Gorbachev's early days, was one of the Moscow initiatives which was widely despised in the minority Union republics. Excessive drinking was viewed as a particularly *Russian* problem and not theirs. I shall return to these points in a moment. By the time Gorbachev came to power, following Brezhnev's so-called 'period of stagnation', alcoholism in Russia had already reached an alarming level. The 'bread and circuses' attitude toward the 'toiling masses', which had apparently condoned the selling of cheap alcohol as a means of pacifying the hard-pressed population, had encouraged unprecedented levels of absenteeism. At the time, this absenteeism, and the alcohol to which it was officially deemed to be due, was seen as one of the important causes of the backwardness of the Soviet economy. The government had not yet addressed itself to other, and more fundamental, causes of economic failure.

Gender

Drinking among Russians was mainly a male preserve. One of the measures brought in to curb consumption involved the direct payment of factory wages to the wife so that her factory-worker husband would not spend it all on drink. Research soon showed evidence of improvements in children's diets; women had more access to the family income and could spend it on food instead of its disappearing on men's alcoholic beverages.

Nevertheless, measures such as making alcohol harder to buy in the shops, or handing over wages to wives, were never going to succeed in eradicating the problem. For those defined as 'alcoholic', help was not easily available. Complaints about what some saw as 'the root causes of alcoholism', such as the difficulties of working conditions, were not tackled. The social constructions of alcohol were such that some men tried to drink themselves into positions of relative status and power, into greater male camaraderie, or into the prestige of a wage-earning, socially worthy, drink-buying man amongst men; they became officially deviant, 'alcoholic' and a problem in the process. It was easy for a situation to develop in which credibility sank at home and outside it, and seemed to require yet more drink and drinking to restore it. Such drinking could also become its own form of resistance. Sugar disappeared almost completely from open purchase since it was bought in bulk to be used illegally for home-brewed alcoholic beverages. Some resorted to drinking eau-de-Cologne.

Western studies of women in the Soviet Union have been mainly of Russian women, mostly in their workplace, and often studies have concentrated on women's inequality of status and their unprestigious location in social ranking, despite official commitment to sexual equality.

Alcoholism has been, with some exceptions (mainly of women marginalised into prostitution and homelessness), largely a male problem. The relatively low extent of female drinking can be partly accounted for by their choice to retain control within the domestic domain. The harsh economic conditions did not include official unemployment. This was very different from a situation in which suburban non-earning housewives might drink their way, alone, into new modes of existence (one scenario which, real or not, has been imagined to exist in the West).

It has been tempting for outsiders to interpret the observation that women drink less alcohol than men as an indication that women are more repressed in Soviet society, a society that is officially very prudish and, unofficially, very sexist. Such an explanation risks being either misplaced or inadequate, however. Due to difficulties of access, there are few studies of women's positions in the domestic context for the period that concerns us. Urban Russian homes have been marginally more accessible to Western researchers than those of rural women. From observations that have been made here, it seems that power for women in the domestic context derived partly from the fact that they were income-earners themselves, partly because most domestic tasks were deemed to be in the female domain and under their jurisdiction, and partly from the fact that, in families where there was frequent intoxication on the part of the males, then the men *de facto* abdicated control of the household to their level-headed partners. There were frequent reports that at weekends one could see women supporting the arms of their inebriated spouses as they travelled home on the Moscow metro. However, in urban Russian homes where women drank as much as their men, I noted that they lost the domestic authority they had habitually exerted.

Ethnicity

When Gorbachev brought in anti-alcohol laws in 1987 and 1988 that restricted production of alcoholic beverages, the republics, including those with a Muslim population, were resentful. Under Brezhnev, the local population had in some instances – such as Azerbaijan – been forced to relinquish their garden produce and to grow grapes on the land instead. Brezhnev and his allies had ordered this plan in order better to integrate all the republics into their system of All-Union interdependence. These minority populations were therefore required to grow grapes for the alcohol-drinking population of Russia and not for themselves. The subsequent Gorbachev decree from Moscow which cut down production acted directly against a newly acquired source of income for some Soviet republics.

In Georgia, there was anger among the population as well, not about production levels in a traditionally wine-producing country, but about restrictions on retail purchases. Resentment grew to the point that most of the laws concerning the sale of alcohol in shops were ignored. They were especially indignant that laws with relevance for other cultures should be applied to their own nation as well. Most alcohol in Georgia is drunk at table, ritually integrated and regulated (see Dragadze 1988 and forthcoming). The table rituals provide a meeting-point for affirming Georgian identity and celebrating ideals of conviviality, dignity and chivalry. They offered a focus for resisting Russification and for celebrating what was seen to be a traditional, Georgian social order.

The style of consumption of alcohol in Georgia was determined less by where it took place – a ritual banquet might be set up at an open picnic site, for example, or in a closed domestic space – than by the degree to which the various elements of the community were represented. The social locations of alcohol consumption in Georgian society can be analytically summarised briefly, if somewhat crudely, by setting them out in a continuum, with the use of alcohol in church at one end of the continuum and casual drinking in the street at the other. This would give the following general picture:

1) CHURCH COMMUNION RITUAL

Community presence: all the community; heterogeneity – both sexes and all ages.
Control of consumption: strictly regulated.
Regulator: the priest.

Differentiation of quantities consumed by individuals: equal among all participants.
Location: unique, inside church.

2) CEREMONIAL FEASTING

Community presence: all community; heterogeneity – both sexes and all ages.
Control of consumption: regulated.
Regulator: the toastmaster.
Differentiation of quantities consumed by individuals: unequal, according to sex and age.
Location: restricted location, within domestic space or in specifically designated banquet location.

3) CONSPICUOUS DISPLAY FEASTING

Community presence: not all community; both sexes but not elders.
Control of consumption: weakly controlled.
Regulator: the toastmaster.
Differentiation of quantities consumed by individuals: unequal according to sex.
Location: restricted location, within domestic space or in specifically designated banquet location.

4) COMPETITIVE DRINKING

Community presence: young males only.
Control of consumption: quantities equal among competitors until end of game.
Regulator: the toastmaster, chosen among peers.
Location: unrestricted.

5) CASUAL DRINKING

Community presence: males only, any age, any ethnic group.
Control of consumption: none.
Regulator: none.
Location: street only.

The different forms of drinking in Georgian society are not a simple social continuum, in the sense of one form leading to another. They are distinct contexts in that they would be recognised as requiring different behaviours, but they can nevertheless be presented as a continuum, with some features shared between adjacent categories.

The first context listed above is the highly ritualised Church communion (important in people's minds but not exemplified in everyday life in the Communist period); this embraces a universal community of heavenly and earthly members. The Church is also involved in the ceremonial feasting which accompanies rites of passage or any solemn occasion. The presence of men, women and children, of young and old, and the regulation of drinking by the toastmaster, echo the importance of wine as does the communion service in church.

Important in determining the social use of alcohol is the presence or absence of women, children and elders. 'Alcoholism' is associated entirely *with a life style where female members of the community are absent*. Prostitutes are assumed to drink and to encourage drinking, but in Georgia are assumed to be non-Georgian. The end of the continuum I have outlined is the urban street, open to non-ethnic or non-Georgian community intervention. It represents the collective nightmare of many Georgians: the friendless, kinless, homeless destiny of social outcasts.

Locations for drinking may be qualified by strong claims of custom. A picnic spot, for example, may be said to have been chosen by local ancestors because of its proximity to a shrine or holy tree. Most ritual feasting, however, takes place inside the domestic space of the house and courtyard. Conspicuous consumption is often involved, with the sheer number of guests an element of display. In urban settings, a large banqueting hall might be hired for the purpose. A few apartment blocks built for the élite had such halls on their ground floor. Foreign makes of cognac, and the presence of drinks such as whisky, were intended to impress the participants. Women are deemed to prefer sweet wines to dry wines or spirits and their tastes are also catered for in this boasting exercise. These visible displays of consumption openly defied Communist egalitarianism.

All drinking, however is regulated by a toastmaster. Men were expected to be able to rise from the table at the end of the feast and walk home. Georgians liked to contrast this with the perceived behaviour of their Russian masters whom they accused of drinking to excess, without regulation. Using both ethnic and gender imagery, they considered that a man was 'more of a man' if he was Georgian, because he could better hold his drink than could Russians. Similarly, although neither Georgian nor Russian women were expected to drink like men, it was thought by Georgians that their own women could be 'more of a woman' because they did not have to carry their men home from a drinking binge. In short, questions of modes of drinking and gender had special significance here. They were used to support the general nationalist idea that Georgia should be a self-regulating, sovereign country, not ruled by Russia.

Conclusion

In the Soviet period, ethnic assertiveness through local evaluations of the use of alcohol was instrumental for Georgians in maintaining a defiant self-identity. The use of alcohol was integrated into self-images at once ethnic and gendered. Positive evaluations depended on the orderly regulation of drinking according to ethnic custom in which the presence of both sexes and all age-groups of the community was emphasized. This ordered social drinking was contrasted with the all-male outcasts in the street who were 'alcoholics', and deemed to be no longer properly men or Georgian. The laws restricting alcohol consumption, decreed in the early days of Gorbachev's rule, were seen by non-Russians such as the Georgians as not being devised for them. Decrees which did not take account of ethnic variations could not, therefore, be properly implemented throughout the Soviet Union. It was not that Georgians wanted to drink more, but they believed that their own forms of regulation were sufficient. In their view, Gorbachev's 'alcoholic' was not part of Georgian society; his 'alcoholic' was, by definition, 'Russian'.

The role of gender constructs in assertions of ethnic identity and in the social context of alcohol-drinking is important here. Women drink less than men, in urban Russia as in Georgia. Urban Russia does not have the close-knit communities of Georgia, in which moral pressures might encourage conformity to the view that it is unseemly for women to be drunk. Yet, in Russia as in Georgia, women would usually forgo any perceived over-indulgence in alcohol in order to maintain overall authority and control – in the domestic domain at least.

The authoritarian regime of the Soviet period provides many tales of missed opportunities. Sufficient control of the economy and the amount of human resources at its sole disposal could have given the government unique opportunities to single out those deemed to be severe alcoholics, and give them access to supportive therapy. This, however, was not possible because the very presence of these perceived deviants ran counter to the positive image the regime wanted to create of Soviet society. Even when this society explicitly entertained notions of 'treating' rather than punishing alcoholics, in practice the alcoholic nevertheless continued to occupy the space of moral and political deviant. To the authorities, such deviance might appear throughout the Soviet Union and the decrees were therefore applied everywhere. To many non-Russians, however, this deviance was most likely to be Russian. As a consequence, an apparent paradox arose in which Russian women could be, and were, viewed as having an unenviable fate in comparison with women living in the lands subordinated to Soviet Russian rule. They had to work harder to obtain control at home and this control seemed all the more necessary and all the more elusive. At the same time, their plight allowed others to pity them, a pity that was politically apt, and allowed Georgians – and especially Georgian women – their own oppositional self-definition of moral integrity.

References

Dragadze, T. (1988), *Rural families in Soviet Georgia*. London and New York: Routledge.

Dragadze, T. (forthcoming), 'Banqueting in the Republic of Georgia'.

7

The Drinker as Chief or Rebel: Kava and Alcohol in Fiji

Christina Toren

In Fiji, the drinking of *yaqona* is central to *na cakacaka vakavanua* (lit. 'work in the manner of the land') an expression which encompasses ritual and tradition. *Yaqona* is a mildly intoxicating but non-alcoholic drink made from the ground roots of *Piper methysticum*, commonly called 'kava' in other South Pacific countries. In presenting, making, serving and drinking *yaqona* participants at once constitute and express social relations as ordered and hierarchical. By contrast, relations between those drinking alcohol together seem to be characterised by egalitarian disorder. This apparent antithesis ideally pits 'the Fijian way' against 'the European way' – or 'the way according to money'. But the two forms of drinking (like the two 'ways') also implicate an endemic antithesis between hierarchy and equality that has to be negotiated continuously in the daily round of Fijian lives.

Hierarchy takes shape in the exchange relation of tribute and redistribution which in part constitutes chiefly power and authority. However, tribute and redistribution themselves rest on a transformation of balanced reciprocal exchange between people who are relating to one another as landspeople and sea-people, as men and women, or as affines. This transformation can never be final; rather it has to be effected in ritual on a daily basis, again and again, and *yaqona*-drinking is crucial to this process. (Some of the points about hierarchy and exchange are set out in more detail in Toren 1990.)

Today *yaqona* is both crucial to ritual and a valuable commodity – its commercial value being largely derived from its ritual value. However, money and *yaqona* are allowed to be exchangeable in entirely different ways depending on the form of the *yaqona* (as root or prepared drink) and the way the context of exchange is categorised. The difference is such that 'the Fijian way' is seen to

153

emerge intact from a confrontation with 'the European way' (or 'the way according to money') (see Toren 1989). In the present paper I largely ignore the status of *yaqona* as a commodity to concentrate on the antithesis that is offered by the drinking of *yaqona ni vavalagi* – drink that is both alcoholic and foreign (i.e. associated with Europeans). This antithesis turns on Fijian villagers' ideas of *yaqona*-drinking as expressive of hierarchical relations where elderly male chiefs have the highest status, and of alcohol-drinking, on the other hand, as an anarchic challenge by young men against the traditional status quo.

Yaqona-Drinking

For the villagers of Sawaieke, on the island of Gau, central Fiji, where I did fieldwork (18 months 1981–83, four months in 1990) *yaqona*-drinking was virtually an everyday affair[1]. Gau is fertile and villagers grew *yaqona* for sale as well as for everyday and ceremonial use. On less fertile islands *yaqona* may be drunk only for important occasions such as weddings, funerals and other life-cycle ceremonies, but in Sawaieke it was possible – if one wished – to drink *yaqona* every day. All one had to do was find out in whose house people were drinking and, taking a small *sevusevu* (an offering of *yaqona* root), go and join in.

Yaqona is prepared by squeezing the pounded root through water to produce a pleasant, astringent and mildly intoxicating brew – pharmacologically classified as a 'barbituric narcotic' (Lebot and Cabalion 1986:61)[2]. On important occasions the very gestures of the man preparing the drink are highly ritualised and orchestrated by a traditional chant given out by the men. Once the drink is prepared, it is served in bowls of polished half-coconut shells one after the other to the assembled people according to their status in the local hierarchy – the highest-status person present being served first. This ordered drinking emphasises the ordered seating above and below the *tanoa* (the large central bowl in which *yaqona* is mixed and from which it is served). The paramount chief sits above and centrally, flanked by the clan chiefs and other high-status men; below and facing them are married men, the young men who look after the preparation and serving of *yaqona*, and finally women; here 'above' and 'below' refer to areas of the same plane – no one is literally above anyone else. People's seating positions in *yaqona*-drinking seem to suggest that hierarchy is given in the fundamental conditions of existence. Indeed, this kind of ritualised behaviour is of crucial importance for children's cognitive construction over time of a hierarchical principle which is understood to order people's status according to an interaction between rank, gender and seniority (Toren 1990).

In short, the presentation of *yaqona* in its root form as *sevusevu* together with its preparation and drinking are central to the continuity of 'the Fijian way' – another general term for which is 'the way in the manner of the land' (*na i vakarau ni bula vakavanua*). This has three main aspects: 'the chiefly way' (*vakaturaga*), 'the way according to the land' (*vakavanua* – here the term may have a narrower application and refer to commoners in contradistinction to chiefs), and 'the way according to kinship' (*vakaveiwekani*). So, in the proper ritual setting, under the aegis of the land chief (the chief of the landspeople's clan that 'makes the chief'), the drinking of *yaqona* installs a paramount; it gives him *mana dina*, 'true effectiveness', whose source is the ancestors in their benign aspect by virtue of the power of the Christian god. *Yaqona* is drunk only in company with others. To say that someone 'drinks alone' is an idiom for witchcraft. It implies that he or she is pouring libations to an ancestor for evil, selfish ends – the point being that *yaqona*-drinking is always *mana* ('effective') in that it gives either legitimate or illegitimate access to ancestral power[3].

So the drinking of *yaqona* is, under any circumstances, hedged about by ceremony. It is prepared and drunk under the auspices of chiefs and someone must always sit above the *tanoa* so that it may be described as 'facing the chiefs' (*qarava na turaga*) even when the drinking is at its most informal. For instance, if young unmarried men and women are drinking together, packed into someone's kitchen with one kerosene lamp shedding a dim light, and having fun, they make the highest-status young man of their number sit in the top central position above the *tanoa*. There may be a lot of giggling and perhaps exaggerated ceremony in the way the drink is served. The server may clap his cupped palms loudly and cry '*maca!*' ('empty!') in a parody of extreme respect when the 'chief of the hour' finishes drinking his bowl. But this parodying of the best form seems to arise from a degree of embarrassment rather than from any desire to rebel; the young people are constrained by their consciousness of *yaqona* ritual itself to behave to one of their peers – all of them at the lowest end of the status hierarchy in terms of adult seniority – as if he were chief. The parody recognises both that the young man is not really, or not yet, a chief and that, at the same time, someone has to be.

Yaqona has been important as the chiefly drink throughout what we know of Fijian history. Indeed, its importance was recognised by Christian missionaries who saw it as inimical to their own teachings. In the early part of this century, the Fiji Methodist Synod made strenuous efforts to persuade its congregation to pledge abstinence from *yaqona*-drinking. They were singularly unsuccessful and 'gradually retreated to the point where they asked only that ministers limit themselves to strictly ceremonial drinking, whereas ordinary church members could do as they pleased' (Forman 1982:114).

Today, while some ministers adhere to this principle and go so far as to preach against overindulgence in *yaqona*-drinking as detrimental to family life (*na bula vakamatavuvale*), others routinely drink *yaqona* at gatherings in their own houses and elsewhere. However, it is comparatively recent that drinking *yaqona* has become an everyday matter for all adult members of the community. In the nineteenth century and, in many areas, until the 1950s or so women and young men did not drink; women were not admitted to the company of *yaqona*-drinkers and the young men were there merely to look after its preparation and serving[4]. Consumption of *yaqona* appears to have risen dramatically even during the past thirty years or so, with the plant becoming a valuable cash crop. When I left Fiji in March 1983, *yaqona* root was fetching the equivalent in Fijian dollars of English £3.50 to £5 a kilo; by mid-1990 it had risen to £7.50 a kilo. This increase in the consumption of *yaqona* and its concurrent development into a valuable commodity have been accompanied by an increasing monetarisation of the village economy as a whole. Fijian villagers still depend very largely for their day-to-day needs on subsistence agriculture, fishing and the keeping of a few livestock. However, money is as necessary to comfort in the village as it is in the town. One thing which contributes to comfort – at least for men – is alcohol.

Drinking Alcohol

The following details concerning the consumption of alcohol (known as *yaqona ni vavalagi*: literally, foreign or European *yaqona*) are culled from observation at a distance and second-hand reports. As a respectable woman I could not be seen to drink alcohol, nor be in the company of men who were drinking. To be the only woman sitting with men who were drinking *yaqona* could just about be countenanced (in large part because I am not Fijian); to be in the company of men who were drinking beer would be to lay oneself open to the severest moral censure. Moreover, both men and women considered this situation to be a dangerous one for a woman.

Alcohol is entirely disapproved of by all representatives of the Methodist Church (ministers, lay preachers, church elders) and – at least in public – by the chiefs. Sawaieke and the majority of the surrounding villages were 'dry', beer not being sold in any village store. During the period 1981–83 beer was available only from the Gau Co-operative in Qarani, a village some three kilometres from Sawaieke where clinic and post office are also situated and where the administrative officials appointed by central government have their living quarters. In 1990, it was not available even there and at this point men relied on kin who returned to the island from a visit to the capital, Suva, to bring with them a bottle of gin or whisky or rum. Young men performed the same service for each other when the opportunity arose, but also resorted to 'home-brew'. I was told several times by different people that the chiefs had not always banned alcohol-drinking in the villages; the rule had only come into effect around 1976 owing to the influence of a persuasive visiting preacher. Women with whom I discussed the matter all approved of the rule and most men – especially elderly men and fathers of large families with teenage boys – did so too. People associate alcohol-drinking with fighting among young men, and with wife-beating, sexual licence, general disorder, and disrespect for village values – with, in short, 'the European way'. The following speech from a married woman of twenty-nine with two young children, separated from her husband, is representative of married women's opinions as I heard them expressed in both public and private during my first fieldwork period:

> Today, all the young men want to be Europeans. They're always going off to Qarani to drink beer until they're drunk. When they return here they make a lot of unpleasant noise, fight each other and I don't know what else. It looks bad, it is not respectful, they neglect [the reputation of] the village. It would be better to forbid beer-drinking altogether so that it may not be sold in Qarani. The preaching of Italatala [the Minister] is absolutely right when he says that alcohol injures family life. Look at So-and-so; he used to be a good young man – hardworking, church-going, respectful. Today he is not. He has changed – because of his beer-drinking. Last night he came back here drunk, went at once to his wife. His wife remonstrated with him and he punched her and kicked her. This is really bad behaviour.

The man referred to here was by no means an habitual drunkard. His usual behaviour was that of an exemplary family man who took his obligations seriously and was good to his wife. One implication of the above story is that alcohol is seen to have aroused his sexual appetite and then his anger, when his wife refused his demands. This man's drinking, like that of most other village men so far as I could tell, took the form of an occasional binge – usually during the Christmas and New Year holiday season or on the occasion of a wedding or suchlike. However, when a man did go on such a binge women tended to talk of him later as if he was a confirmed drunkard. This was especially so if drunkenness occurred more than once during, for example, the two weeks spanning Christmas and New Year – even though this was the period when it was most to be expected.

Alcohol was preached against in the pulpit, especially if young men had recently been seen to be drunk in public; for example:

> It shames all of us here in the village when you young men come back here drunk. Don't! Don't do it! Take hold of Jesus Christ so as to prevent drunkenness, so that your sins of this kind may be over and done with. With your permission, I'll just tell you a little story. One day, in the capital [Suva] a gang of young men went to drink beer. With them was nice young man called Tevita...

Here followed an account of Tevita's fall from grace and his ending up in prison with a long sentence for theft committed under the influence of alcohol. It is noticeable that virtually all accounts of crime in Fijian newspapers, both English language and Fijian, say that the defendant offered in extenuation of his crime the excuse that he was drunk. This is particularly true of Fijian men accused of assaulting women or of rape, and it is part of the Fijian male folklore of drunkenness that when drunk one has to have a woman and that this urge cannot be denied, that it is not under the control of the man concerned. This is why it is thought dangerous for a woman to be in the company of men who are drinking alcohol and I have heard a girl described as 'stupid' (*lialia*) who was gang-raped under these circumstances. This over-whelming sexual urge is ascribed only to young men and is only implicit (as in the story above) with respect to settled married men who are presumed to satisfy themselves with their wives. 'He was drunk, he's a young man, he wanted a woman' goes the line of reasoning and it seems to be largely accepted.

Too much *yaqona*, on the other hand, is said to weaken a man's sexual desires and perhaps his prowess. Moreover, one of the virtues of *yaqona* is that it is said to induce a dreamless sleep; dreams may entail encounters with devils (*tevoro*, the ancestors in their malevolent guise) and sexual dreams are especially disturbing because they denote possession.

To be drunk on either *yaqona* or alcohol is to be *mateni* (lit. 'dead of'). In pharmacological terms, *yaqona* is a soporific and while a great deal of it may affect the use of the limbs, it does not entail any other behaviour that we might morally and medically expect of, or associate with, being drunk on alcohol – e.g. slurring of the speech, incoherence, loss of inhibition etc. Villagers themselves make their own explicit contrast between the two forms of drunkenness: they say that their gatherings are relaxed and very lively for the first hour or two and then become quiet, while European parties are quiet and stiff at first but get more and more lively as they go on.

On those occasions when young men made home-brew (which seemed to be, chemically and morally, of a higher alcohol content than bottled beer) they would be castigated by the chiefs during the weekly village meeting in much stronger terms than were ever used in church. On one such occasion the young men (those over the age of nineteen or so and unmarried) were called together under the eyes of the chiefs who, one after the other, lectured them on the evils of alcohol-drinking; for example:

> You hooligans! You give our village a bad name. The name of our chiefly village smells bad through the whole of Gau. We have told you before not to make home brew. Don't! Don't do it! If it is done again then the police will be called to take the young men concerned into custody... We the chiefs have spoken before about this matter. Do you want to make the name of our village smell bad? Your behaviour looks ugly to us...it is both unfitting and disgusting...

This extract from one of the chiefs' speeches is typical of what is said on such occasions. But it was only young men who were thus castigated and once, when it was presumably common knowledge that the majority of those involved had all been in their mid-twenties, three 'little young men' (*cauravou lalai*) in their mid- to late teens were made public scapegoats for the behaviour of all. The behaviour of married men who get drunk was never a matter for a public lecture, despite the fact that older men are more likely to drink alcohol regularly since they are more able to afford it; the drunkenness of two highly-placed married men who were habitual drinkers and often defied the ban on alcohol within the village environs was a matter of gossip only when it could not be ignored.

This association of young men with alcohol is at least partly due to the fact that young men tend to get drunk in spectacular fashion in fairly large groups whereas older men do so more quietly. However, it also seems to be connected with the continuing constitution of 'the Fijian way' in contradistinction to 'the European way'. It is young men who are accused of the desire to be Europeans, and this accusation is always a contemptuous one since it virtually always refers to perceived aspects of European behaviour that are either amoral or highly immoral in terms of Fijian conventions. Older men, simply by virtue of being senior, of being perhaps elders or chiefs, should embody in their own behaviour 'the Fijian way'. Thus even if they are known to drink whisky in the privacy of their houses, they are not publicly accused of violating *na i tovo vakavanua*, 'customary behaviour', even when their behaviour is frowned upon, as it usually is by women and those men who are earnest church elders. Young men's drinking behaviour is held to violate 'the way in the manner of the land'; that the young men's behaviour is itself customary is not usually admitted. The point is that the manner and style of young men's drinking seems to offer an almost perfect antithesis to 'the Fijian way' as exemplified in *yaqona*-drinking, and as such might appear to be a form of ritualised rebellion.

To begin with, young men maintain that they actually need to drink beer after a long session of *yaqona*-drinking. All ceremonial drinking of *yaqona* – at a wedding for instance – lasts for at least four nights. During my first fieldwork period, it was usually on the morning that followed a long night's ceremonial drinking that a group of young men got together, pooled whatever money they could lay their hands on and went off to Qarani to buy beer to 'wash down' the *yaqona*. One has to be able to buy enough to get drunk; there is no point in buying just a few bottles. In 1990, under similar circumstances, young men prepared home-brew (a concoction of yeast, sugar, water and the liquid of green coconuts) in readiness for the end of a given ceremony. The necessity for 'wash-down' – and it is this English expression that is used – is represented by young men as being an inevitable physical demand that has to be met, much as a man who is hungry has to eat.

As a woman, my access to details of the organisation of beer-drinking was limited on some points, but as far as I could tell, it was necessary to be able to contribute money to the buying of the beer in order to take part. Otherwise a young man might be invited to drink by a cross-cousin on the implicit understanding that he would reciprocate in turn some time in the future. The beer having been bought, the young men retire to a convenient and comfortable place in the bush or, at least, on the very outskirts of the village, to drink it. Home-brew, too, is prepared and drunk in the bush. Sometimes a glass will be laid on, more often one drinks straight from the bottle.

The drinking goes in rounds, the bottle being passed from hand to hand and about a glassful being swallowed in one go. If a glass is used, it is drained (much as one drains a bowl of *yaqona*) and passed to the next drinker. The timing of the next round is the prerogative either of one of the young men who provided the drink or of the one who is most senior; the young men sit in a circle with all the bottles or container of home-brew nearby, and the drink goes from hand to hand round the circle; thus conventional status distinctions are not observed in the seating arrangements and only minimally in the order of the drinking. But here it is important to realise that if one is able to provide alcohol for one's peers, this in itself invests one with a certain higher (if only temporary) status. The drinking continues until all the alcohol is finished. There is much joking and laughter and *fakawela* – the giving away of clothes to a friend, usually a cross-cousin, as a sign of friendship and respect. Often, too, fights flare up and a pair of young men have to be separated from each other. Indeed, fighting seems almost to be *de rigueur*. If no fighting breaks out while the drinking is going on then it is likely to occur at some later point when it is over and the young men have returned to the village.

Young men saw little point in drinking alcohol unless they could get drunk. When drunk, the young men might return to the village and make their condition known in what amounted to a public display – fighting and/or rowdy and boisterous behaviour on the village green or in the store. Once, during the Christmas/New Year period of 1982/83, when perhaps twelve or so young men were clustered together drunk and high-spirited outside the village store, a good fifty men, women and children came out to watch their antics. At that time the rowdiness and fighting seemed as much an expected response as an expression of genuine aggression. This is not to say that serious fighting never occurs, and occasionally severe injury results when someone uses a broken bottle or other weapon. However, on all the occasions that I witnessed drunken behaviour, there was more bravado than anything else.

This was especially true of drunkenness at the dances that were held every year to raise money for the local sports teams' annual visit to Suva for competitive games. These dances were held in a 'rubbish hall' – again, English loan words were used. The rubbish hall was always built on the outskirts or actually outside a village, made in the same style as what, inside the village, is called a *vakatunuloa* – a temporary shelter erected for ceremonial or other purposes. However, unlike the *vakatunuloa*, the rubbish hall had no dried coconut fronds covered with mats on the floor, and the space itself was not treated as is internal space in other buildings. That is to say, the internal space of the rubbish hall was not accorded any value in terms of the above/below axis that describes the space inside any house, church or village hall. Moreover, because the floor was just earth, with no mats or other covering, one did not and could not behave inside the rubbish hall in anything like a proper Fijian manner; one did not take off one's shoes before entry and sit down on the floor near the door; nor did one move across the space on one's knees or walk with one's body bent over in the manner described as *lolou* – as one does when passing amongst others in house, *vakatunuloa*, village hall, or kitchen. At a *soqo vakavanua*, 'gathering in the manner of the land', it is disrespectful to stand upright in the presence of one who is of higher status that oneself. So dancing can take place only by special permission of the chiefs, and is confined to the area of the village hall or *vakatunuloa* that is described as *i ra* – below; there, young women invite apparently shy and reluctant young men to dance.

But at rubbish-hall dances there were no elders or chiefs, only a young couple who coached the men's rugby and the women's basketball teams and perhaps two elderly ladies; they acted as chaperones. The rubbish hall was built outside the village proper and the space inside it was not valued in terms of above/below because virtually all those present were one another's peers from the point of view of the chiefs and adults back in the village – peers among whom there were no distinctions to be made. Here the young men, feeling emboldened by beer or home-brew, invited the girls to dance and often used the opportunity to suggest illicit meetings later, outside. There is a convention that one need not remember what one has done when drunk, so a young man is able to urge his suit with some passion and retire unashamed if it is not successful. The same behaviour when sober would be humiliating unless it was successful. Some young men assert that approaching a girl is impossible without the aid of alcohol.

That young men should be at least a little drunk seemed to be required for the success of a rubbish-hall dance, since girls too say that a dance is only really lively when the young men have been drinking. Provided the drunkenness was not too spectacular, adults in the village generally turned a blind eye to it. However, at my first rubbish-hall dance in 1982 (which was also the first of that season) an extraordinary number of young men interrupted or transformed the dancing several times to engage in free-for-all fights. It was after this dance that chiefs in all the villages involved threatened to refuse to allow them to take place if drunkenness on the same scale occurred again. The dances that followed were markedly more sedate.

Rubbish-hall dances were nothing new, for men of fifty to sixty years old sometimes referred to them in talking of their own youth, but in general people were vague about how long they had been going on, and when I first attended these dances I supposed them to be an innovation. It was as if young people had only recently won this privilege from their elders – but in fact I think it was a privilege that was lost and rewon more or less every year. In 1990, however, there were no rubbish-hall dances and I was told the chiefs had banned them.

Yaqona Versus Alcohol

The material above reveals the antithesis that Fijians understand to exist between *yaqona*-drinking and alcohol-drinking[5]. *Yaqona*-drinking encompasses all adult members of the community and takes place *inside* the village in properly appointed surroundings (be they village hall, house, kitchen, *vakatunuloa* or even a few mats under a mango tree). All these spaces are valued on the above/below axis so that order and stratification are manifest in people's disposition with respect to one another, and also in the order in which they drink. Virtually all life-cycle and other ceremonies take place around the *tanoa* (the large central bowl of *yaqona*) in the presence of chiefs. *Yaqona* is the chiefly drink and the drinking of it takes place under the auspices of chiefs; it is the quintessence of everything Fijian and thus the behaviour proper to *yaqona*-drinking is redolent of respect for rank and seniority.

In explicit contrast, alcohol drinking is associated with 'the European way', and with young men only; it takes place *outside* the village 'in the bush' (*mai na veikau*, that is, in someone's gardens), where there are none of the appointments of properly conducted social life. The association of alcohol-drinking with rubbish-hall dances is a case in point. Order and stratification are denied by alcohol-drinking, by the circle in which the beer-drinkers sit and the haphazard order of their drinking and, because alcohol-drinking only occurs amongst peers, it is in its nature egalitarian. Thus, although young men *do* rank themselves internally in terms of their birth as chief or commoner and their relative seniority, from the outside they can be seen as a group of peers – *cauravou*, 'young men'

– and particularly because, as a group, they are at the bottom of the scale of men's statuses.

So one arrives at an ideal antithesis which, schematically presented, looks like this:

yaqona-drinking	alcohol-drinking
Fijian	European
moral rectitude	crime
inside the village	outside the village
valued social space	asocial space
all adult community	young men only
hierarchical order	egalitarian disorder
ritualised	haphazard
dignified behaviour	rowdiness and fighting
controlled sexuality	uncontrolled sexuality
time honoured tradition	modern innovation
under the auspices of chiefs	castigated by chiefs

It should be evident from details already given that these are not neat empirical distinctions, although they were talked of locally as if they were. Thus married men probably consume as much alcohol as do young (i.e. unmarried) men; alcohol-drinking is itself ordered and ritualised and confers status – albeit in a different way; fighting is not an inevitable accompaniment of alcohol-drinking; chiefs also drink alcohol (though in a less public and spectacular fashion than do young men); men whether or not they are drunk on alcohol, importune women, and it is not only young men who do so; and so on. It should be noted too that a 'rubbish hall' cannot be treated as a traditional space even though the addition of dried coconut fronds and a few mats would make it one; it is not *allowed* to be treated as traditional space. Similarly, alcohol could not be drunk under socially acceptable conditions since its consumption within the village was banned by chiefs and church. Moreover, no one seemed seriously to consider it possible that alcohol-drinking would cease, and both adults and young people of both sexes tended to view drunkenness as a phase that almost any young man was bound to go through. Young men themselves talked of the time when, as fathers of children, they would naturally give up their wild ways and lead a sober and respectable existence. Then it seemed the necessity for 'wash-down' would disappear of its own accord. I once pointed out to a group of young men that if 'wash-down' was a physical need then all the men in the village should be off drinking beer in Qarani;

they laughed immoderately and one said, 'It belongs to us young men alone' (*sa neitou ga na cauravou*), well aware that he spoke of a convention that suited him.

The fact is that young men do not generally challenge the status quo. Whatever grumbling and bravado occurs among themselves with respect to traditional authority, their public behaviour towards their elders virtually always shows acceptance of traditional values as being only right and proper, values that they themselves will come to embody as they get older and settle down. In this connection a young man of twenty-two who had been lectured severely by his elder brother (the age difference between them being about ten years) said to me of the experience: 'My elder brother lectured me. He said that I get drunk too much and neglect my work...he said I'm getting a bad reputation because I go after girls too much. He was very upset about it because my bad behaviour brings shame on the name of our house... He was crying, we both were.' He went on to tell me that he was determined to change his behaviour and that perhaps he would get married soon.

In other words, alcohol-drinking is talked of as if it constituted a real challenge to the status quo, but the conditions under which it is allowed and its association with the 'wildness' of young men make it into a challenge that has effectively been institutionalised.

This becomes more obvious when one considers how kin-relations enter into the behaviour appropriate to alcohol-drinking and *yaqona*-drinking respectively. Exchange between affines within the same generation and more specifically between young men who are cross-cousins, is always competitive and fundamentally egalitarian. Groups of alcohol-drinkers are typically cross-cousins and much of the behaviour associated with beer-drinking – the comradeship, the joking and high spirits, the exchange of clothing, and even the fighting – are all traditionally appropriate between them. In other words, the behaviour of alcohol-drinkers with one another is, by definition, only possible between cross-cousins, for the exchange relation between them is that of balanced reciprocity. This equal relation between potential affines (i.e. brothers-in-law) within the same generation, with its inherent challenge to a hierarchy whose authority is in part constituted in tribute and redistribution, is assimilated to alcohol-drinking and 'the European way'.

By contrast, *yaqona*-drinkers behave in ways appropriate to hierarchical kin relations. In Fiji, all relationships can be conceptualised and referred to as kin relations. At its widest extension, one's kin include all other ethnic Fijians. And with the exception of the equal relations between cross-cousins, *all* Fijian kinship relations are hierarchical and require varying degrees of respect and avoidance.

Here then is an old antithesis between non-marriageable kin (where the paradigmatic reference is to the hierarchical household and the clan) and marriageable kin (who as cross-cousins relate to one another as equals across households and clans), and an old observation that it is before marriage that young men are most free from hierarchical kin obligations and most bound by peer relations with potential affines.

The tension between hierarchy and equality given respectively by relations between kin within the household, and kin relations between affines of the same generation across households, can be historically related to the nature of chiefship in Fiji. High chiefs are associated on the one hand with kinship within the household and on the other with affinity. A properly installed high chief becomes the leader of the community – here conceived of as 'the household' writ large. At the same time, in both myth and history, a high chief is represented as a foreigner from over the sea who stayed to marry a daughter of the land chief and was later installed by him as paramount. However, the high chief and his descendants rule thereafter only by consent of the people of the land; thus the power that lies with the land chief as head of the clan who can 'make the chief' is crucial. He can, and often does, refuse or delay the installation of a putative paramount.

A similarly competitive (rather than clearly hierarchical) tension can be seen in the ceremonial exchange that takes place on marriage between 'the side of the man' and 'the side of the woman'. Both sides give large quantities of whales' teeth, mats, blankets, cloth and so on, but 'the side of the man' must be seen to give more. One might suppose that, in giving more, the man's side establishes superiority over the woman's but this is not so. In Gau I was told that the man's side gives more because if it did *not* do so it would be shamed. This indicates that the bride herself is part of what is given by her side, and this most valuable gift can only be balanced by the groom's kin giving far more in goods. In other words, people who are acting as affines (cross-cousins) compete with one another for precedence.

Putative high chiefs may similarly be seen implicitly to compete for precedence with those who will make them paramount. By virtue of the initial marriage between the incoming stranger chief (associated with the sea) and a daughter of the land, paramount chiefs are sometimes spoken of as *vasu* (sister's son) to their people (to those who are *tamata*, commoners) who thus stand to them as mother's brother. In day-to-day kinship terms, the *vasu* can take what he or she wants from the mother's brother's clan but the mother's brother has authority over the *vasu* and is owed the utmost respect and strictest degree of avoidance by the junior relative. The paramount chief, like the *vasu*, mediates between affinity and kinship within the household. So his status as paramount cannot be given by birth alone, but depends on his being installed by the land chief, who thereby constitutes the paramount's precedence in ritual[6].

In other words, *yaqona* ritual is a crucial, constituting feature of Fijian chiefship – not merely because it installs a chief but because on a day-to-day basis, it constitutes the chiefship as apparently unequivocal. This is possible because *yaqona*-drinking seems to present us with an image of any level of community relations (clan, village, chiefdom) as the household writ large. As is suggested by the myth of the in-marrying stranger chief, the earlier exclusion of women from *yaqona*-drinking, and the image of the paramount as sister's son, gender is important here.

Gender and Drink

Today village women drink *yaqona*, but ideally they do not drink alcohol, and I never saw a Gauan woman do so in the village[7]. However, during the period of my second fieldwork in 1990 I was told that there had been an occasion at Christmas, when a chiefly lady had introduced the other women to wine. They had all ceremoniously taken a small glass, but I was told that most expressed their dislike of it and that one had asserted (to the amusement of everyone else) that it tasted like the smell of cow's urine.

Women's admittance to *yaqona*-drinking is explicable in terms of their admittance to Methodist Christianity on the same general basis as men (see Toren 1988)[8]. However, women's seating position at the pole below (*i ra*) in *yaqona*-drinking makes their presence effectively irrelevant. In relation to the men who are present, they take the position below as wives who are subordinate to their husbands, rather than as sisters who may formally rank above their brothers. That the *vasu* (sister's child) may take without asking from the mother's brother's clan is an acknowledgement of the natal rights (both material and spiritual) that a woman gives up when she marries into her husband's household. Marriage is exogamous to the clan (*mataqali*) and often to the village; residence is virilocal and on marriage a woman becomes axiomatically subservient to her husband. This relationship transforms an ideal equality between cross-cousins (for one is by definition cross-cousin to one's spouse) into the hierarchy of marriage[9].

The marital relationship is pivotal to the constitution of the hierarchical household, and in terms of their relation to men, adult women are much more visible as wives than as sisters. Women are 'paths of kinship' (*sala ni veiwekani*) and 'carry the blood of posterity' (*kauta na dra ni kawa*); in other words, they literally contain within themselves 'the Fijian way'. So alcohol is seriously polluting to women in a sense in which it is not polluting to men.

The notion that alcohol increases sexual desire to the point where it is uncontrollable implicitly links alcohol-drinking with heat, since the strength of a man – especially his sexual strength – is deemed to be manifest as heat, which is thought to be dissipated by sexual activity. Women's sexuality is ideally represented as passive and, with respect to sexual partners of the same age, the woman's sexuality is considered to be weaker than the man's. On the one occasion when I heard one of the village young women accused of drinking alcohol with young men, she was called 'a bad young woman' (*gone yalewa ca*) and it was immediately suggested that she was sexually promiscuous (*dau lako vakaveitalia kei na cauravou*, 'in the habit of going as she pleased with young men'). The process by which women's sexuality is rendered subordinate to men's is crucial to the continuing constitution of Fijian hierarchy (see Toren, in press). Were alcohol-drinking to be implicitly condoned for women, as it is for men, women's sexual passivity would inevitably be called into question.

However, if women are not allowed to drink alcohol because it is too 'heating', pregnant women are not supposed to drink *yaqona* because, as I was told, it is 'too cold' (*rui batabata*); that is, it may damage the foetus by upsetting the balance between heat and cold that is fundamental to health in Fijian indigenous medicine. Sahlins (1985) takes the water that is mixed with *yaqona* root to be an analogue of semen, the root itself to be a female analogue because it is a product of the land, and equates the *tanoa* (the bowl in which it is prepared) with the womb. I am not convinced by this analogy, if only because both men and women are associated with both land and sea in complex ways; so the root vegetables produced by men (e.g. yams, taro etc.) are explicitly associated with male genitalia, while other land products (e.g. the pandanus used to make mats) are associated with women. That the feet of the *tanoa* are called 'its breasts' (*sucuna*) makes the analogy with the womb convincing enough, but *yaqona* itself seems to be a male analogue. The ritual of the chiefly *yaqona* is compelling because, having effectively excluded women from the reckoning, men are able to rank themselves against one another; so, in offering to chiefs their own male product they at once constitute and express their allegiance by virtue of their status-ordered submission. One could argue perhaps that the drink as a transformed product of male (i.e. ancestral) fertility is contained in a female vessel (the *tanoa*) just as the child is contained in the womb. Indeed this interpretation would seem to fit better with the earlier exclusion of women from *yaqona*-drinking and thus from direct access to the ancestors, with Hocart's accounts of the origin myth of *yaqona* whereby it sprang from the body of a sacrificed child or of a young chief, and with certain aspects of Sahlins's own analysis (e.g. that the drink is the sacrificed product of the landspeople and an analogue of their children, (see Hocart 1952:127, Sahlins 1985:73–103, Toren 1988).

The 'living water' (*wai bulabula*) of the *yaqona* chant is certainly an analogue of semen, but within the set of land/sea distinctions, freshwater is classified as belonging to landspeople, whose women's prerogative it is to fish for all freshwater species. This living water, when added to the *yaqona* in the *tanoa*, 'is like the dropping of the rain'. Rain fertilises the land and brings forth *yaqona* by virtue of ancestral power mediated by men's labour; both freshwater and the *yaqona* plant are analogues of ancestral (male) fertility; brought together, they are transformed into the child that is contained in the womb represented by the *tanoa*. Note that children belong to their father's clan and are conceived by virtue of the power of the husband's ancestors; Fijian kinship is reckoned bilaterally and women carry the blood that comes from their own male ancestors and which is also necessary for the conception of children. But, with respect to my argument that *yaqona* cannot be an analogue for female fertility, it is important to realise that in Fijian cosmology, all fertile power is essentially male, even if women may be the vehicles of it.

Given the association of alcohol-drinking with young men rather than with men in general, it is apparent that alcohol is polluting not only to women, but to chiefs (*turaga*) – a term that is politely used in reference and address to any married man. Marriage is understood to entail sobriety, and it is women as 'mothers of children' (*tina ni gone*) who inveigh against alcohol and its deleterious effects on family life. So, too, chiefs who sometimes drink alcohol can never be publicly acknowledged to do so and have to be heard to oppose it[10].

Conclusion

One can demonstrate a transformation of an old opposition between hierarchy and equality in the antithesis offered by *yaqona*-drinking and alcohol-drinking. However, I think it would be wrong to accept this as constituting an explanation of that antithesis, just as it would be wrong to take at its face value the villagers' view of it as an opposition between traditional values and degenerate innovation. We have to recognise that social change is far more complex than we might be tempted to suppose. Today the chiefs of confederations (*vanua* – literally 'countries') come under the control of central government and the administration of a given village is a matter for various elected committees, which do their best to encourage 'development' while not offending the chiefs or appearing to encroach on their authority. So administration by committee is seen to take place under the auspices of local chiefs and would appear to depend on them even where it does not. Similarly the form of *yaqona*-drinking that takes place today differs significantly from its historical form – a change that is linked to Christianity. Not only is it more or less an everyday matter, but women and young men drink too, and *yaqona* is no longer solely a prerogative of chiefs and married men.

This is not to say that the old order has 'really' disappeared or that it will ever do so, but rather that we have to recognise that change is an inherent condition of existence. Drastic change can occur even while it may be expressed in an idiom that is fundamentally traditional. Indeed, it is the strength of far-reaching ritualised behaviour and the symbolic concepts it helps to constitute that it *appears* that, even though ritual is inherently dynamic, behaviour 'in the manner of the land' is powerfully resistant to change. What we find in *yaqona*-drinking and alcohol-drinking is an antithesis whose significance is at once material and symbolic, and which is thus able both to manifest far-reaching change and to deny that it ultimately makes any difference.

Notes

1. Research was supported by funding from the Social Science Research Council and from the Horniman Trust. The June 1981

census for Gau Island showed the population as 3,119; the population of Sawaieke *vanua* (country) of which Sawaieke is the chiefly village was given as 1,242. My own census taken in 1983 showed Sawaieke village as having 46 houses and a population of 257.

2. This classification is taken from Lebot and Cabalion (1986) who give an encyclopaedic account of kava, its uses and effects; other pharmacological analyses include Buckley *et al.* (1965); Gajdusek (1979), and Meyer (1979). Brunton (1989:5) summarises the most recent research as follows: '*Piper methysticum* contains a number of active alpha-pyrones whose properties include soporific, anti-convulsant, muscle relaxant and local anaesthetic effects.'

3. For analysis of the meaning of *yaqona*-drinking and its connection with transcendent power, see papers by E.Bott and E.Leach in J.S.La Fontaine (ed.) (1972); also Sahlins (1985), Turner (1986), and Toren (1988) and (1990:90–118).

4. *Yagona*-drinking was considered unfitting for women in Deuba, Viti Levu, in the 1940s and was still so in Fulaga in the late 1970s (see Geddes 1945:18 and Herr 1981:344). For an analysis of historical shifts which allowed women and young men to drink *yaqona*, see Toren (1988).

5. That Tongans conceive of a similar antithesis between kava and alcohol is suggested in a paper by A.A.Perminow, University of Oslo, delivered to the 1991 Conference on the Pacific, Hawaii.

6. For a discussion of the significance of Fijian wedding exchanges, the *vasu* relationship, the relations between spouses and the valuation of space, see Toren (1990:52–64, 85–86, 238–244); the analysis differs from that proposed by Sahlins (1976:26–46).

7. Urban middle-class Fijian women do occasionally drink alcohol but usually only in their own homes. In a paper presented to the Institute of Commonwealth Studies in 1983, Chris Griffin described alcohol-drinking in town, i.e. in Suva, the capital of Fiji, and discussed its connection with crime and violent behaviour towards women.

8. Women are still excluded from kava-drinking in various other countries. Along with an analysis of the distribution of kava throughout the Pacific, Roy Brunton gives an account of kava ritual on Tanna, Vanuatu. In local explanation, women were excluded from kava-drinking because, given that kava is supposed to have originated in the first place from a woman's vagina, both men and women would feel shame when they saw the kava being chewed in preparation for drinking (Brunton 1989:107).

9. Where no kin relation can be traced between a married couple, the in-marrying woman learns to address her husband's kin as if she was known to be cross-cousin to her husband; for example, anyone he calls mother, she addresses as mother-in-law, anyone he calls female cross-cousin, she addresses as sister, and so on. This also holds for the man in respect of his wife's kin.

10. Marshall and Marshall (1990) give an historical and ethnographic account of how women in Truk, supported by both church and chiefs, have fought for prohibition. Trukese women's views (p.61) are very similar to those of Fijian women as reported here. In their conclusion, Marshall and Marshall point out that, at least in terms of women's traditional obligation to care for the community, the women's unprecedented political activity 'was not a "revolutionary" gesture...but rather a new behaviour brought into accord with the conservative canons of Trukese culture' (p.146).

References

Buckley, J.P., Furgiule, A.R. and O'Hara, M.J. (1967), 'The pharmacology of kava' (Shorter Communications), *Journal of the Polynesian Society*, 76:101–102.

Brunton, R. (1989), *The Abandoned Narcotic. Kava and cultural instability in Melanesia.* Cambridge: Cambridge University Press.

Forman, C.W. (1982), *The Island Churches of the South Pacific: Emergence in the Twentieth Century.* Maryknoll, New York: Orbis Books.

Gajdusek, D.C. (1979), 'Recent observations on the use of kava in the New Hebrides' in Efron D.H. (ed.) *Ethnopharmacologic Search for Psychoactive Drugs.* New York.

Geddes, W.R. (1945), 'Deuba: A study of a Fijian village'. Wellington (N.Z.): *Memoirs of the Polynesian Society*, vol. 22.

Griffin, C.C.M. (1982), 'To booze or not-taboos: alcohol and gender in Fijian society', paper presented to the Institute of Commonwealth Studies Postgraduate Seminar, May 1983.

Herr, B. (1981), 'The expressive character of Fijian dream and nightmare experiences', *Ethos*, 9:331–52.

Hocart, A.M. (1952), *The Northern States of Fiji.* London: Royal Anthropological Institute.

La Fontaine, J.S. (ed.) (1972), *The Interpretation of Ritual.* London: Tavistock.

Lebot, V. and Cabalion, P. (1986), *Les kavas de Vanuatu. Cultivars de Piper methysticum Forst.* Paris: Editions de l'Orstom.

Marshall, M. and Marshall, L.B. (1990), *Silent Voices Speak. Woman and prohibition in Truk.* Belmont, Ca.: Wadsworth Publishing Co.

Meyer, H.J. (1979), 'Pharmacology of kava' in D.H.Efron (ed.) *Ethnopharmacologic Search for Psychoactive Drugs.* New York.

Perminow, A.A. (1991), 'Recreational drinking in Tonga: kava and the constitution of social relationships', paper presented to the Conference on the South Pacific, Hawaii.

Sahlins, M. (1976), *Culture and Practical Reason.* Chicago: University of Chicago Press.

Sahlins, M. (1985), *Islands of History.* London and New York: Tavistock Publications.

Toren, C. (1988), 'Making the present, revealing the past: the mutability and continuity of tradition as process', *Man (N.S.),* 23:696–717.

Toren, C. (1989), 'Drinking cash: the purification of money through ceremonial exchange in Fiji' in J.Parry and M.Bloch (eds) *Money and the Morality of Exchange.* Cambridge: Cambridge University Press.

Toren, C. (1990), *Making Sense of Hierarchy.* London: Athlone Press.

Toren, C. (in press), 'Transforming love: experiencing Fijian hierarchy' in P.Gow and P.Harvey (eds) *Sexuality and Violence.* London: Routledge.

Turner, J.W. (1986), 'The water of life: kava ritual and the logic of sacrifice', *Ethnology,* Vol. XXV, no. 3:203–14.

8

Drinking and Gender in Japan

Joy Hendry

The consumption of alcoholic beverages is very popular and widespread in Japan, among women and, increasingly, among under-age youths, as well as among men. In general, social drinking is a regular and frequent activity, quite hard to avoid, and there are clearly defined expectations for the participants. Unexpectedly perhaps, alcoholism and social problems of alcohol consumption are not subjects which are much discussed. Organisations which deal with some aspects of 'drinking problems' were instituted in the mid-sixties and have been growing, but official sources are not forthcoming with information[1], and it is much more difficult to obtain figures on this subject than for drug abuse[2].

This chapter will not focus then on the question of alcohol consumption as a social problem, although the information that is available will be discussed. Instead, it will examine drinking customs and their history, attitudes to drinking and its religious associations, and how drinking relates to gender issues. It will thereby attempt to demonstrate reasons for the apparent lack of concern. The aim is to provide some of the social context of alcohol consumption and to suggest why alcoholism is apparently not an issue as prevalent in Japan as it would appear to be elsewhere[3].

Customs, Availability and Quantity

There are many social occasions when alcohol is consumed in Japan as a more or less compulsory part of the proceedings. As one anthropologist has noted: 'It is impolite to be sober when others are not, so newcomers to a party are encouraged to get drunk as soon as possible' (Dalby 1983:140). The consumption of alcohol is often ritualised, rather in the manner of drinking a toast, and participants will follow a fixed order of proceedings, perhaps involving a move, together, through as many as three different types of drink[4]. These

175

drinks may well be decided from the outset by the organisers of the occasion, so that the participants will have little choice about what they drink.

The customary form of drinking also makes it difficult to refuse drinks. People drinking together express their conviviality by pouring drinks for those around them. It is considered rude to pour oneself a drink, so the routine is usually for one person to offer a drink to another who receives that drink and pours one back for the first[5]. Since this offer of a drink is an expression of friendship and opens the way for further communication, it is not only difficult to refuse but also difficult to control one's consumption. With *sake*-drinking, the partners in such an exchange also use each other's cups for this event, so it is not easy to leave the drink in its container, as sometimes happens with beer and other drinks. There are, of course, various subterfuges, such as pouring the drink away into the ashtray, but on a normal occasion this would be considered strange when the object of the exercise is patently to get drunk.

Alcoholic beverages are also abundantly available in Japan. They are sold at restaurants throughout the day, there are liquor shops in almost every street, and certain drinks are available in grocers' and other shops too. It is even possible to buy most drinks in vending machines (cf. Randle and Watanabe 1985:56), although this tends to make a mockery of the legal drinking age, which is twenty. According to the National Tax Administration, Tokyo, the Japanese drank 6.3 litres of pure alcohol per person in 1987, and this is a figure which has been rising steadily for more than twenty years[6]. Nevertheless, an international comparison based on 1981 figures ranked Japan only thirtieth among forty-eight nations with Luxembourg and France in first and second places (Smith 1988:44).

Sake is the local drink, made from rice. It was reported in 1983 that Japan had 3,870 breweries producing four hundred million gallons of *sake* in five thousand brands (Seward 1983:108–110), but the same commentator noted that it accounts for only 30 per cent of the total liquor consumption (ibid:109). Other drinks consumed in large quantities are beer, whisky (both local and imported[7]) and a much stronger local brew entitled *shôchû*. Whisky and *shôchû* have a higher alcohol content, but they are frequently drunk with water and ice in a concoction known as *mizuwari*. More recently popular are other Western drinks such as wine, sherry and brandy, but these are still drunk in much smaller quantities[8].

Drinking in Japanese History and Mythology

The introduction of Western alcoholic drinks has been very successful in Japan, but this should not be taken to imply that alcohol was not consumed in great quantities previously. One nineteenth-century commentator reported that *sake* was said to have been made in Japan for 2,600 years (Bird 1900:223), and two breweries still in operation claim to have been producing since 1331 and 794 respectively (Seward 1983:108). The first mention of Japanese drinking in a written record is in the Chinese *Wei chih*, a third-century text, which describes the ancient Japanese as fond of liquor which they drank at funeral ceremonies while they sang and danced (Oto 1983:46). There is also much mention of *sake* drinking in Japan's earliest anthology of poems, written down in the eighth century, but containing more ancient poems (ibid).

By this time, the Japanese court had set up a *Sake* Production Bureau within the palace, which made rice wine for court use. *Sake* was made by women, who also took part in the banquets. Soon after this, sake was being produced at Buddhist temples, some of which gained considerable reputations for the practice. In the country, people had made their own *sake* for festivals, but by the Edo period (1600–1868) it had become a commercial activity associated with particular towns and regions, and with particular times of the year. Women in some classes were more inclined to drink than others. In rural areas, it was quite common, whereas in the city it was generally confined to women employed in the entertainment business.

Religious and Ritual Associations

In the two most ancient books of Japanese legend, written in 712 and 720, accounts appear of the gods who created Japan enjoying sake of one sort or another (Seward 1983:108). There are three deities associated particularly with the drinking of *sake*, and these have shrines dedicated to them, one in Nara and two in Kyoto (Oto 1983:46). Bird's nineteenth-century work on Japan also notes that 'to drink for the gods' is the chief act of 'worship'. She writes of drunkenness and religion as inseparably connected since, for the Ainu, the more *sake* one drank, the more pleased would be the gods and the more devout one was thought to be (Bird 1900:326).

Sake is much used now in both religious and secular ritual. It is invariably presented to the gods as part of the offerings made before a Shinto ritual begins, it is sometimes shaken around as a part of the ritual, and it is usually shared by the participants at the end. The crux of a wedding, for example, is a sharing of three cups of *sake*, with three sips taken from each cup, not only by the bride and groom, but also by the bride with the groom's family, the groom with the bride's family, and, more simply, between the two families. *Sake* is used to celebrate many other occasions such as the birth of a new baby, the building of a new house, or an annual shrine festival. A French commentator suggests that there is something spiritual about the consumption of *sake* at any time (Random 1987:23).

In fact, there is a distinction made at weddings, for example, between the cold *sake* of the ceremony, and the warmed *sake* which is drunk afterwards at the reception. There is generally a conceptual and behavioural difference between the two. The first may be seen as having ritual efficacy to accomplish the object of the occasion, in this case to bind the couple and their families into a long-term agreement, somewhat resembling a contract. The second, on the other hand, is more in the nature of aiding enjoyment, oiling the social wheels and helping people to enjoy the occasion together. There is little condemnation of those who drink so much at a wedding reception that they fall asleep at the side of the room (usually men).

There is a similar indulgence towards rough and rowdy behaviour at local festivals, when young people of both sexes pull or carry portable shrines around the whole community. This is seen as heavy, thirsty work, and sometimes the bottles are pulled along behind the procession so that those taking part can stop at regular intervals for refreshment. The shrines rock and sway as they proceed, usually to the accompaniment of rhythmic chanting, or flute and drumming music, and there is said to be an element of ecstasy in this corporate exertion, supposedly supported by the gods themselves.

The Symbolic Use of Sake

Sake is made from rice, and, like rice, it is used as a form of currency to forge and express social relations. The exchange of cups has already been mentioned, but bottles of *sake* are also presented at various times to express links in social life. For example, when one house in a community decides to rebuild its premises, all the neighbours will send round a bottle of *sake* on the day the roof is finished. At this time, too, the owners of the new house hold a ceremony on the roof and throw down rice cakes to anyone who cares to come and stand below. There is usually a scramble to pick up the cakes, some of them made with coins inside, and generally everyone in the community is made to feel part of the affair. A drinking session in the evening allows the proprietors and their helpers and employees to relax after the day's work. Bottles of *sake* are also sent round when a family suffers a misfortune, for example if their house should burn down.

More specific significance is attached to the *sake* sent round as part of the betrothal gifts, for this time it must be two bottles, bound together, as a symbol of the new union to be formed. A more elaborate version of this gift consists of sending two small barrels of *sake*, suitably decorated for the betrothal with objects of further symbolic value. At an earlier stage in the proceedings, more subtle use of a bottle of *sake* is made. A go-between who has suggested a possible match will call on the families involved after the first tentative meeting has taken place. He carries a bottle of *sake* with him, and though no definite answer may be given immediately, the opening of his bottle is a better sign of a future match than if the family produces their own.

In modern times, Western liquor has taken on some of *sake*'s ritual and symbolic meanings, and at New Year and the summer festival of Bon, it is often bottles of whisky that are presented. This may well be a gift from an inferior to a superior but in any case it is more likely to be an exchange expressing personal relations, perhaps within or between companies, rather than the household links more commonly expressed by the movement of bottles or barrels of *sake*. The type of whisky may again have its own symbolic value, since certain brands are valued more highly than others, even within the same price bracket. Duty-free shops throughout Europe have caught on to these Japanese preferences, as travellers may readily witness.

Some Pragmatic Aspects of Drinking

In a more mundane but no less important way, drinking in Japan has some vital applications in everyday life. It is now widely known that Japanese company employees spend a lot of time drinking after work. This has been reported as a mostly male occupation, said to deprive wives of their husbands' company at home, but women working at the same office are also expected to attend, and there are very often female hostesses or barmaids in the bars concerned. The event is not entirely social, however, and many men claim that they feel obliged to attend these drinking sessions after work. The aim is to relax with one's colleagues, but the 'relaxed' behaviour is fully expected to bring out underlying tensions and offer a venue for communication of a kind unacceptable in the office (cf. Smith 1988:169; Vogel 1971:105).

An employee who fails to attend these occasions is aware only of the behaviour of the workplace, therefore, and cannot come to know his colleagues as well as do those who drink together. This knowledge is felt in Japan to be vitally important for the communication of non-verbal messages, the general well-being of a group of colleagues, and the smoothest possible running of an outfit (Rohlen 1974:ch.4). This principle applies to members of different companies doing business together. A formal agreement in the office is held to be insufficient for good future co-operation, and drinking or eating together brings the partners into a more acceptable long-term relationship.

According to one author, there may be an even more clearly pragmatic reason for drinking with potential future business partners, for drinking is also an opportunity to play a gambling game by the name of *marjon* (sic). During this game, it is not unknown, according to this same author, for the wooing company casually to lose a large amount of money to the representative of the company they hope to entice into a contract, probably using business expense money for the purpose, in a form of what the author describes as 'semi-sophisticated bribery' (Befu 1974:197–8).

A country version of the pragmatic role of drinking has been discussed in detail by the anthropologist Moeran in an account of *sake* drinking in a pottery community in rural Kyûshû. He argues that whereas there is an ideal that one may relax completely during drinking sessions and open one's heart to one's neighbours because all will afterwards be forgiven and forgotten, in practice 'local residents not only remembered what was said during drinking sessions; they stored this information away, to use for their own political ends' (Moeran 1986:227). Thus, it is vitally important in order to have power and influence in village affairs to attend the drinking sessions, and to stay the course through the five stages of the proceedings, as identified by Moeran.

The point is also made that it is not in fact absolutely necessary to drink alcohol in order to participate in these events. Moeran gives as an example the case of a politically active man, claiming to be unable for medical reasons to consume alcohol, who attends with a supply of tomato juice (ibid:239). According to Moeran, 'the fact that Shigeki chose to remain to the bitter end shows the importance he attached to the way in which community affairs were discussed during these gatherings' (ibid:240). Interestingly, however, Moeran also notes that Shigeki even went so far as to feign a certain drunkenness (ibid:239); acting too soberly could change the context of communication.

This would support the more general contention that men who do not drink are marginal in Japanese society because 'it is difficult for them to participate fully in the socialising that forms a part of occupational life' (Valentine 1990:43). Other commentators have gone further on this point. Stephen Smith, for example, describes non-drinkers as 'highly stigmatized' (1988:150). He argues that alcohol is used as a 'social cue', designating an interactional arena to be governed by what he describes as 'Time-Out rules of behaviour', and he asserts that it is the act of drinking, 'taking the first sip', which renders Japanese 'socially drunk' rather than the entry of the ethanol into the blood-stream (ibid:161).

This dividing line between drunkenness and sobriety is also illustrated by Seward in his account of drinking with a man who suddenly received some news, vitally important to his work, which required immediate action. He took a taxi to the bar where his boss was engaged in apparently drunken games with a geisha, and on attracting his attention, transmitted the urgent message. The man in question apparently returned to 'stone-cold sobriety' within minutes, issued a complicated and detailed set of instructions and then returned, entirely undaunted, to the drunken behaviour he had left behind (1983:115–6).

An article by an Austrian sociologist suggests that the bars and small restaurants which men visit on their way home from work also provide an important 'zone of evaporation', as he describes it, a place where men can 'reduce the accumulated feeling of stress after a long working day' (Linhart 1986:206). These bars are clustered around the stations, particularly those where people change trains. Most men have one or two favourite bars where they are known to the proprietor and where they can be assured of a welcome and a sympathetic ear. The role of women in this context is to work in the bars, to provide the listening ear and perhaps to make an independent living.

Gender and Drinking

Linhart is quite clear that *sakariba*, or drinking zones in the big cities, are predominantly for men (1986:203). They are the guests who pay for the amusement, Linhart writes, while women's role is to serve the men and to earn money. 'Women add an erotic touch to the place and give lonely, motherless men a feeling of belonging.' On the other hand, he notes, these women are among the most emancipated, even if it is, in his view, 'out of pure necessity'. Linhart does concede that modern young people of both sexes amuse themselves in 'pubs and discos', and that some Japanese women with careers have adopted a 'more or less male life- and leisure-style', but he maintains that 'the *sakariba* is by and large a place for the male sex' (ibid:203–4).

This, I would argue, is a fair, if one-sided view of much of the public drinking scene, particularly in urban Japan. It is usually parties of men who drink together, although there is no taboo against women joining them, and they are all usually entertained by women. From the point of view of the women involved, the men's co-workers may be quite happy to escape; but they will be unlikely to reach dizzy heights of promotion if they do. This is one of the ways in which women who try to combine company careers with marriage will almost undoubtedly fail to make a success of both, since the need to be around for the informal, relaxed side of work relations would preclude almost any input into the home at all.

On the other hand, the propensity of male company workers to spend time drinking after work does provide a great deal of employment for those women who are, for one reason or another, not committed to creating a home life as well. The fact that most men when drinking prefer to be attended by women rather than men actually means that this is an occupation from which men are excluded. Devos has even suggested that it is sometimes more the 'ego boost' provided by female waitresses than the alcohol which is sought. 'One of the attractions of drinking at a bar is the attendance of professional waitresses who cajole and inflate the customer's ego' (Devos 1984:18), he writes of the commuters who drop off at a bar on their way home. This is a man's world then, and one largely commented on by men, but it could hardly exist in its present form without women.

There are various levels of employment available. In large establishments, such as restaurants, night-clubs or beerhalls, there is plenty of opportunity for casual employment. The smaller bars are very often run by their proprietors, who may have been set up in the establishment by a male patron at some point. The kind of attention required by male drinkers can vary from the simply serving of drinks, through the provision of a sympathetic ear, to various forms of quite lavish entertainment including dancing, singing, the playing of deliberately silly games and the provision of sexual services. At the top of the hierarchy of this service industry are the traditional geisha, whose quality of service requires some years of specialised training.

In most of these cases, women are also expected to consume quite large quantities of alcohol, so that Dalby writes of geisha that this can be considered an occupational hazard. She also notes, however, that some geisha will now help to disguise one another's lack of drinking if there are deemed to be 'health' reasons why one of them should refrain (Dalby 1983:318). Dalby's work generally strives to present the female side of the situation. She discusses only the highest-quality geisha and does so in a way that sometimes suggests that, from the point of view of some of the women who are providing these various services for their male clients, it would not be completely ridiculous to describe the whole scene as an example of gross female exploitation of men.

In the countryside, the situation is rather different, since there are many occasions when men and women drink together. Smith and Wiswell's book on the women of Suye Mura devotes some considerable attention to describing parties and more formal gatherings at which the women, often in male company, became quite drunk and disorderly (1982:e.g. 4,74). Weddings have already been mentioned, and country weddings have a tendency to become particularly bawdy, especially at the parties which take place in the homes of the families involved after the official event is concluded. Other local celebrations may call for much mixed drinking, and there is certainly no taboo here on the drinking together of married couples, although at the same event men and women may well separate into different groups. There are also events exclusively for male or for female participation.

Gender-specific domains are in some ways more clearly distinguished in the country. Although male and female members of the same family drink together, there are events which actually exclude members of the opposite sex. The meetings of the firefighters' group, for example, usually involves some fairly serious drinking afterwards, and in many parts of the country there are women's groups and young wives' groups who meet for social occasions without the presence of men. The young wives, in particular, find only rare occasions when they can be free of their household duties together, and one reported to me that the main aim of their get-togethers was to get very drunk. In Kyushu, where I carried out fieldwork, on the other hand, groups of age-mates meet regularly to drink together as husbands and wives.

A more recent phenomenon, but one which intermeshes with the absent husband syndrome, is that described as the 'kitchen drinker phenomenon'. This can refer to any women who drink at home, but generally refers to women who are said to drink at home alone, perhaps while preparing meals, and it is said to have led to problems of alcohol dependence. In my own research experience, housewives would gather together during the hours when their children were at school, or sometimes even with their children after school, and it is certainly not uncommon for them to drink alcohol together. The middle-class women of my research experience had rather sophisticated and much more varied tastes than their male counterparts in the bars. They would try out a variety of wines and light spirits, as well as liqueurs and harder spirits if the fancy took them. It seemed to give a housewife some kudos with her friends if she discovered a new drink, or a new way of serving it. However, she would then produce the same old well-tried beverage if her husband came home with his friends to drink.

A novel by Tanizaki Junichiro, translated into English as *The Key*[9], describes rather poignantly the case of a housewife presented as totally dependent on alcoholic stimulation. However, there is little in the way of condemnation expressed by the protagonist's family, despite some quite extraordinary behaviour, and, in general, the Japanese public is rather tolerant of drinking in both men and women. A foreigner who is relaxed enough to become inebriated in Japan, whether male or female, seems to be a delight to his or her Japanese hosts, who may well interpret the behaviour as a compliment to them and their skilful attentions (cf. Seward 1983:115).

Acceptability of Drunkenness

All this consumption of alcoholic beverages in Japan is for the most part quite an acceptable pastime, and there is relatively little disapproval of drunken behaviour. Indeed, drunken behaviour itself is rather different from that expected elsewhere. Outside commentators have been struck by this. Devos writes, for example, that generally speaking the Japanese do not become aggressive when drinking, rather they become maudlin, or express an affectionate childishness (1984:48)[10]. Befu points out that 'socially defined rules of drunken behaviour, varying from situation to situation, dictate how drunk one should appear' (1974:201). When the party is over, Befu claims, everyone except a few who have fallen asleep will regain sobriety almost instantly, 'like a group of actors leaving the stage after the curtain comes down' (ibid:202).

According to Seward, the leniency is extended to anyone who is drinking and drunk, whatever behaviour this might involve. They can 'curse, cry, dance, cackle, sing, fight and talk dirty without much fear of punishment, or even a mild scolding', he writes (1983:112). On the contrary, he argues, 'failure to get looped when the opportunity presented itself was viewed with suspicion and distaste' (ibid:115). Ben-Ari (see Ben-Ari et al. (eds) 1990) describes the ability to engage in expressions of 'social nudity' through deliberate violations of conventional manners and etiquette as an aspect of Japanese 'manliness'. Substances other than alcohol have been historically unable to occupy or maintain this moral space. 'Drug-taking', for example, on a largely imported model, is subject to strong disapproval by the authorities and the general public alike.

Alcohol-Related Problems in Japan

'Alcoholism' is little discussed in Japan. The Japanese vocabulary in this area is one of loans or adaptations from English – giving *arukôruisumu*, for example, and also *arukôru chûdoku* (alcohol poisoning) or *arukôru izonshû* (alcohol dependency). A recent article would suggest that there is, as such importations might suggest, increasing concern about the consumption of alcohol in Japan. A 'self-help group for sobriety', *Danshûkai*, inaugurated in 1963 along the lines of Alcoholics Anonymous, now has seven hundred chapters with forty-eight thousand members all over Japan. There are also some 76 specialised treatment units in hospitals, offering approximately three thousand beds (Suwaki 1989). Some first-hand ethnographic description of both the activities of *Danshûkai* and the hospital treatment are to be found in the unpublished thesis of Stephen Smith (1988).

Smith points out that 'alcoholism' is not usually diagnosed by doctors unless there is a disruption of social relations (for example, involving violence). In that case, patients will very often be classified as psychotic and sent to a mental hospital where they will be 'treated', alongside other psychiatric patients, with tranquillisers. The treatment is custodial rather than therapeutic, he argues (1988:186, 202). Otherwise, 'drunks' are dried out and discharged. The specialised treatment units, mentioned above, are an exception to this, but people are quite reluctant to accept government-assisted treatment because of social stigmas attached to being diagnosed as alcoholic. Those who claim medical insurance will make reference to ailments such as liver disorders (ibid:197–9). 'Alcoholism' tends to be seen as a moral rather than a medical label, Smith argues, and it carries implications of being 'weak-willed' (ibid:180). These are serious implications, and help to explain the relative lack of figures.

Paradoxically perhaps, the branches of *Danshûkai* have done away with the anonymous aspects of the American AA which inspired them, and members meet regularly, with others in their families, to enjoy themselves without alcohol. They do have confession sessions and a resocialization process, with pledges, but the *Danshûkai* is very much a Japanese version of the original model. There is a Japanese-style hierarchical structure, and the groups tend to form new in-group sobriety circles for those who have overcome their dependency problems. Smith's work in several chapters of this organisation found virtually all the members to be male, however (1988:210–249).

Concern has been expressed recently in the Japanese press about the alcohol consumption of high-school students (some 25 per cent) and university students (83 per cent of male and 91 per cent of female) (*Japan Times* 1988:13 April). Smith comments that the present law limiting the sale of alcohol to those who are over twenty years of age is 'virtually unenforced' (1988:126). In 1986 a journalist writing in *Business Week* quoted a Japanese psychiatrist's estimate that 3 per cent of Japanese men were alcoholics by American standards, less than half the proportion of American men, but the article also noted that 'in Japan every effort is made to conceal the problem' (Helm 1986:31). There may, however, be less a question of concealment here than a perception amongst the wider population, including politicians, that drinking is benign and alcoholism rare or non-existent (cf. Smith 1988:200).

Some Western observers who have tried to offer reasons for this apparent lack of concern have clearly been convinced of the ontological priority of their own notions of 'alcoholism'. Fields (1985:152), for example, has argued that Japan is not a nation of alcoholics, despite drinking throughout meals, because of the practice of diluting the abundant whisky they consume in the form known as *mizuwari*. Seward has a more complicated argument, claiming that there are fewer alcoholics in Japan (than in the US) because the Japanese become inebriated more quickly due to a lesser consumption of animal fats and flesh and 'because of the binding behaviourial restrictions...which produces a compensating need for release. Given lesser actual consumption of alcohol and faster reactions to it, their bodies seldom reach the point where they require continual infusion of spirits' (1983:112).

Devos, on the other hand, argues from research carried out in the sixties that alcoholism is prevalent in Japan but receives less attention there than in the US. He describes several specific cases of acknowledged problems related to drinking (1984:111, 143, 148–50, 241, 248), and relates the lack of concern to the fact that 'tensions over dependency, which often underlie alcohol problems, are considered more "natural" by Japanese' so that as long as the problems do not lead to violence, they are accepted (ibid:232). Devos's study of delinquents' families in urban Tokyo uncovered a significant correlation between the drinking problems of parents and grandparents and the delinquency of their children (ibid:95–6, 156, 180–2).

In practice, 'the problem' is inevitably a matter of definition. In mainstream Japanese society there is evidently considerable tolerance for behaviour attributed to the consumption of alcohol. Indeed, according to Smith, 'drinking and drunkenness are essentially good and desirable' (1988:253). Deliberate violations of conventional manners, in social drunkenness, are allowed to both women and men; the business context overrides gender distinctions in this sense. However, women more generally seem to be more susceptible to problematisation where drink is concerned. This would be especially true of housewives. The larger number of acceptable social outlets for men, particularly in urban areas, may have exacerbated the notion of the 'kitchen drinker' as a 'problem'. It is, in any case, not acceptable to be drinking alone. Suicide statistics (quoted in note 1) are suggestive of this problematisation process, and in turn they have helped it along.

Women can get together and drink. It may be that, denied a suitable place for social relaxation in the outside world, usually more readily available in the rural areas, some lonely urban women – and especially urban housewives – are beginning to drink themselves into the imaginary friendship of sophisticated women or into the world of career relations which home commitments preclude. Industriali-sation and modernisation seem to have carried along with them the relatively relaxed attitudes to drinking which Japan seems for long to have had. In practice, however, these attitudes are not evenly distributed between the sexes nor between social contexts. Recently imported models of problematisation, already gendered, are helping to turn attention to the 'kitchen drinker'. Alone or not, she may well become a serious problem.

Notes

1. An enquiry to the Information Centre of the Japanese Embassy in London, for the purpose of writing this chapter, revealed only one statistic related to alcohol consumption, namely that 27.6 % of housewives' suicides in 1985 were related to drinking problems. This percentage had increased by a factor of two since the previous year (information from the *Nihon Keizai Shinbun*). It was also reported by a member of the Embassy staff that a foreigner who had decided to take up alcoholism in Japan for a research topic ultimately felt forced to abandon it altogether because of a lack of data on the subject. Stephen Smith (1988) of Columbia University had more success in this respect, although entirely from the point of view of male drinkers. His thesis includes first-hand reports about hospital care and the activities of the Japanese version of Alcoholics Anonymous, *Danshûkai* (discussed later in this chapter).

2. See, for example, the entries in the *Kodansha Encyclopedia* on 'drug abuse' and 'alcoholic beverages'. The former lists various periods in the history of drug addiction with considerable detail, whereas the latter makes no mention whatsoever of problems related to alcohol consumption. For details of drug related issues, see also Hirai 1989:25–7. An article on the drug problem in *The Japan Times Weekly* noted that while social taboos about drug abuse remain high in Japan, alcohol consumption is a comparatively acceptable form of relaxation (Saturday, 30 September 1989).

3. Mary Douglas has, of course, noted that anthropologists, in general, do not necessarily treat alcohol as a problem (1987:3).

4. This procedure is reminiscent of a formal dinner in Western countries, where, for example, sherry precedes two or three varieties of wine, and port or brandy is served at the end. There may be more choice in the Western case, perhaps at the beginning and end of the proceedings, but there is also a starker difference in type in the Japanese case, which would perhaps include sake, beer and whisky or shôchû.

5. A detailed description of the rules and etiquette of drinking exchanges is to be found in Befu 1974:200–201, and in S.R.Smith 1988:112–126.

6. Figures, courtesy of the Scotch Whisky Association, can be found in *Hoeveel alcoholhoudende dranken worden er in de wereld gedronken?*, published by Produktschap voor gedistilleerde dranken, November 1988. Consumption in 1963 was only 3.6 litres of pure alcohol per person.

7. An interesting and quite moving account of the efforts of one

Japanese scientist, son of a sake brewer, to extract from the Scots the secrets of whisky brewing, appeared in a special report in the magazine *Industria* (October 1988).

8. Accurate and detailed figures about the production and consumption of alcohol in Japan are available in, for example, *The Japanese Liquor Market* (Shokuhin 1989). They break down into different categories of alcohol, and currently show an increase in the consumption of *shôchû* and a decline in that of sake, an increase in the consumption of wine and general fluctuation in the rates for whisky and brandy.

9. One version of this novel in English was published in 1960 by Berkley Publishing Company, New York, translated by Howard Hibbett.

10. Smith discusses a Japanese classification of drinkers into three types depending on whether they laugh, cry or become quarrelsome under the influence of alcohol. The vast majority fall into the first type, he claims (1988:129).

References

Befu, H. (1974), 'An Ethnography of Dinner Entertainment in Japan', *Arctic Anthropology*, XI-Suppl.

Ben-Ari, E. (1989), 'At the Interstices: Drinking, Management and Temporary Groups in a Local Japanese Organization', *Social Analysis*, no. 26, pp.45–65.

Ben-Ari, E., Moeran, B. and Valentine, J. (eds) (1990), *Unwrapping Japan*. Manchester: Manchester University Press.

Bird, I.L. (1900), *Unbeaten Tracks in Japan*. London: John Murray.

Dalby, L.C. (1983), *Geisha*. Berkeley: University of California Press.

Devos, G. (1984), *Heritage of Endurance*. Berkeley: University of California Press.

Douglas, M. (ed.) (1987), *Constructive Drinking: Perspectives on Drink from Anthropology*. Cambridge: Cambridge University Press.

Fields, G. (1985), *From Bonsai to Levis*. Chicago: Mentor.

Hendry, J. and Webber, J. (eds.) (1986), *Interpreting Japanese Society. Journal of the Anthropological Society of Oxford*, Occasional publication no. 5.

Helm, L. (1986), 'Japan, the Price of Success', *Business Week*, 24 March, pp.28–32.

Hirai, T. (1989), 'Japan's War on Drugs', *Journal of Japanese Trade and Industry*, March/April, pp.25–27.

Linhart, S. (1986), 'Sakariba: Zone of "Evaporation" between Work and Home' in Hendry and Webber (eds) 1986, pp.198–210.

Moeran, B. (1986), 'One over the Seven: Sake Drinking in a Japanese Pottery Community' in Hendry and Webber (eds) 1986, pp.226–242.

Oto, T. (1983), 'Alcoholic Beverages in Japanese Society' in *Kodansha Encyclopedia of Japan.* Tokyo: Kodansha.

Randle, J., with Watanabe, M. (1985), *Coping with Japan.* Oxford: Blackwell.

Random, M. (1987), *Japan: Strategy of the Unseen.* Wellingborough: Crucible.

Rohlen, T.P. (1974), *For Harmony & Strength: Japanese White-Collar Organization in Anthropological Perspective.* Berkeley: University of California Press.

Seward, J. (1983), *the japanese.* Tokyo: Lotus Press.

Shokuhin S. Shibun-sha (1989), *The Japanese Liquor Market 1989.* Tokyo: Ishii Tsutomu.

Smith, R.J. and Wiswell, E.L. (1982), *The Women of Suye Mura.* Chicago: University of Chicago Press.

Smith, S.R. (1988), Drinking and Sobriety in Japan, Unpublished Ph.D. Thesis, Columbia University, New York.

Suwaki, H. (1989), 'Addictions – What's Happening in Japan: Alcohol', *International Review of Psychiatry*, vol. 1, parts 1 and 2, pp.63–70.

Valentine, J. (1990), 'On the Borderlines: The Significance of Marginality in Japanese Society' in Ben-Ari, Moeran and Valentine (eds) 1990.

Vogel, E.F. (1971), *Japan's New Middle Class: The Salary Man and his Family in a Tokyo Suburb.* Berkeley, Los Angeles and London: University of California Press.

9

Women and Wine in Ancient Rome

Nicholas Purcell

Introduction

In the Roman period, which may be taken here as meaning roughly the period from 150 BC to AD 150, wine – fermented grape juice and pulp – was a comestible of complex associations. Psychotropic effects were explicitly discussed and prized, but the cultural significance of wine both took up and went beyond the interpretation of physiological consequences. Wine was regarded as the normal intoxicant to such an extent that other fermented products were either ignored or marginalised. Wine was one of the chief indicators of the élite life style which gave cultural coherence to the systems which we know as Greek and Roman civilization. Beer, on the other hand, fermented from grains, was a characteristic sign of ethnic, geographical and political marginality. It should be added that the ancient sources show no awareness of the psychotropic properties of any other foodstuffs, and that reinforcement of the effects of fermentation by distilling was not practised.

Wine was, however, assessed by a purity-related criterion of 'strength', and this was crucial to establishing its place in the value-system of consumables. There was a hierarchy of fermented grape-products ranging from mildly alcoholic vinegars to wine made sufficiently carefully and (in practical terms) to a sufficient strength of ethanol to enable it to be kept from vintage to vintage (Tchernia 1986:11–19). In the following paragraphs, I use or allude to the concept 'strength'. This may seem a vague term in the context of modern biochemistry, pharmacology or oenology. We might, for example, consider many of the effects that the ancients associated with 'strong' wine to be proportional to its alcohol content, but they themselves operated with no sense whatsoever that wine was a compound in which there was an isolable active ingredient. That

191

they do not seem to have been tempted to postulate such a substance on the evidence of other fermented foodstuffs is strong corroboration of the very special regard in which wine was held.

For male members of the Roman élite, the practice of diluting wine was a normal part of a highly ritualised consumption of wine with food, as it had been for their Greek forerunners. Dilution was the main mode of articulation of the different 'strengths' of wine. The addition to the wine before drinking of various quantities of water (and sometimes of other things too: sea-water is, for example, quite frequently attested) to provide varying degrees of dilution offered a very intricate system identifying the status and cultural nuance of a meal, or a part of a meal, and of those who partook (Villard 1988). There was at work here a cultural chemistry which has nothing to do with molecules. The principles on which the dilution was thought to work were those of ancient physics, in which the interaction of the hot and the cold, the wet and the dry, and the properties and associations of the ingredients of foodstuffs, were the basis for understanding the process. The mixing was not regarded as the dispersal of a powerful principle in a neutral medium: water itself was too complex and characterful a substance for that.

It is not too much to propose that the occasions on which the ceremonious, sociable consumption of wine took place constituted the central communal acts of the ancient aristocratic system. Far-reaching claims about their relationship to the political and intellectual development of the early Greek *polis* have been made (Murray 1990).

Drinking Constructs the Roman World

The cultural centrality of wine went beyond the rituals of the dinner-party. Cultivation of the vine and the process of vinification both had a special place in the network of production relations which supported ancient societies. Viticulture belongs in the more general category of Mediterranean arboriculture which, although extremely widespread, represents the careful and labour-intensive production of non-staples for redistribution. Olives, figs and other fruit offer many parallels, but the demands of viticulture, especially if 'strong' wine is to be produced, are particularly great. The process of growing grapes and making wine is one which is therefore nearly as rich in cultural and social implications as that of consuming it.

This is instantly perceptible in the enormous range of viticultural motifs and allusions in ancient art. The status of viticulture is also reflected in Roman religion, most prominently in the two ancient wine-festivals, the Greater and Lesser *vinalia*, but in numerous other ways too. The priest of Jupiter (*Flamen Dialis*), a senior priest whose movements were particularly subject to prohibitions and constraints, was not allowed to come into contact with unpruned vines (Aulus Gellius, *Noctes Atticae* (Rolfe edition, London 1927): X, 15, 3). In some sacrificial rituals, likewise, it was forbidden to use wine made from the grapes of unpruned vines (Pliny, *Natural History* (André edition, Paris 1958): XIV, 88). The careful management of the plant is thus given formal recognition as an auspicious and desirable end; the prohibition reinforces the distinction between the wild vine and the cultivated plant, domesticated and improved with skill and labour and requiring attention to stop it reverting to the wild state. The agricultural complexity and the need for great skill and ingenuity which are necessary prerequisites for good wine were accepted as contributing to its high status as a sign of élite power and achievement, and were of importance in defining its nature as a commodity.

All that said, it would be wrong to assume that wine served as a simple indicator of the high standing of a tiny topmost élite. It was an essential feature of the use of wine that it was various and calibrable. It acted as a differentiator, even within exclusive high-ranking circles. It was a focus of eloquent choices. Those choices concerned not only the pattern of the consumption itself in relation to the process of mixing and the quantity consumed over time, but also the moral repertoire of responses to intoxication – and reactions to those responses. If wine itself was a cultural identifier, and certain types of wine characteristic of particular groups, occasions or places, cultural excess of wine was a hallmark also – of certain social groups, like the irresponsible young adult higher aristocrat, or of particular barbarians or ethnicities (such as the 'Celts' (see McDonald, this volume) or, in the Greek tradition, the Macedonians or the Egyptians).

Through its calibrability, moreover, wine-drinking could serve to indicate many gradations of status below the ruling élites. As we shall see, whole communities come to share in an echo of élite behaviour as a sign of their privilege; by the second century BC, access to some form of this wine culture had become very widespread in the cities of the Mediterranean world, and that fact is not without a bearing on the attitudes of élite consumers themselves. It is important to bear in mind, however, that what we are talking about here are statements made about attitudes to wine by the élite, and by male members of the élite at that. There is no doubt a theoretical history of consumption habits among the low in status, or the agricultural producers, tracing fluctuations and changing fashions and preferences: but we will never be able to write it. We are, on this subject, in the hands of the literary aristocracy.

Another point to bear in mind is that, if the material discussed here seems to have a diachronic form, that is not because we are perceiving real change through time. Drinking, to quote Mary Douglas (1987:11), 'constructs an ideal world', and the construction of such worlds in antiquity was a profoundly historicising activity. In the Roman literary tradition as we have it, there is a sense – because of the accidents of the survival of the texts – in which 'now' is the age of Cicero and the next two or three generations, say 80 BC to AD 70. Behind that, the writers of this period constructed a heroic age of *causes célèbres* and great achievements, which we usually think of as the Middle Republic; and before that was an Age of Origins, the time when prescriptive decisions were taken by the heroes of early Rome. Our vision of the Roman evidence also adds a 'Greek background' and a Christian postscript, the period of the taking up and appropriating of the ethical and normative opinions of Roman civilisation. These four phrases constitute an interpretative framework conveying structural relationships among the propositions which I will be discussing. It would be rash to take them as real periods or see change between them as happening in real society in real time. They are aspects of the way in which the morality of social behaviour was used by the writers of the Roman world as a way of making sense of their own times, and it is in this discourse that much of the evidence for the prohibition on women's drinking is located.

Women and Wine: The Roman Picture

The discourse of social morality was not wholly a matter of written literary texts. The decorative panoply of both élite Roman residences and public spaces included comment on and allusion to relevant themes. One statue type, originating in a Greek context and found in more than one example from the Roman world (Zanker 1989), represents an old woman, well-dressed, in an advanced state of drunkenness, clutching a decorated wine-jar. It belongs in the company of a wide range of images (literary as well as visual: note the portrait of the drunken Lesbia in Terence's play, *Andria*, ll.228–

31) which represent the boundaries of the normal and the acceptable in the moral and social world of Roman high culture.

In this particular case, the crazed abandon of an emphatically aged and presumably élite woman becomes the subject of a virtuoso display of realism. Other invectives against deformity, old age and lack of self-control, especially in relation to the female, and both literary and artistic, are common in the Roman milieu. We might note the contrast with images of male drunkenness, images such as the well-known type of the drunken Hercules: the male figure is a god, not an ordinary anonymous human, and his drunkenness, as he urinates towards the spectator, is presented as boisterous and unashamed. The sexual undertones are clearly that the old woman is passively out of control, whereas Hercules retains a certain bravado; he is still an agent, and if he is a figure of fun, it is a temporary and tolerant joke, not expressed with disdain. He is, moreover, naturally a type of strength and vigour, and this is undiminished by his intoxication, whereas the virtuoso presentation of age in the female case makes the piece a study in infirmity. Both images are in some senses Hellenic, but both were relocated in contexts that culturally and politically can only be called Roman. This theme of Roman decorative art is consonant with a prohibition which is the subject of this paper, a moral tradition summed up in the gnomic formula sternly proclaimed by Cicero: 'Carent temeto omnes mulieres', or 'women shall not partake of pure wine' (*On the state* (Ziegler edition, Leipzig 1960): IV,6) for the sake of '*verecundiae disciplina*', the discipline of modesty.

Cicero's aim in this work is overtly prescriptive, and it is not surprising that he puts the prohibition in so legalistic a form. But in one form or another this prohibition is widely attested in the sources, and its principal aspects must be examined before we attempt to move towards an explanation.

The most detailed account is to be found in the encyclopaedia of Pliny the Elder, the *Natural History* (xiv, 89–90):

> It was not permitted to women at Rome to drink wine. We have found among the collections of useful examples the case of the wife of Egnatius Maetennius who was clubbed to death by her husband for drinking wine from the jar: he was acquitted of her manslaughter by Romulus. Fabius Pictor wrote in his *Annals* of a lady who broke the seal on the cupboard in which were the keys of the wine-cellar, and was compelled by her relatives to starve herself to death. Cato wrote that this was the reason why close relatives give women a kiss – to see if they smell of wine... Cn. Domitius ruled as judge that a woman appeared to have drunk more

wine than could be excused for medicinal reasons, without the knowledge
of her husband, and fined her of her dowry.

Two of these instances were well enough known to feature in other
collections. Egnatius Maetennius' act is regarded with surprise by an
author of the early first century of our era, since the fault was so
minor, but he concedes that whenever a wife 'likes drinking wine
without restraint, she closes the door to all virtue and admits the
vices', (Valerius Maximus *Facta et dicta memorabilia* (Kempf
edition, Leipzig 1888): VI 3, 9; see also Tertullian's *Apologeticus*
6, 4–5, which derives literally from Pliny's *Natural History*). He
makes the same point about the general prohibition in an earlier
section: the use of wine was once unknown among Roman women,
to prevent them falling into some dishonour, since from 'Father
Liber [the god of wine] it is but a short step of indiscipline to illicit
sex' (Valerius Maximus II, 1, 5). But chastity was not all grim, in the
view of this author, since women had always been allowed a certain
amount of personal ornament. The 'first step on the slippery slope'
explanation is also favoured by a Greek author of the same date
(Dionysius of Halicarnassus II, 25, 6) who is still more startled by
the law, which he too attributes to Romulus, who made it
punishable by death, 'this thing [being caught drinking wine] which
would seem to be the very least of peccadilloes to a Greek'. The
opinion of Cato, one of the principal culture-heroes of Roman
austerity, was quoted in full from his speech *On Dowry* (Aulus
Gellius (Rolfe edition, London 1927): X, 23, 4–5): 'When a man
makes a divorce he judges his wife as if he were Censor, and has the
equivalent of magisterial power if something irregular or evil has
been done by the wife: she is punished if she has drunk wine; she is
condemned if she has done anything worthy of reproach with
another man.' Again the commentator is surprised to see this
equation of adultery and drinking, and comments that women were
allowed to drink the lesser and sweetened wines *lora, passum* and
murrina (though how the smell on the breath was distinguished he
does not say).

These instances belong in the early second century BC, at the time
when the Romans, fresh from their defeat of Hannibal, did most to
secure the complete subjection of the Mediterranean world, and
began to formulate their own self-image through the creation of a
national literature and with it a new culture and ideology. Cato was
Censor in 184 BC; the judgement of Domitius is probably to be put
in his praetorship of 194 BC or his consulship of 192 BC. Fabius
Pictor's *Annals* are a work of the same generation. Shortly after, the

Greek historian Polybius, describing Roman *mores*, also talks of the ban: the control of the Roman wife over the domestic arrangements of the household does not extend to the cellar, and he too talks of the *ius osculi*, the right to test for the consumption of wine through a kiss of greeting (*Historiai*, Bütner-Wobst edition, Leipzig 1889:VI, 11a, 4).

The timing is important. The whole issue was tied up with Roman self-definition. As they emerged on to the stage of public scrutiny in the Mediterranean world, the Romans had to ask themselves the questions which others asked of them: how did their city work, what was the role of the household within it, what way of life was expected of the men who controlled both the public sphere of the city and the private domain of the family, and how did those ways of life relate to each other? The diversity of social custom from one part of the Greek world to another meant that there was a good deal of material available for imitation or formal rejection, and Rome's process of self-definition in relation to what was available had already been going on for centuries by the time a tradition of Roman distinctiveness became canonical. Restrictions on the drinking of wine by various sections of society, and on Greek women's movements and activities in general, were extremely common, and were in many cases attributed to the most highly reputed law-givers of the Greeks. Restrictions for women could range from a prohibition on eating lettuce-hearts (Plutarch, *Questions concerned with banquets, Moralia* (Babbit edition, London 1936) 672) to wholesale bans on walking at large to avoid being stolen by pirates (see Mendoni 1989 for examples of other restrictions). Women were forbidden wine specifically at Massalia and at Miletus (Athenaeus, *Deipnosophistai* (Kaibel edition, Leipzig 1887): X 33, 429a). The Romans ended up with a complex set of aetiologies and prescriptions, emphasising old practices or creating responses *ex novo*, and expressing the cultural approval of certain parts of the Greek tradition at the expense of others. In particular, they rejected social forms that were associated with the complex urban societies of the Greek world, whether democratic Athens or a contemporary Hellenistic metropolis like Alexandria. The paradox is that for all the rejection of the mores which formed the prevailing Greek attitudes (attitudes which we have glimpsed in their surprised reaction to the Roman custom about women and wine), Rome experienced both a plebeian society which enjoyed and was moulded by the tradition of Attic New Comedy, and an aristocracy which could not and would not pass up the opportunity of surpassing the luxury of the Hellenistic royal cities. Hence the realistic statues of drunken old women in the Hellenistic taste.

For the definition of a Roman austerity, it was the moral rigour of Sparta or the Pythagorean societies of South Italy that appealed. The formulation of the Roman ban on women's drinking was part of the domestic rigour which characterised the ideal picture of a Roman citizen. It is important to locate the prohibition in a wider social context, too. Despite the selectivity of the sources, the ban was not restricted to the aristocratic élite, let alone to one particular aspect of their behaviour, such as the formal meal. (Murray (1985:48–9) sees the insistence on the ancient tradition of restraint on women as an apologetic reaction to Greek disapproval of the fact that Roman women were allowed at feasts at all.) The Roman ban on women's drinking was not restricted to wives either, though the issue features prominently in discussions of Roman marriage and its institutions (MacCormack 1975; compare Treggiari 1991: 461 n.120). Available anecdotes make it a feature of the admirable customs of Rome the citizen-state. It was the business of the mainstream of Roman rhetoric, and the scholarly tradition which fed it, to propagate and elaborate ideals of this kind; and that is neatly reflected in the type of literary work that I have been drawing on in these paragraphs. In one later source, in which we might see this tradition surviving, the Roman restrictions on women's access to wine are set alongside good Greek practice, and it is asserted that formerly slaves and the freeborn until their thirtieth birthday were equally excluded from drinking (Athenaeus X 33, 429b). This is the 'moral rationality' argument, and if this was a consistent account of Roman behaviour, there would be much less of interest in it for us. It would be easy to list similar instances from the debate between the formal cause of Roman virtue and that of adopting the hallmarks of the way of life of the political élites of the Eastern Mediterranean; this is the background to the portrait of Cato the Censor which has come down to us, moral guardian and opponent of the foreign, and it is likely to have genuinely informed the political discourse of the period.

Cato's rigour impinged on the lives of élite women on another occasion, in a celebrated debate on the mitigation of sumptuary legislation controlling female display (Livy, *Ab urbe condita* (Leipzig 1939): XXXIV, 1–7; Haury 1976:427–36). This type of occasion is clearly the context for many of the anecdotes and observations about women and drinking. As presented in the sources, the debate was characterised by a display of arguments of the 'moral rationality' type from the Roman politicians involved. But from the same period comes material which shows that the issue was more complicated than any question of the nature of Rome's pick-'n'-mix from the uplifting precepts of well-governed Greek states. In these years, the place of the matron within the home was a source of deep anxiety and the focus of repression in the form of a series of prosecutions for poisoning. These were explicitly associated with the great crisis of 186 BC in which Rome and her South Italian dominion were threatened by the disorder of the Bacchanals, an affair which combined religious and social control with issues of Roman self-definition. The religion in question – labelled as alien, disordered and immoral – was the cult of the god of wine (Pailler 1987 and 1988). In the fears explicitly expressed by the Roman government at this time we see linked with women the principal dangers that wine was deemed to exacerbate: sexual licence, alternative social groupings, and threat to health. Women's ideal role as the mothers of legitimate offspring, a role threatened by unchastity, was seen alongside their role as household-managers, in which they could corrupt the sustenance of the present generation. The punishment for unchaste Vestals, as for other erring women, was starvation, which was deemed to fit the crime.

The setting of the crisis of 186 BC in a firmly religious context is important. Religious explanation, and the interpretation of an elaborately arcane religious tradition, were important ingredients in Roman self-definition, and the third century BC had seen the reflection in the cults and sacred topography of the city of a number of incidents which were retained in moral memory as prescriptions on the practice of upper-class women. Wine naturally formed a central element in Roman religious ritual, since that had an obviously alimentary core. The libation of wine was a normal ritual act, part of the sacrificial rite. There were exceptions: a cult of Sober Mercury is attested in the city of Rome; a supposedly early law forbade the pouring of wine on a funeral pyre (Festus, *De verborum significatu* (Leipzig 1933): 382 L; Pliny, *Natural History* XIV, 88 – this was sumptuary in intention), and these were exceptions which do indeed prove the rule, by showing how universal and unexceptional the religious use of wine normally was. The exclusion of women from participation in the consumption of wine should be seen as a – not by any means unparalleled – exclusion of women from religious rites which were for the most part, whether private or, still more so, public, the domain of men. But there was a role in Roman religion for women, both as a deliberately interstitial ingredient in observance, as for the Vestal virgins (Beard 1980), and in a representative sense, since women did form part of the community. In at least one example of female religion, it is clear that the prohibition on wine was to some extent relaxed.

This example is the ritual of the Good Goddess (*Bona Dea*), an important and exclusively female rite performed – in its most significant manifestation as far as the state religion was concerned – by the wives of the chief magistrates, in privacy and secrecy, in the house of the chief magistrate or high priest. On this occasion, we are told, the wine-bowl was always referred to as a honey-pot, and the wine itself was called milk (Plutarch, *Roman Questions* 6, cf. 20; Macrobius, *Saturnalia* (Leipzig 1933): I, 12, 25). The ritual substances were labelled with a deliberately false and inconsistent taxonomy, suggesting a consciousness of ambiguity and danger. It is reasonable to compare this with the predictable response of a satirical, cynical and misogynistic literary tradition to such festivals, that they resulted in drunkenness on the part of the women participating. The unusual and abnormal in the cult, which is what helps to render it efficacious, and which is naturally related to the general view that women should not normally consume the pure wine used in sacrifice, is not for that reason free from accusations of abuse and self-indulgence; indeed the licensed exposure of the participants to this sort of opprobrium may be part of the way in which the sanctity of the occasion is pointed up.

The opprobrium fits into a widespread tradition on the subject of female drunkenness, in which the effect of wine is usually to lead to sexual abandon: 'When she is drunk what matters to the Goddess of Love? She cannot tell her groin from her head' (Juvenal 6 300–1). What I earlier referred to as the 'moral rationality' argument was founded on this principle, which is illustrated by several of the texts already quoted. MacCormack (1975) sees the wine ban as symbolic of unacceptable behaviour in general, taking this strand in the Romans' exegetic tradition at face value. The Roman medical tradition reinforces the moral system with accounts of how wine inspires strange fantasies (Minieri 1982). It also offers a whole series of more or less 'common-sense' claims for the ill-effects of wine on women.

Drunkenness, for instance, prevents the retention of semen (Caelius Aurelianus, *Gynaecia*, ed. Drabkin and Drabkin (Baltimore 1951): I 59, 493). It affects digestion in the days after conception, when it produces *violentes* or *percussibiles nutrimentor-*

um in corpore retributiones (Cael. Aur. I 60, 507). It exacerbates the state (technically called *kissa* in Greek) of alternate craving and disgust for particular foods during pregnancy (Cael. Aur. I 67, 571–2). For the author who drew these passages to modern scholarly attention (Durry 1955), these are the real reasons for prohibiting women's wine-drinking:

> au moins est-ce une explication simple, matérielle, médicale. On m'excusera de la préférer aux explications par la sorcellerie ou la mystique, dont abusent peut-être depuis quelques décades pour maint problème les savants qui se penchent sur le passé le plus lointain de Rome.

This is precisely the problem: we are meant to be persuaded by the 'simple, material, medical' explanation, but we should be cautious about it. It is our job to attempt to explain not just the elements of antiquity which appear most consonant with our own world-view, but also those awkward things such as magic for which we have little sympathy. That the Romans used a functionalist explanation for this prohibition is interesting in itself; it is part of what we must take into account rather than a satisfactory answer to adopt ourselves. Durry was reacting to theories like those of Pierre Noailles (1948), for whom all the Roman anxieties about marriage were connected with ideas about blood; and in our case, wine can indeed be readily assimilated with blood. More recent work (see Villard 1988: 28) has considered concepts of what wine was thought to be in a more sophisticated way, and demonstrated that wine was not seen in a way so close to our own medical/moral rationality as might appear at first sight. Behind the simple ethical reasoning is a whole complex of beliefs about the person and her or his reaction to the environment, and the place of diet in expressing that reaction. Some of these will emerge in the last section.

Towards an Analysis: Women in the City

The Greek doctor Soranus of Ephesus, writing in the early imperial period, describes a condition of children involving malformation of the lower limbs which is typical of the city of Rome. It seems likely that – 'simply, materially, medically' – this is rickets. But despite a lively tendency in the classical medical tradition to attack the bad dietary practices of famous cities, no dietary explanation is offered. In accordance with normal practice, however, Soranus gives a series of misguided explanations and then the correct one in his view

(Soranus II 16 (Burguière et al. edition, Paris 1990)), forming a sequence of constructions about health at home that are valuable to the social historian.

The three wrong aetiologies are i) that the city is perched up on open spaces through which cold water runs; ii) that the women have sex too frequently; iii) that the women are accustomed to make love when drunk. (The explanation that Soranus prefers is that, through inexperience and lack of affection, Roman women do not swaddle the infant in the proper way.)

In these wrong explanations, we have an instance of the normal medical disapproval of women's drinking, but in addition to the straightforward concern for the practicalities of procreation, there is a very telling context: the behaviour which damages the health of the infant is characteristic of the privileged city where a way of life normally enjoyed, even if to their moral disadvantage, only by the wealthy élite, is available more widely. Explanation i) focused on the wonderful 'hanging' architecture of Rome and its famous water-ways, an ingredient in the copious tradition of 'praises of Rome' here being turned, not without a hint of sour grapes on the part of inhabitants of the Eastern provinces, into a cause of illness. (The 'ailments of Rome' seem to form something of a tradition in the medical writers, antithetical to the city's praises; see Galen's *Commentary on Hippocrates*, Kühn edition (Leipzig 1821–33): vol. 17, 1: pp.121–2; vol. 17, 2: pp.159–60.) Explanations ii) and iii) likewise take their starting-point from aspects of life in Rome which were widely regarded as part of the felicity of the city which had conquered the world. The life of the tavern, with its lubricious entertainments and its abundant low-priced wine, was central to this view as it was central to the 'shopping-list' of perks that formed the political agenda of the urban populace. In an invective against drunkenness, the encyclopaedist Pliny the Elder attacks the conspicuous inebriation which is made a prize and a commodity; wine being 'so pleasurable that a great part of the population thinks that there is no other reward in life' (*Natural History* XIV, 140).

These rewards and benefits – the *commoda*, as they were known – occupy an overlapping territory between public and private. They concern such domestic matters as food, and such civic benefits as participation in the great festivals with their exciting spectacles of hunting, gladiators or chariot racing. The tavern, a meeting-place which was neither forum nor private dwelling, like – on a larger scale – the baths, had an ambiguous position between the two. The ambivalence of these activities derived in addition from the paradox that these social forms, which were bestowed on the populace by the rich and which became characteristic of the life of the lowly, never quite lost their connection with the life style of the élite and retained a fascination for members of the upper status groups in Roman society, a kind of *nostalgie de la boue*.

Ambiguities of status, then, as well as of location in the social geography of the city, characterised the world of the *commoda*. The moral tradition about all these things – *balnea vina Venus*, baths, drinking, sex, food distributions, spectacles – seems to articulate these anxieties, and it is instructive to see how the construction of gender proprieties is intrinsic to the layout of both the overall ambiguities and the moral discourse which reflects and shapes them. Two further examples may help to make this clear.

The *popina* or *caupona*, which we usually translate as 'cookshop' or 'tavern', is, as I have already hinted, central to the ambiguous world of the *commoda*. It is a place of very dubious moral status and is the object of revealing legislation. It has strong associations with the world of public entertainment, and is a principal setting of the very important games of chance which played a defining role in Roman urban life. The tavern is also a location for a cluster of gender statements. Most obviously, the tavern has strong overtones of the brothel about it, and it is one of the main contexts of prostitution visible to us in the evidence. Prostitution was an urban phenomenon which had strong links to the ideology of the *commoda* anyway. More unexpectedly – given the usual patterns of thought in Antiquity – women played a significant managerial role in the *popina* (the *locus classicus* is the poem *Copa* in the collection of minor works attributed to Virgil). This is linked both with the sexual life of the tavern and with its special function as an extension of the food-processing activities of the domestic hearth and kitchen. The preparation of meat was one of the activities picked on in anti-tavern legislation; the other was the serving of hot water, which was presumably for combination with wine. The duplication of the *mores* of the home, particularly where the life style of the well-to-do citizen's home was transmitted to a limited extent out into the street, made the tavern a dangerous place. In this process women, whose functions in the home were being extended *pari passu*, were central, and the character of the *Copa* is an important emblem of the process. The phenomenon naturally reverberated both ways, and just as the tavern cast a sidelong light on the life of luxury that was being imitated, and held an attraction for some at least among the élite, so the place of women in the tavern, perceived or actual, no doubt fed back into the prescriptions which affected the *matrona* and what was expected of her.

Something related can be seen in the attitude – as far as we can reconstruct it – to the interaction of women and public spectacle, particularly the violent games of the amphitheatre. Here there are various commonplaces about the sexual excitement which prevailed at gladiatorial displays, and the particular effects that it had on women – in close parallel with what is asserted about the action of wine (compare the recent publication of an erotic/gladiatorial jug from Campania: Landwehr and Hönle 1987). More importantly, there is a particular response to more active involvement of women in spectacles. At one level, this fits into the life of the tavern – the *Copa* is the dispenser of wine and food, and sexually available, but she is also an entertainer and her activities blur with those of the actress or the mime artiste. The Romans saw this as closely connected with the wish to take part in the violent spectacles of the arena. This taste used to be documented principally by the satires of Juvenal, and seemed so alien to our own preconceptions that it was considered, like other constructions of women in satire, a sordid fantasy. Within the last decade, however, a tablet has been discovered which contains a decree of the senate against upper-class female gladiators, and on the principle that the Romans did not forbid things which could not take place, this must be considered decisive evidence (Levick 1983).

The measure in question, promulgated in AD 19, prohibits appearances on stage and sets this, and being a gladiator, alongside the offences of prostitution and procuring. All these prohibitions were for those who were members of the two topmost status-categories in Roman society. The explanation offered is in terms of the dignity required in people of this social position, and the document can be seen as testimony to the anxiety felt about behaviour which blurred the demarcations of power and stations within the State. There was a widespread association – traceable behind much of the copious legislation on what we would regard as 'moral' subjects – between civil war and breakdown in status barriers. Roman society was one, partly for demographic reasons, in which upward mobility was relatively pronounced, and this fact generated a repressive backlash. As we have seen, the parallel phenomenon of the extension of the symbols of élite culture in Roman city-life created many new occasions for status ambiguity. No group was more able to express the fragility of the boundaries on which so much emphasis was put than women. The involvement of women in the public spectacles was perhaps inevitable, but certainly – and above all in the case of the arena with its overtones of the male world of the hunt and the battle – dangerous for the preservation of the façade which proclaimed the stability of the State. This is a stronger example of the phenomenon than the ban on wine – that does not seem ever to have been enshrined in legislation in the historical period, just attributed to laws of Rome's founder in the imaginary past – but the pattern of problem and response has many points of similarity. And the savage suppression of the Bacchanalia, as we have seen, suggests how seriously the connection of women with the world of wine and its celebration was taken by the Roman authorities in an earlier period.

In conclusion then, the aristocratic consumption of wine was at the centre of Roman élite concerns for the household and its healthy and proper management, for norms of dignified behaviour, and for the relationship of both to the public sphere of life in the city. Women were perceived as central to these concerns, and the control of their behaviour was central to both male and Roman self-definition. The wife was in charge of the running of the household and its tasks, and the healthfulness of its inhabitants; in the restriction on her access to wine the same sort of concern is apparent which we find in cases of women – purveyors of restorative and healing potions – accused of poisoning (Pailler 1987; Purcell 1986 for the case of the Empress Livia). The deportment of women was a fundamental indicator of the moral good order of the household and the effectiveness of the authority of the *paterfamilias*. Drunkenness was a disgrace in élite males, but more dangerous in their female relatives because of the implications of sexuality. We note that when Augustus' daughter Julia was exiled for the disgrace which her alleged adulteries had brought to the images of family power on which her father in his later years founded his authority, she was for some years forbidden the use of wine (Suetonius, *Life of Augustus* (Ihm edition, Leipzig 1967): 65, 3).

Finally, the issues of the boundaries of the household, the healthfulness of the community and the authority of the élite were all tested to the utmost in the cities of the Empire. This was especially so in the capital, where the signs of aristocratic felicity were deliberately made available to a privileged populace with the accompanying risk of the blurring of social stratification with upward social mobility. The role of women in exemplifying and responding to these circumstances was particularly sensitive. Against this background, the wine ban begins to emerge in all its complexity.

It is part tradition, a rhetorical construct of a normative past; but we need not doubt that real women actually suffered as a consequence. Equally, it was not all-pervasive; Cicero's mother herself was praised by her sons for the skill with which she devised a system for sealing wine-jars to circumvent pilfering by household slaves. This shows us not only a woman whose discretion in household management was allowed to extend, against Romulan practice, to the keys of the wine-cellar, but a *materfamilias* whose virtue is actually constructed through her relationship to the control of this commodity (Cicero, *Letters to his friends* (Shackleton Bailey edition, Cambridge 1977): XVI, 26). And if the ban operated both in the breach and in the observance, it deployed in its defence a highly flexible series of ethical modalities – veneration of tradition, fear of the foreign, physiological and moral pragmatism, religious awe, anxieties about nutrition and purity, social status and – last but not least – the need to control a commodity of real potency in ancient systems of value, economic and symbolic.

The wine ban is, of course, more about gender than about wine. The focus of the shifting set of concerns that I have outlined is the changing and problematic place of women in a complex, mobile and rapidly changing society. As a consequence, women's freedom of response was constrained in a number of ways – concerning morality, health, and status – which might, in some respects, seem all too familiar. Nonetheless, the period covered by this chapter, the period in which we hear most of the wine-ban, is one in which some have seen a slight degree of 'liberation' for Roman élite women. There may be a connection between the two phenomena, of a wine ban and possible 'liberation', or moral laxity (depending on the viewpoint).

At the time under discussion, wine itself – one of the principal calibrators of honour and status in ancient society – was becoming ever more carefully classified for use in public occasions which reflected and reinforced the order of society (compare Purcell 1985, Tchernia 1986). In this, élite women played their part, hosting public distributions of food and drink as if their households embraced the whole community. At Acraephia in Boeotia, in the middle of the first century of our era, a local magnate gave a series of elaborate feasts and public entertainments to the whole community, as a part of which his wife hosted the children, slaves, wives, female slaves, and maidens of the town – as well as the performers, 'which had never been done before' (*Inscriptiones Graecae* VII 2712). The inclusion of the female in a system patterned by public entertainment revolving around food and wine was both delicate and precise. Neither the limited overturning of the system which the evidence of hostility suggests, nor the positive participation of women like the wife of Acraephia, should make us optimistic, in modern terms, about female independence or 'liberation' in the Roman Empire. The reality for the Roman élite women was probably one in which the subtle intermeshing of these and other forms of social control made self-determination even more difficult than we might guess from the solemn strictures about consuming wine.

Note on Greek and Latin Literary Texts

Editions referred to are specified in the text. All translations are those of the author. Roman numerals have only been used to refer to *book-numbers* in the ancient texts. All other numerals are chapter or section references, line-numbers, where applicable, being prefixed with a 'll'.

References

Beard, M. (1980), 'The sexual status of Vestal Virgins', *Journal of Roman Studies*, vol. 70, pp.12–27.

Douglas, M. (ed.) (1987), *Constructive Drinking, Perspectives on Drink from Anthropology*. Cambridge: Cambridge University Press.

Durry, M. (1955), 'Les femmes et le vin', *Révue des études Latines*, vol. 33, pp.108–13.

Haury, A. (1976), 'Une "Année de la femme" à Rome, 195 av. J.-C.', in *Mélanges offertes à Jacques Heurgon. L'Italie préromaine et la Rome républicaine* (Rome), pp.427–36.

Kempen, N. (1981), *Image and Status. Roman working women in Ostia*. Berlin: Gebr. Mann.

Landwehr, C. and Hönle, A. (1987), 'Ein Reliefkrug aus Lucrino', *Römische Mitteilungen*, 94, pp.223–40.

Levick, B. (1983), 'The *Senatus Consultum* from Larinum', *Journal of Roman Studies*, vol. 73, pp.97–115.

MacCormack, G. (1975), 'Wine-drinking and the Romulan law of divorce', *Irish Jurist*, vol. 10, pp.170–4.

Mendoni, L.G. (1989), 'More inscriptions from Keos', *Annual of the British School of Athens*, vol. 84, pp.289–96.

Minieri, L. (1982), 'Vini usus feminis ignotus', *Labeo*, vol. 28, pp.150–63.

Murray, O. (1985), 'Symposium and genre in the poetry of Horace', *Journal of Roman Studies*, vol. 75, pp.39–50.

Murray, O. (ed.) (1990), *Sympotica: a symposium on the symposium*, Oxford: Clarendon Press.

Noailles, P. (1948), 'Les tabous de mariage', *Fas et ius. Etudes de droit romain*, Paris, pp.1–27.

Pailler, J-M. (1987), 'Les matrones romaines et les empoisonnements criminels sous la république', *Comptes-rendus de l'Académie des Inscriptions et Belles-lettres*, pp.111–28.

Pailler, J-M. (1988), *Bacchanalia. La répression de 186 av. J.-C. à Rome et en Italie*, Rome.

Purcell, N. (1985), 'Wine and wealth in ancient Italy', *Journal of Roman Studies* vol. 75, pp.1–19.

Purcell, N. (1986), 'Livia and the womanhood of Rome', *Proceedings of the Cambridge Philological Society*, vol. 212, pp.78–105.

Purcell, N. (1993), 'The city of Rome and the plebs urbana in the late Republic', in *The Cambridge Ancient History*, vol. IX.

Tchernia, A. (1986), *Le vin de l'Italie romaine. Essai d'histoire économique d'après les amphores*, Rome.

Treggiari, S. (1991), *Roman Marriage*, Oxford: Clarendon Press.

Villard, P. (1988), 'Le mélange et ses problèmes', *Révue des Etudes Anciennes*, vol. 90, pp.19–33.

Zanker, P. (1989), *Die trunkene Alte. Des Lachen der Verhöten*, Frankfurt.

10

Gender, Community and Confrontation: Power Relations in Drunkenness in Ocongate (Southern Peru)[1]

Penny Harvey

Introduction

It was Jorge's birthday. The women had spent all morning preparing the special festive meal. Jorge had taken the cows up to the higher pastures, the other men were similarly occupied elsewhere, but by about two o'clock everyone had gathered inside the little kitchen. We had a few shots of *trago*, an alcohol-and-water mix, and Juana had handed round some *chicha*, the specially prepared corn beer. Nothing was drunk with the meal but after we had eaten our way through the massive portions of the festive *merienda* we sat outside, talked and continued drinking. Juana's brother and sister-in-law were there, and Jorge's brother had also come by. Maria, Jorge's daughter-in-law, arrived a bit later with her youngest children, and a neighbour who is also a *compadre* (a spiritual kinsman) had been called to come and eat the meal, which his wife had been helping to prepare since early that morning.

Each guest had handed Juana a bottle of *trago* and somebody had even brought beer. By four o'clock in the afternoon, the sun was going down and as it began to get cold we moved back into the house.

The atmosphere had changed quite dramatically from the quiet, somewhat subdued meal. We'd gone beyond the jokes and animated talk; people were dancing. Jorge began to cry, calling me his daughter, telling me that he was nothing but a poor Indian – then he burst out laughing and shouted, '*Pero soy vivo*' ('but I'm spirited' – an apt pun). He continued laughing and crying in this vein for a while. Juana had started muttering in Quechua about me and about

209

how mean I was, not paying her enough for my keep. Other people told her to be quiet and reassured me that she didn't mean what she said because she was drunk. She then turned her attention to Jorge and told me that it was lucky that I was there because he always hit her when he got drunk but he wouldn't do it when I was around. The neighbour kept falling over while he was dancing but nobody took much notice; his wife was singing loudly in the corner in unison with the tape-recorder, whose batteries were running a bit low by this stage.

Maria told me that I should watch out with Juana as it was she who was really mean and she'd use me and never give me anything in return. She assured me that she had only come to the party because she loved her father-in-law and that she would never come back to this house once he died. At some stage I was aware that the children were attempting to light the fire to reheat the left-overs of the meal. I woke up the next day feeling a bit stiff and muddy – the children were delighted to inform me that I'd staggered out of the house and fallen over at some point the night before. I didn't remember[2].

As this example suggests, social life in Ocongate, a small town in the Southern Peruvian Andes, is marked by heavy drinking[3]. In this paper, I will be exploring how the people in this village think about drinking, and examining their own notions of use and abuse. For the outside observer, drunken behaviour appears superficially to offer a few cross-cultural similarities. In many cultures, drunkenness can be said to be associated with the breakdown or redefinition of social convention[4]. The drinking of alcohol is widely reported to lead to increased sociability, as conventions of appropriate behaviour are more flexibly interpreted, and as drinkers' perceptions of their own practical competence increases[5]. People dare to do, say and even think things when drunk that take them beyond the norms of their own sober interaction[6]. It is this aspect of drunkenness that can also generate conflict and social disorder.

The potential for social disruption is reflected in the various ways in which drunkenness is often separated from everyday social practice. Drinking behaviour tends to be bound by rules relating to appropriate occasions and ways of drinking; the disruptive effects of drunkenness are also thereby contained. Laws and moral sanctions exist to enforce these norms. The social impact or significance of excessive behaviour may be further reduced by attributing diminished responsibility to the drinker[7].

Some aspects of the drinking behaviours described in this chapter are familiar both in Western cultural experience, and in the literature on other non-Western societies. Price (1975), for example, in an analysis of North American Indian drinking patterns from the Arctic to New Mexico refers to social integration, increased social animation, 'time-out', release from inhibitions, transcendence of the physical to obtain spiritual experience, joking, quarrelling, depression and heightened sexuality. These behaviours may seem to occur in different combinations and with different emphases in a whole range of societies described in the wider literature; however, although certain manifestations of drunkenness may seem, to the observer, to occur in cultures as distinct as the North American Indian and the English rugby club, the local meanings that construct and are associated with these behaviours, and the norms and customs that distinguish acceptable from unacceptable drinking practices, are less immediately available and are culturally and historically specific. As an outsider you have to learn what your actions mean to those you are drinking with. This is one thing you try to understand by finding out how to drink, when to drink and even whom to drink with. At the same time you have to find a way to understand the meanings and implications of other people's words and actions.

The following paragraphs outline ways in which acceptable drinking is distinguished from unacceptable drinking in Ocongate, and the sense in which getting drunk in this community necessarily involves making a strong statement about one's identity. While these statements may be explicitly formulated, they are also implied by the fact that drinking sessions in this area emphasise sharing and social interaction and generate a sense of ideal social cohesion. This social cohesion, an experience of a sense of sameness or of shared interest, has to be abstracted from a range of other possible orientations, and it is this process of abstraction which could be said to constitute the statement of identity (Spivak 1988). Negotiations are required for a mutual recognition of shared interest or sense of sameness, and drunken behaviour in Ocongate allows a more explicit demonstration of this activity.

I discuss this and related issues firstly in terms of ethnic identification, showing how gender difference is used to emphasise ethnic difference, and secondly in terms of how gender differences are themselves constituted and negotiated in drinking practices.

Socially acceptable drinking in this part of Peru could be said to be about promoting or negotiating some form of social cohesion or sense of sameness, and it is in this process that drunkenness generates conflict. Much of the violence associated with drinking is directed at women. To understand why this should be so, we need to look both at the distribution of social power and the relative ability to impose definitions of acceptability, and at how this power is reproduced or challenged in the drinking sessions.

I start off by looking very briefly at the history of alcohol use in the Andes. This history both informs present-day attitudes and provides a clear example of the potentially political nature of both the classification and enactment of drinking practices.

Drinking in the Andean Region – An Historical Overview

During the period of Inka rule (c. 1440–1532) alcohol and drunkenness were associated with the realm of the sacred, and by extension with the powers of the ruling élite, the divine Inka lineage. This ruling group strictly controlled the production and distribution of alcoholic maize beer (*chicha*) and coca leaves, and the mass of the population only participated in their consumption during state-sponsored festivals. Given the sacred status of the Inka élite, these festivals were necessarily religious, ceremonial and public occasions.

After the Spanish conquest there was a general secularization of many aspects of life, including the circulation of both maize and coca, which had now become general trade items and were thus more widely available. The Spaniards had introduced vines and sugar into Peru by the 1540s and the wine industry was well established in the colony by the turn of the century, with brandy soon becoming as commercially important as the wine itself (Brown 1978, Cushner 1980).

However, links between the sacred and the state of drunkenness remained important, and drunkenness was closely linked in the minds of the Spanish Catholic authorities with idolatry and continuing political opposition. In keeping with European ideas about the nature of pagan belief and the influence of the Devil, drunken behaviour was also thought to be indicative of moral inferiority, particularly laziness and sexual promiscuity[8].

It is also important to note that the secularization of daily life which took place during the colonial period, particularly the overt separation of production from religion, dictated new standards for the acceptable usage of alcohol. While the Inka had required that drinking and drunkenness be a public event, the colonial authorities stressed the separation of public and private spheres. Drinking came to be more acceptable in private than in public, while drunkenness was synonymous with excess and therefore reprehensible on any occasion (Saignes 1989).

The historical experience of Andean people has thus produced a range of distinctive practices and evaluations in relation to drinking and drunkenness. Some writers have associated drunkenness with an intrinsically degenerate and uncivilized indigenous culture. Others have attributed widespread drunkenness to the influence of outside forces. In this view, drunkenness is associated with escapism, a desperate response to poverty and political marginalization. These views have vied with each other since colonial times and are still frequently voiced today[9].

From the outside, drunkenness is still generally considered problematic, an obstacle to nationalist programmes for modernization and integration. The recently established Protestant Evangelist Churches prohibit the use of alcohol among their congregations, associating it with alcoholism, laziness, backwardness and a lack of self-control that necessarily leads to the waste of human potential. As in the colonial period, drinking practices are thought to be archaic and primitive customs that tie people to their past and thus inhibit contemporary political projects. Alternatively, they are integrated as a sign of desperation, as an inability on the part of Andean people to embrace fully the modern world of which they have been forced to become a part.

My interest is in looking at how the people of Ocongate themselves discuss their use of alcohol. While they draw on these negative discourses, they also stress the social importance of drinking and drunkenness, especially in relation to ritual activity and the realm of the sacred.

Socially Acceptable Alcohol Use

Drinking is still very important to the ritual life of many Andean people. Indeed, the relationship between the use of alcohol and sacred activity provides one of the few cultural continuities through both space and time in the Andean region.

Particular drinking practices and experiences of drunkenness are therefore associated with the continuity of a distinctive indigenous culture and community, and also with those relations of production, with both humans and supernatural beings, that ensure the regeneration of crops and herds[10]. There is a social expectation that both men and women will drink in agricultural, domestic, Catholic and state festivals because, ideally, people establish and maintain good relationships with others by offering and receiving drink. Drinking sessions can involve very intense interaction and the refusal to accept a drink can imply a lack of trust and a denial of mutual respect and affection. Similarly, it is difficult to leave a drinking session, and those who leave usually promise to return, even when they have no intention of doing so. Drinking is thus seen as an act of sharing and collaboration through which the community is created and sustained, community projects for progress realised, and continuing care from the supernatural powers ensured (cf. Allen 1988, Wagner 1978).

Corn beer (*chicha*), watered-down industrial or cane alcohol (*trago*) and commercial beer are the most commonly consumed drinks. *Chicha* is the drink associated with the indigenous powers, principally the mountain and earth spirits who ensure the continued fertility of land and animals and thus permit the continuing reproduction of the social group in the locality. It is served to legitimate the ritual importance of a social event but in Ocongate it is very rarely consumed on its own and has a low alcohol content. Commercial lager-type beers are available but expensive. *Trago* is the most widely consumed alcoholic drink. Other commercial wines and spirits are available in the village but are not commonly drunk in any quantity; there is a poor correlation between price and alcohol content. They thus tend to be used either in offerings to the spirits or as an indication of refined taste and sensibility.

Given that drinking is a social affair, the style of drinking is extremely important. Before raising your glass to drink you must always involve others present in the act by wishing them good health in Spanish (*salud*) or exhorting them to drink together as a group in Quechua (*tomasunchis/machakusunchis*). Everyone is served in turn from the same mug or little glass. The supernatural powers are also drawn into the drinking circles. They are always invited to drink the first glass of *chica, trago* or beer and people often additionally offer the first drops of any subsequent drink passed to them. The degree to which these rules are followed is indicative of the extent to which the drinker concerned is asserting his or her ties to the locality. The way you drink thus both constitutes and reflects your commitment to an insider as opposed to an outsider identity.

Drinking sessions fall into two basic stages. There is no striking moment dividing one stage from the next but there is a qualitative change in the purpose of drinking and in the rhythm of consumption. Initially people drink to 'liven up' (Spanish. *para animarse*; Quechua. *kausachikunanpaq*). Drinking to 'liven up' involves the idea of building yourself up, encouraging yourself to do something outside of the normal. To work, sing or dance with enthusiasm encourages others to do likewise and also, most importantly, allows the drinker to fulfil the purpose for which the drink is being provided. Conversely, a lack of drink can ruin a social event. It was in these circumstances that the following complaint was voiced to me concerning the inadequate performance of two dancers acting the role of disruptive ancestor spirits (*machus*) in a local festival[11]: 'In other years they made out with the women or played with the adults and not just the children, bothering the Mistis (local notables) as a joke. When you've had quite a bit of alcohol you're not afraid, they would have livened up and played with the adults and nobody would have had the right to take offence.'

The search for autochthonous power in the form of potency and energy is an explicit aim of drinking, expressed in the concept of 'livening up'. People try to create a community base for this energy by passing alcohol and coca around and by inviting both humans and supernatural powers to join the drinking circle. This community base is also created verbally. As people begin to get slightly drunk, communication increases. They lose their shyness and reserve, and begin to talk, joke, laugh, shout and swear.

Once the technical aspect of the specific task has been fulfilled, such as the performance of a ritual, the roofing of a house or eating a festive meal, the rhythm of drinking changes and people drink to get drunk in celebration of the fulfilment of social duty (Sp. *para emborracharse*; Q *machananpaq*). At this stage people are expected to drink until they lose consciousness, or are dragged away by a caring child or spouse. It is also at this later stage that people establish the closest contact with the forces of the animate landscape and with the dead. Allen (1988) has stressed the ways in which drunks can act as conduits for Andean supernatural power[12]. The power of the landscape can thus enter the sphere of human activities through drunkenness although the drinkers themselves are not acquiring enhanced knowledge as would be the case here with hallucinogenic drug use. I have frequently heard drunken people declare that they are dead – and that the dead are drunks. Drunken men are believed to engender deformed babies who rarely survive the first few weeks of life. The complex relationship between the dead and the supernatural powers of the locality is also invoked here, especially in this context of drinking as an integral part of ritual activity. It could also be argued that drunks establish an essential link between the supernatural powers of the landscape and the community through their loss of consciousness[13]. As Gose (1986b:296) has described, sacrifice is a central 'image of social cohesion and power in Andean culture'. Regeneration of life in the locality is ensured by the continual offerings of plant or animal 'food' to the spirits of the landscape. Human sacrifice, offered during the Inka period and still offered in ritual form today, is the highest form of offering. Thus, in a state of 'death', drunks become the ultimate sacrifice on the part of the community and thereby dramatically increase the potential for positive interaction with the supernatural world.

It was this deliberate orientation towards self-transcendence and loss of consciousness which gave rise to many of the comments and adverse judgements about Andean drinking practices made in the colonial period. These judgements, which failed to appreciate the total meaninglessness of drinking in moderation, was and is paralleled by a negative attitude towards drinking *within* the community which condemns excessive drinking by persons whose drunkenness is not harnessed to the regeneration of community[14].

Socially Unacceptable Alcohol Use

Drunkenness *can* be thought of, therefore, as antisocial behaviour. People whose drinking is deemed to be antisocial are said to drink from bad habit (*por vicio*) and are most commonly mentioned in the following circumstances:

a) when not drinking with the appropriate rhythm and when failing to distinguish between drinking in moderation, in order to fulfil a social duty (drinking to 'liven up'), and drinking less moderately in celebration of its fulfilment (drinking to get drunk);

b) when drinking without a motive (Sp. *por gusto*; Q. *yanga*).

The line between socially acceptable drinking and the disapproved drinking as *vicio* is changing and contextual. Attempts to label others as *viciosos* occur particularly when drunks start voicing tendentious opinions and ignoring social hierarchy. Drunks often seem to operate rather like Shakespearean fools, uttering truths that nobody else dares mention, or voicing complaints to social superiors that sober norms of respect would prevent them from raising. Thus the old woman in my initial example criticised me for being mean and talked in public about her husband's violent behaviour. On other occasions I have heard drunks disrupt community meetings by making direct accusations of theft or fraud on the part of the town officials, or ridiculing those in positions of authority by using diminutive forms of address.

Apart from physical removal, there are several ways in which people attempt to silence drunks: they may be threatened by superior coercive force, and if able to assess their weak position, they may leave a drinking session of their own accord. Kin, especially wives and sisters, often try to silence drunks by telling them off, almost under their breath, speaking quickly and sharply and pulling disapproving faces. Such disapproval usually serves to quieten a quarrel in the initial stages. Trying to establish the drunk concerned as a *vicioso* is also an important strategy to ensure that they are not listened to. The comments of a *vicioso* can always be discounted.

Ethnic Identity

The people of Ocongate constantly negotiate their ethnic identity among themselves and with outsiders, playing off the positive and negative implications of an indigenous insider identity and a mestizo national identity. The former is basically associated with the animate Quechua-speaking powers of the local landscape, with autonomy from the Spanish-speaking powers of the state, and with a legitimation of local values, morals and knowledge. The positive side of this identity is kept alive through the frequent small offerings made to the earth and the hill spirits to ensure the well-being and fertility of land, animals and close kin. And it is in terms of this identification with the landscape itself that people distinguish themselves from the dominant forces of the wider society. The negative side to this identity is its implication of ignorance, backwardness and political vulnerability. They refer in these terms to the defeat of their people by the colonial powers and their subsequent history of exploitation at the hands of outsiders – the large owners and the agents of the State (Harvey 1987a, 1987b).

Mestizo national identity reverses these concepts and is associated with education, material comfort, progress and political power. However, it also has overtones of the abusive, immoral social position of the powerful outsider with no legitimate claim to authority in the local context.

We have seen that legitimate drinking sessions take place on those occasions which stress indigenous values and identities; it is the powers of the animate landscape that are sought and with whom communication is established. As might be expected, participants in such ritual events continue to negotiate their ethnic identity in the above terms, always aware of the negative implications of an over-indigenous identification. Drunks do this in an exaggerated fashion, and the juxtaposition of two irreconcilable options, the indigenous and the mestizo identity, is made quite explicit as the extended social competence which drink allows here enables people to identify with the two possibilities much more directly than would usually be the case.

For example, people who knew very little Spanish would nevertheless express pride in their indigenous identity in Spanish rather than Quechua – using phrases such as '*soy indio de la puna – pura inkaica*' ('I am an Indian from the *puna* – a true Inka'). In the same vein, those who hardly ever spoke Spanish could be heard assertively claiming '*yo sabo todo*' ('I know(s) everything'), unconstrained by the fact that such a pronouncement also demonstrated their rudimentary knowledge of standard Spanish grammar. Men and women boast of their strength of character and ability for hard work. They talk about how much they own, how many animals, their own successful achievements and the achieve-ments of their children. The strength which they seek through drinking is manifested in these boasts and positive assertions about themselves.

However, drunken speech also dwells on how hard life is and how much one has to suffer. People cry about being alone. It is something that women feel most acutely. In Ocongate more women than men marry into the community and these women feel the lack of support which only close kin can provide. Men and women cry as they reflect on their poverty and the ways in which they suffer as a result. They think about the low productivity of their fields, and of animals that have been stolen or killed in accidents.

This discourse of despair centres on an explicit realisation that ideals of reciprocity and co-operation, which define close kin relations and provide the basic moral validation for an indigenous identity, do not pay. However hard they work, however much support they offer and receive, they continue to live in poverty. This language of despair is marked by crying in contrast to the swearing and defiant attitude which marks the expressions of pride.

In any drinking session, people are likely to move between these forms of speech but it is most striking when an individual swings violently from one to the other and back again. I was often struck by how drunks would laugh loudly, proclaiming some positive statement about themselves, and then swing into crying and talking despairingly, and then back again to laughter and pride. These swings could continue for an hour or so, with people continually repeating the same phrases. The swings usually only emerge at a late stage of drunkenness when people seem no longer concerned with any kind of linear communication and instead repeat their preoccupation of the moment.

The swings from pride to grief emphasise a strong sense of insecurity in social identity; the people prone to this discourse are those in the most ambiguous position socially. This can be seen above all during festivals when their 'Indianness' is suddenly proclaimed to be the source of their authority. This authority in the ritual context lies uneasily with their paramount lack of power in the economic and political sphere, and with their feelings of solitude, poverty and suffering.

The relationship between drinking and an uneasy negotiation of ethnic identity is reflected in norms concerning age and gender. Growing into an adult involves initiation into drinking and into sexual relationships, both conducted outside the control of the domestic or household group – in fact, outside the social space of the village. Young men and women get drunk and make their liaisons in the fields and pastures above the village, at festivals such as Carnival and All Saints and All Souls, particularly associated with the wild powers of the dead and of the animate scape. Once married, drinking patterns for men and women should ideally reflect the harmonious complementary difference in duties and obligations that distinguish men from women – in which men carry the main responsibility for community affairs, for communal working parties and for village politics. Married couples most commonly drink together during the household-based life-cycle rituals of baptism, marriage and death. Widows and widowers are freer from family obligations and often become heavy drinkers.

Married women drink less than men because their responsibilities are deemed to be of a more continuous nature (Harris 1978). They are expected to look after the home, prepare meals, and take care of their husbands – work which is not deemed to require an initial 'livening-up' process. On the other hand, tasks which men most commonly perform, such as roofing, sowing or the communal work party (*faena*), are seen to require particular collaboration, strength and/or supernatural intervention and thus involve drinking to 'liven up'.

This is not to say that women do not drink heavily. Many of them do, especially in cases where they have children whom they can rely on to watch the house against thieves, to cook for themselves if necessary, and to bring their drunken parents home to bed safely and watch over them to prevent them getting into fights. However, drunkenness in women is thought to be particularly indicative of an indigenous identity, an image associated with indigenous dependence on the supernatural powers of the landscape and also with mestizo male fantasies about the natural promiscuity of female peasant women.

The greater the cultural orientation towards the city, the less a woman is likely to drink and thus the richer, more powerful women in the village are very rarely drunk in public. When they do drink they do so in hiding, both from their own male kin and from the judgement of others in the village. Their discretion also prevents them from being identified with others in the village. By not drinking in public, these women maintain a separation between themselves and the rest of the community. The male kin of these women enforce these practices although they themselves frequently get drunk in public, with each other and with people whom they would identify as indigenous peasants. Richer women are thus used, and indeed use themselves, to create concrete images of class distinction within the village. Their not drinking holds meaning only in terms of an opposing category of female drinkers, and thus reproduces the stereotype of the drunken peasant woman.

Certain unambiguous outside groups, notably the police and the schoolteachers, can achieve a degree of assimilation into the village by drinking with villagers but it is very hard for such outsiders to negotiate an acceptable insider identity in this way. They tend to drink according to their own norms and etiquettes to maintain a degree of separation but as a result they soon get classed as *viciosos*. Not drinking, however, does not make life much easier. The Jesuit priests, Spaniards who have lived in the area for the past eight to ten years, seldom drink with the villagers and this failure to drink is often cited as proof that they are not real Catholics and are probably Evangelists. The small number of non-drinking Evangelists in the village are viewed with great suspicion, are equated with devils and are perceived as generally antisocial. Their not drinking entails a non-participation in the affirmation of the community in communal drinking and in the celebrations of festivals.

In practice, the Evangelists who are tolerated are either those who drink despite their religion, or those who go out of their way to participate in other ways in the drinking sessions, joking and laughing and demonstrating overt sociability. Drinking and the creation of community exert a very strong moral force over those who wish to constitute themselves as members of the locality.

Gendered Identity

Ethnic identity is constituted in drinking sessions and gender plays a role in this process, but gender categories are themselves explored and constituted in drinking. People are aware that there is more than one acceptable way to be either male or female, and drunks explore both the possibilities and limitations of gender, experimenting with identities that they would not normally adopt, for fear of ridicule, of giving offence or simply of not successfully embodying particular positions.

I have already mentioned the complementary unit that a husband and wife ideally form. This relationship is one of interdependence, joint responsibility and a division of labour that corresponds to naturalised constructs of male and female qualities. The issue of hierarchy is not addressed in this perspective, which stresses collaborative difference. Parenthood confers adult status on a young couple and places them into this world of sexual differentiation. Women are represented as having the closest bond with and responsibility for their children and for providing the environment in which the children are raised, and a respectable woman must show herself to be hardworking and responsible. Men are generally thought of as incapable in the day-to-day maintenance of the home; they cannot cook or serve food properly. A lively, clever woman will represent the interests of her household behind the scenes in informal networks and in the subtle manipulation of the men over whom she has some influence. While both men and women hold responsibilities for the household economy, men are seen as more capable in the representation of the household at the level of community.

A variation on this model is the division of home and street into female and male domains, respectively. This particular representation of appropriate domains of male and female activity appears to draw on dominant, broadly 'western' notions of public and private. These do not actually fit the reality of Andean village life, but they provide a standard whereby a woman should not question why a man spends time outside the house, just as a man should accept a woman's decision to be at home. There is no simple or necessary ideal here of male dominance, and women are often seen as the ultimate authority in all domestic affairs.

However, there are also powerful models of male dominance in this community according to which, to be worthy of respect, a man must not only show effective engagement in the public life of the village but also exert authority in his role as head of the household, the guardian of order and discipline. This is the model reinforced in school and Church teachings and in the visible male control of all public agencies, but it also fits with views held more generally across the population concerning hierarchical kinship relations which mark status by gender and age.

Marital relations should ideally embody similar principles of trust and respect. A husband thus has an acknowledged right to discipline his wife and it is a right which women recognise. For example, a woman reacting to an insult from a man once said: 'I'm not your wife, you have no right to talk to me like that.'

Men are expected to display heterosexual virility and women can easily insult them by suggesting that they are no longer sexually active or that they are homosexual. When linked to the positive evaluation of the autonomous spirit of the man of the street, the association between masculinity and sexual virility leads to a general acceptance of the inevitability of male sexual infidelity. However, notions of acceptable female sexuality are quite different.

Female infidelity is far more threatening to men than male infidelity is to women, because it cannot be reconciled with that particular model of masculinity in which domestic authority ultimately rests with the man. Since marriage is most frequently virilocal, a man can carry on sexual relationships with other women without disrupting the hierarchy of his domestic unit, especially when his affairs are conducted away from the village, and away from his wife's kin. A woman's sexual infidelity, on the other hand, automatically challenges the man's position in the domestic hierarchy as it places him in a disputed relationship not only with his wife's kin (an inevitable consequence of affinity) but also with his wife's male lover.

Young people's sexuality stresses the complementary model of male/female relations. Women are expected to be active, even aggressive, rather than submissive or reticent. However, such notions again coexist with hegemonic Western models, backed by the Church and the State education system, in which women are encouraged to suppress active sexuality and seek a monogamous relationship in which sexual activity is directed towards the conception of children.

When drunk, however, people frequently refuse to abide by the limits of these sometimes contradictory ideals of masculinity and feminity. Thus it is that drunken men often adopt a gendered identity that pushes beyond the limits of their own, normally accepted, cultural biology. They talk about their own menstruation or pregnancy for example. Such identifications are always interpreted as jokes but are nevertheless extremely common in the speech of drunks and seem to imply a cultural fascination with aspects of gender normally denied to them. Drunk men also frequently feel empowered to live up to models of dominant heterosexual virility. Drink constructs men able to perform the exploits of daring required to impress a loved one, or to engage in the animated verbal banter through which desire is properly expressed. Many women joke that men are only capable of expressing this masculinity when they are drunk.

Women also associate drinking with sexual activity. They fight and joke better when they are drunk and their first sexual experiences are nearly always described by them as occurring during drinking sessions. They say that men get them drunk and then deceive them. This way of talking about their early sexual experiences meshes with the way in which some men associate drunkenness with female promiscuity.

Women do not experiment to the same extent with optional biologies but they do adopt attitudes beyond the limits of normative social relations. They stop looking after the household, neither cooking nor caring for children. Evening meals are never prepared when both men and women are drinking and children are expected to fend for themselves. It is also particularly women who talk openly when drunk about the limitations and hardships of their position as wives and mothers – thus openly challenging the values on which their daily lives are based. Men, however, are more likely to identify their *Indianness* as problematic rather than their masculinity.

This dramatic extension of possible ways of being for both men and women generates considerable tension. It is around the legitimacy of particular positions that disagreements arise, although these disagreements may well be expressed as disputes about the legitimacy of particular drinking activities.

One such tension which often causes disputes between men and women arises over the relationship and relative priority of household and wider community concerns. Given that women have the major responsibility for the day-to-day tasks necessary for the regeneration of the household, the tension between household and community can often become a tension between men and women. It is also a tension closely associated with drinking practices. Men justify their participation by appealing to a sense of moral and reciprocal obligations between households, while women complain that these community tasks are not important but are arbitrarily imposed by the authorities, to the benefit of nobody except themselves.

The household/community tension concerns the allocation of labour and money. Involvement in community festivals takes a minimum of one day's, and often several days', labour away from the household. For this reason, women and older children in particular may not want the male members of the household to get involved. When the man in whose house I was living was elected to the position of Community President (*Presidente de la Comunidad*), his wife was adamant that he should not take up the job. His main task would have been to organise communal work parties. She said that he only wanted the job because he was *vicioso* and would be able to indulge his bad drinking habits without compunction.

Heavy drinking is also seen as potentially dangerous. Death and illness occasionally occur as a direct or indirect result of drinking. People fall into the river and drown, they sleep in exposed places and catch pneumonia, and they are also more likely to sleep in places where they are vulnerable to the dangerous spirits of the dead. I was told of one woman who had had seven children of whom four had died because she drank every day instead of taking care of her family. Drinking sessions also lead to forgetting one's responsibilities. It is in these circumstances that houses are often left unguarded and possessions are stolen.

Although men and women can and do drink together without problems, tensions arise in terms of conflicting orientations and men and women, particularly husband and wife, then accuse each other of illegitimate alcohol use, attempting to label the other as *vicioso*. The strong associations that exist between drinking and a particular kind of femininity that stresses sexual availability, and an orientation away from spouse, family, and domestic responsibility, makes married women especially vulnerable to criticism.

Alcohol Abuse and Physical Abuse

Drunkenness allows people to articulate some of the contradictions under which they live, and leads them to explore those aspects of their own subjectivity that are usually subordinated in the interest of continuing sociality. These fragmented aspects of self are ideally merged in the final stages of drunkenness when drinkers pass out or fall asleep. Occasionally, however, drinkers attempt to impose a particular self-identity through the use of physical force. Men in these cases tend to hit their wives, their children or their subordinate kin; women hit their children and occasionally their husbands.

There is an acknowledged connection in Ocongate between alcohol and the possible misuse of the strength and power with which it endows the drinker. On certain ritual occasions intended to enhance the strength and fertility of domesticated animals (sheep, cattle and horses), libations are poured over models of animals, as offerings to the hill spirits. Many people in the village will not use the industrial or cane alcohol for the libation as they say it might make their animals dangerous and aggressive. They prefer to use wine as it is seen to be less potent.

The frequency with which drunks use physical force to assert positions of authority within the domestic unit appears to be connected to fundamental contradictions at the heart of domestic life, generated by the particular configurations of available masculinities and femininities. Disputes often arise between husband and wife as he asserts his dominance as household head and she asserts her orientation towards the regeneration of the household in opposition to the community. Women become especially vulnerable as in-marrying spouses, often with no kin of their own in the village to defend them and to take their side. Relations with female affines are unstable and cannot be relied upon. For example, I witnessed a case of two sisters-in-law who were very close and most of the time lived together as sisters. The husband came home drunk and abusive one night and the two women between them managed to knock him out and thus force him to sleep – acting according to the principle that women are expected to be the guardians of drunken men. They were extremely pleased by their collaborative enterprise. However only a few days later when the man again came home drunk, his sister accused the wife of mistreating him, although the wife's unaided attempts to get him to rest when drunk could be said to have been far less physically damaging than on the previous occasion when the two women had acted together.

However, the issue which most frequently leads to the use of force concerns female sexuality and male sexual jealousy, or *celos*. This sexual jealousy is aroused in men by female sexual infidelity, real or imagined. Women are often beaten for their past sexual experiences and may also be punished for the deeds of others. A woman once told me that she had been severely beaten by her husband and when

I pushed her to tell me why, she said that the wife always suffers, that he had beaten her for all the faults of his other lovers, even calling them by name as he did so.

There are plenty of stories of crazy female jealousy in which women are accused of practising witchcraft against men, or lying in wait in order to inflict severe physical injury, but such violence is always presented as abnormal and illegitimate. The acceptable, and indeed common, way for a woman to deal with such cases is through the courts. Men, on the other hand, very rarely use the courts for dealing with their feelings of sexual jealousy, not least because their passions are seldom based on real infidelity on the part of the woman concerned.

Women are also in a weak position symbolically. Legitimate drunkenness involves an approximation to supernatural power. This supernatural power is ultimately more accessible to men than it is to women for it is marked as conceptually male in opposition to the subordinate, conceptually female human community. Gendered representations of both political and affinal hierarchy are also marked in this way. In the metaphor of relatedness which is applied in the conceptualisation of an affinal relationship between the supernatural domain and the community, maleness and political dominance are associated with the superior position of the wife-taker, femaleness and political subordination with the inferior position of the wife-giver. This representational dichotomy is particularly stressed on ritual occasions and is thus highly salient at most legitimate drinking sessions where drunken men and women ideally transcend their individuality and operate as a sacrificial link between the dominant supernatural power and the subordinate community. When men drink, they are therefore placed in a very ambiguous position and are likely to experience strong cultural pressure to reassert a recognition of themselves as dominant, and to overcome the negative implications of their subordinate, indigenous, feminized identity. Such recognition is frequently imposed through the use of force. Wives and children are particularly vulnerable both because they can be legitimately subordinated in terms of dominant images of family relations, and also because their subordination allows men to reconcile or overcome the deep contradictions experienced at the later stages of drinking sessions. Men's behaviour may not be seen as generally acceptable but it is understandable in terms of coexisting cultural logics that both celebrate the relationship between maleness and social dominance yet simultaneously associate an indigenous identity with subordination and lack of social status.

Thus while both men and women, when drunk, subject those in subordinate positions to physical abuse, it is particularly wives, subordinated by both gender and affinity, who are vulnerable to male violence. Women who attack men are commonly thought to be crazy. Furthermore, appeals to judicial authorities as an optional course of defence is problematic: firstly, because it requires women to appeal to a particular femininity that stresses 'natural' weakness and dependence; secondly, because while male violence towards women may be seen as reprehensible by the judges, it does not mark particular men as in any way unreasonable. The following case illustrates this point.

A woman complained to the judge that her husband had beaten and insulted her while he was drunk. The judge listened to both sides of the case in which the man's defence basically consisted of his saying that he could not remember anything and thus could neither confirm nor deny his wife's statement. The judge was particularly concerned about any mistreatment of the children in the family and delivered a lecture on child psychology saying that drunkenness was no excuse for violent behaviour. However, having ordered that the man be detained for twenty-four hours at the police post (seen as a calming-down period) the judge turned to me and said that he was impressed by the man's calm acceptance of the punishment, and that he was obviously a good and reasonable man.

Alcohol Use as Illness

Connected to, but separate from, the idea of the unacceptable use of alcohol is the idea of alcohol use as an illness which itself determines the drinker's behaviour. It is older members of the community who are seen as particularly vulnerable to this illness. They are pitied as lonely figures who have nobody to look after them, and in turn nobody to care for – the reciprocal relationship of reciprocity and complementarity that exists at the heart of functioning households is missing. Through heavy drinking, these people live more closely connected to the world of the dead. Indeed the cure involves getting the dead to take the illness of a drinker with them on the journey which all souls must make after burial. Items such as clothing or a stone that have been rubbed over the body of the drinker are thrown into the grave at a funeral and the newly deceased is urged to take the illness away from the community and from the person concerned.

The behaviour of these ill drinkers is not markedly different from that of the *vicioso*. A drinker's status as *vicioso* or *enfermo* is a negotiated one. In both cases the drinker has failed to negotiate the social relations of drinking sessions successfully. All drinkers try to establish an appropriate rhythm, a motive and an increased sense of sociability. If such motives are not recognised or picked up by a sufficient number of suitably influential others however, the drinker can be labelled as *vicioso*. If such failures are common, they are likely to be seen as *enfermos*. The relative possibilities for successful negotiation of drinker status vary according to both age and gender, according to the principles which I have discussed in previous sections. The relative social power of the drinker is also important. To be classed as an *enfermo* is in effect to be given a position of relative powerlessness in the village – ill people cannot help themselves, they are to be pitied but they do not pose a threat to the fabric of social life and thus are less likely to be forcibly controlled.

Conclusions

In Ocongate drinking ideally serves an integrative function: it should generate social cohesion and ensure social reproduction through the integration of human beings both among themselves and with supernatural powers. Such groups are actively created in the process of livening up, and then celebrated and expressed in the later stages of drunkenness. However the abstractions required to achieve this sense of group or sameness are problematic. The process is never completely under the control of either drinkers or non-drinking participants as people operate with conflicting models of the group that is being formed. Thus, drinking often appears to achieve or enforce a particular interpretation of community at the cost of social relations.

Because drunkenness is about creating community from the available relationships in people's social experience, it is also a time when the fragmentary nature of 'society' is revealed. It is revealed precisely as people are frustrated in their constructive aims and as they voice their understandings of the contradictions on which the fictions of social cohesion and community are built. These frustrations in turn reveal that people are not free to choose particular identities. Historical experience has generated a set of coexisting and mutually defining representations of both ethnic and gender identities. They have come into existence as part of the historical process of social relations shaped by particular economic and political conditions that empower some groups and subordinate others. Thus, despite the fact that drunkenness is experienced as empowering by drinkers, it also necessarily places them into new relationships which involve negotiations in which they may be very ineffective. Drunks are frequently silenced and ignored.

The reason that drunkenness can be so problematic is that this renegotiation of a subject's identity is necessarily social; it can never be unilateral since it generates responses, reactions. Even the negative action of forgetting, a frequently stated purpose and result of drinking, itself creates effects. The obliteration of a particular field of meaning necessarily involves a renegotiation of personal social space, and thus will restructure ongoing social relations, often bringing drinkers into confrontation with law, with custom, with personal opinion and with self.

From this perspective, the topic of drunkenness and gender emerges as particularly interesting. An investigation of the processes by which the status of particular drunken behaviours are negotiated reveals those axes of power that allow certain definitions of acceptable and unacceptable practice to become culturally salient. It becomes clear that it is not simply the State-controlled schools, the Church, the courts and the government administration that act upon a community by imposing an alien set of values, but that these values are themselves sustained and reproduced in local kinship and gender hierarchies and particularly in the powerful metaphorical use of gender to describe the relationship between supernatural power and the human community.

Finally, the conflicts that emerge in drunken interaction reveal the ways in which social power and authority are distributed. It is important to remember that it is the drunks themselves who reveal the contingent nature of such power through their ability to challenge its legitimacy and field of appropriate application. The words and actions of drunks demonstrate that it is through normative discourse and social convention that societies and selves are constituted as integrated and natural entities. Drunks may not appear to have the social power to undermine such norms and conventions but by confronting them they reveal the artifice of social life and allow the imagination of alternative forms of social order.

Notes

1. This paper was presented to the seminars at the Institute of Latin American Studies, University of Liverpool, and at the Anthropology

Department, University of Sussex, and I am grateful for the comments and suggestions which were made on these occasions. Particular thanks go to Cecilia McCallum, Peter Gow and Maryon McDonald for their detailed critique of my earliest draft.

2. This example is a composite description of a typical drinking session which combines elements from a number of events in which I participated.

3. Ocongate (3,600 m.) is situated in the Southern Peruvian Province of Quispicanchis on the main road that connects the Departmental capital of Cusco, to the adjoining lowland Department of Madre de Dios. This road is an important trade route for migrant labour, working principally in gold and lumber extraction. The area is also a focus of religious activity lying close to the snow-capped Mountain Ausangate, one of the most powerful hill spirits in Southern Peru, and to a shrine of national importance, dedicated to the miraculous Christ of the Snow Star (*El Señor de Qoyllorrit'i*). See Harvey (1987a and forthcoming) for further information on drinking practices in this area.

4. Dwight Heath has produced three major reviews of this literature: 1975, 1987a, 1987b.

5. The concept of practical competence was put forward by Pierre Bourdieu (1977) and refers to the competence not only to speak but also to be heard. Practical competence is thus the ability to embed utterances in strategies which are tacitly adjusted to the relations of force between speakers.

6. Alcohol and/or drugs are frequently used quite deliberately to enhance consciousness, even to acquire knowledge. I am thinking here particularly of the shamanistic practices found throughout Amazonia involving the use of hallucinogenic drugs (Luna 1986, Gow 1988, Wagley 1976). In the Andean region of the colonial period hallucinogens were still being used, together with alcohol (Saignes 1989).

7. The extent to which such diminished responsibility should be allowed is itself the subject of social negotiation. In contemporary Britain, for example, those who kill others when driving with more than a specified amount of alcohol in their blood are increasingly unable to invoke diminished responsibility as a defence, although the behaviour is still seen as less socially disruptive (unnatural) than premeditated murder.

8. Saignes (1989) cites the following passage from Matienzo, a lawyer writing in 1567:

> The trouble and impoliteness that follows from the drinking sessions are so notorious that there is no reason to waste much time in reporting

them, for these drunks obviously come to commit adultery, and incest with their sisters, daughters and relatives, and in some places the abominable sin itself, and they murder each other. The Devil easily deceives them and they talk with him and get drunk with him to find out about the future, about events in the war, or any other thing. It is also very harmful to their health. Finally it prevents their conversion, which is our main concern in this land (Matienzo 1967:80).

9. See Saignes (1989) for further details of condemnations of drinking practices in the colonial period.

10. 'Virtually every (Andean) ethnography has some allusion to drinking and drunkenness' (Heath 1987a:25). Examples of Andean ethnographies which refer to drinking practices are Allen (1988), Bastien (1978), Carter (1977), Doughty (1971), Gose (1986a), Harris (1978 and 1980), Harvey (1987a), Isbell (1978), Sallnow (1987), Wagner (1978).

11. The festival of Saint Isidore the patron saint of farm-workers was celebrated on 15 May: see Harvey (1987a).

12. Harvey (1987a,b and forthcoming) also discusses the relationship between drunks and the dead.

13. I am grateful to Cecilia McCallum for pushing me to look at this connection.

14. A difference between drinking in moderation and drinking to lose consciousness as distinctive stages in a drinking session is also noted by Saignes (1989) for the colonial period.

References

Allen, C. (1978), 'Coca, Chicha, and Trago: Private and Communal Rituals in a Quechua Community'. Unpublished Ph.D. thesis, University of Illinois at Urbana-Champaign.

Allen, C. (1988), *The Hold Life Has: Coca and Cultural Identity in an Andean Community*. Washington: Smithsonian Institution Press.

Bastien, J. (1978), *Mountain of the Condor*. New York: West Publishing Co.

Bourdieu, P. (1977), 'The Economies of Linguistic Exchange', *Social Science Information,* vol. XVI, no. 6, pp.645–68.

Brown, K.W. (1978), *The Economic and Fiscal Structure of Eighteenth–Century Arequipa*. University Microfilm International.

Carter, W.E. (1977), 'Ritual, the Aymara, and the Role of Alcohol in Human Society' in B. du Toft (ed.) *Drugs, Rituals and Altered States of Consciousness*. Rotterdam: A.A. Halkema, pp.101–10.

Cushner, N.P. (1980), *Lords of the Land: Sugar, Wine and Jesuit Estates of Coastal Peru, 1600–1767*. Albany: State University of New York Press.

De Rios, M.D. (1972), *Visionary Vine: Psychedelic Healing in the Peruvian Amazon*. San Francisco: Chandler.

Doughty, P. (1971), 'The Social Uses of Alcoholic Beverages in a Peruvian Community', *Human Organization*, 30, pp.187–97.

DouglDouglas, M. (ed.) (1987), *Constructive Drinking: Perspectives on Drink from Anthropology*. Cambridge: Cambridge University Press.

Gose, P. (1986a), 'Work, Class and Culture in Huaquirca, a Village in the Southern Peruvian Andes'. Unpublished Ph.D. thesis, London School of Economics.

Gose, P. (1986b), 'Sacrifice and the Commodity Form in the Andes', *Man*, 21, pp.296–10.

Gow, D. (1976), 'The Gods and Social Change in the High Andes'. Unpublished Ph.D. thesis, University of Wisconsin, Madison.

Gow, P. (1988), 'Visual Compulsion: Design and Image in Western Amazonian Cultures', *Revindi*, no. 2, pp.19–32.

Gow, P. (1991), *Of Mixed Blood: Kinship and History in Peruvian Amazonia*. Oxford: Clarendon Press.

Harner, M. (ed.) (1973), *Hallucinogens and Shamanism*. Oxford: Oxford University Press.

Harris, O. (1978), 'Complementarity and Conflict: an Andean view of Women and Men' in J. La Fontaine (ed.) *Sex and Age as Principles of Social Differentiation*, pp.21–40. London: Academic Press.

Harris, O. (1980), 'The Power of Signs' in C. MacCormack and M. Strathern (eds) *Nature, Culture and Gender*, pp.70–94. Cambridge: Cambridge University Press.

Harvey, P. (1987a), 'Language and the Power of History: the Discourse of Bilinguals in Ocongate (Southern Peru)'. Unpublished Ph.D. thesis, London School of Economics.

HaHarvey, P. (1987b), 'Lenguaje y Relaciones de Poder: consecuencias para una politica linguistica' in *Allpanchis*, 29/30, pp.105–131.

Harvey, P. (forthcoming), 'Drunken Speech and the Construction of Meaning – Bilingual Competence in the Southern Peruvian Andes', *Language in Society*.

Heath, D. (1975), 'A critical review of ethnographic studies of alcohol use' in R. Gibbins, Y. Israel, H. Kalant, R. Popham, W. Schmidt and R. Smart (eds) *Research Advances in Alcohol and Drug Problems*. New York: Wiley, vol. 2, pp.1–92.

Heath, D. (1987a), 'A Decade of Development in the Anthropological Study of Alcohol Use, 1970–1980' in M.Douglas (ed.)
1987, pp.16–69.

Heath, D. (1987b), 'Anthropology and Alcohol Studies: Current
Issues' *Annual Review of Anthropology*, vol. 16, p.99–120.

Isbell, B.J. (1978), *To Defend Ourselves: Ecology and Ritual in an
Andean Village*. Austin: University of Texas Press.

Luna, L. (1986), *Vegetalismo: Shamanism Among the Mestizo
Population of the Peruvian Amazon*. Stockholm: Almqvist &
Wiksell International.

Matienzo, J. de (1967), *Gobierno del Peru* (1567) Lima: IFEA.

Price, J. (1975), 'An Applied Analysis of North American Indian
Drinking Patterns' in *Human Organization*, vol. 34, no. 1, pp.17–
26.

Saignes, T. (1989), 'Borracheras Andinas: Por Qué Los Indios
Ebrios Hablan en Espanol?' *Revista Andina*.

Sallnow, M. (1987), *Pilgrims of the Andes: Regional Cults in Cusco*.
Washington DC: Smithsonian Institution Press.

Spivak, G.C. (1988), *In Other Worlds: Essays in Cultural Politics*.
London: Routledge.

Strathern, N. (1988), *The Gender of the Gift*. Berkeley: University of
California Press.

Taussig, M. (1987), *Shamanism, Colonialism and the Wild Man: A
Study in Terror and Healing*. Chicago, University of Chicago
Press.

Wagley, C. (1976), *Amazon Town. A study of man in the tropics*.
Oxford: Oxford University Press.

Wagner, C.A. (1978), See Allen, C. (1978).

Whitten, N. (1985), *Sicuanga Runa: The Other Side of Development
in Amazonian Ecuador*. Urbana: University of Illinois Press.

11

Drinking and the Management of Problem Drinking Among the Bari, Southern Sudan

Guro Huby

This chapter is based on a study which took place among the Bari people, in the Southern Sudan, during the period 1975–9. The original study concerned the construction of gender in a 'tribal' society adapting to a modern nation-state and its market economy (Huby 1981).

Both the production and consumption of various forms of alcoholic beverage were an important part of daily life in Juba, the main urban centre of the Southern Sudan. Juba was the base for my fieldwork. It soon became apparent that Bari drinking customs were intimately linked to questions of gender and urban adaptation, and material about drinking patterns, and about drinking problems and the containment of these, inevitably became part of my study.

This material underlines how drinking patterns are culturally rather than, in any simplistic way, biochemically determined. It also underlines how 'normal' and 'abnormal' drinking are socially defined, and that we cannot understand 'problem drinking' unless we understand the wider social context in which such behaviour takes the form and definition that it does.

Ideas about appropriate and inappropriate drinking behaviour seem to be important symbolic components of gender construction more widely: approved drinking behaviour is commonly different for women and men. The following description of drinking and of drink problems among the Bari portrays gender as constituting, and constituted by, the production and consumption of alcohol, the definition of drink problems, and the institutional arrangements for the containment of these.

According to Mary Douglas (1987:9), '...drinking (is) a medium for constructing the actual world'. What a Bari drinks, with whom, when and with what effect should be seen as more than a cultural by-product. Drinking here is at the very heart of the process whereby crucial social relationships are constructed and defined.

Juba and the Bari

In order, first of all, to understand Bari drinking, we begin with an outline of the social world in which the Bari in question live. The following description of the Bari and of the town of Juba applies to the period 1975–9. After this period came the introduction of Sharia (Islamic) law, which formally banned the production and consumption of alcohol; and also the resumption of fighting between a Southern Sudanese liberation army and the Sudanese Central Government in Khartoum.

The Bari traditionally inhabit areas east of the Nile and around Juba, the main urban centre. They are considered the host population of the town, which has grown up around an old Bari settlement. Many Bari live in villages within a range of distances from Juba. The village Bari are mainly agriculturalists. They keep some cattle and smaller livestock, but agriculture is the main activity. Some produce is sold in town markets, and where these markets are within reasonable reach the cash from such sales is an important part of household management. Some food is grown for own consumption. Contact with the town and its cash economy is also maintained through relatives and family members who work, study or live in town.

A great many Bari, together with other Southerners in the Sudan, have become town-dwellers and make a livelihood in the town cash economy. Juba, which is the centre of modern Southern Sudanese government and administration, can offer a well-paid and prestigious career in the modern state bureaucracy for the younger, well-educated élite of Southerners. Some employment as guardsmen, messengers and labourers is available for unskilled persons, and many with some education work as nurses, teachers, policemen and soldiers.

Alcohol and Violence

However, work is scarce and most jobs do not pay well enough to support a family. Petty trade in the informal town economy is an important economic activity which supplements family income. Among such activities, the women's beer brewing and distilling of liquor are the most important. Brewing and distilling are women's work, and constitute an important part of women's income.

The brewing of beer is legal if it takes place in publicly licensed beer-houses or *andaias*. On payment of a standard fee, women may use the premises of a beer-house to brew and sell their beer. A beer-house may be owned by a man or a woman, but is always managed by a woman. A male owner is never visibly involved in the day-to-day running of the business. The fee paid by women using the beer-houses can amount to a considerable source of income for the owners. Commercial brewing at home is illegal, as is the distilling of liquor from grain or dates. Distilling always takes place at home. Brewing and distilling for sale take place in villages where grain can be bought from town markets and transported out to the village. Home-grown grain is food; it may not be used to produce alcohol for sale.

There are several types of alcoholic beverage. These are classified into two main types: 'white beer' and 'black beer' (or distilled alcohol). 'White beer' is the most important type of fermented beer. It is made from fermented grain (*durra sorghum*) and is considered the traditional Bari beer: 'The beer we have always made'. It forms an essential part of rituals and helps to define important occasions. It is said by some to be both nutritious and refreshing, and is often thought of as a kind of food. It is also made for sale.

While 'white beer' is thought of as harmless and beneficial, distilled alcohol from dates or grain is called 'black beer' and thought of a source of disruption. A person who 'stops drinking' will stop drinking 'black beer' only.

The production and consumption of alcohol occupy an important place in the town of Juba and in Bari everyday life more generally. Looking for the ingredients for brewing (there is a permanent shortage of supplies in Juba), plus brewing and distilling, and selling beer and liquor, take up a large amount of women's attention and time. The *andaia* or beer-house is an important meeting-place and centre of relaxation for a number of Juba citizens, both men and women. Various kinds of beer, but especially 'white' beer, are taken as a cheap lunch by many. Both beer and distilled liquor are freely available at all times of the day.

The sharing of alcohol marks the recognition of social relationships, both on special and everyday occasions. However, drinking is also associated with disturbance and disruption. Violence, fighting and drinking (especially of 'black beer') are associated in a number of situations. Lineage, clan and tribal rivalries can erupt when such alcohol has been consumed. The focus of my original research also drew my attention to an association between such drinking and domestic violence. Women are by no means passive victims in these conflicts.

Drinking, violence and marital disharmony are seen as normal features of life. Drinking turns into a 'problem', however, when it openly threatens a marriage. In these cases, the kin elders will intervene to contain the disruption and modify drinking behaviour.

Drinking and violence form a striking and, at times, disturbing feature of Juba and Bari life. In other contexts, heavy drinking and associated problems have been attributed to a general loosening of traditional social organisation, together with a confusion of values following urbanisation and social change (see, for example, Field 1962, reviewing Horton 1943). The Bari have indeed faced numerous challenges to their social order during the last century. In addition, many Bari and other Southern Sudanese are poor. In town, many live in badly designed squatter areas with inadequate sanitation, and disease is a part of life. It would be tempting, and would not seem unreasonable, to try to see their drinking as a reaction to 'stress' caused by poverty, rapid social change and adverse material living conditions.

However, the Bari have not been passive victims of the social, political and economic changes wrought by the events of the last hundred years or so. In fact, they have maintained a surprising degree and sense of group identity, social cohesion and stability despite considerable disruptions and upheavals in their lives. When the Southern Sudan was opened up to colonial interests at the end of the nineteenth century, the Bari, like other Southern peoples, were exposed to war, unrest and occupation by various powers. The establishment of a national Sudanese State brought political and economic changes, together with a civil war between the Sudanese national government and Southern Sudanese liberation movements. A peace agreement in 1972 brought the conflict to a ten-year halt, but it started again in the early 1980s. The civil war has caused the displacement of large numbers of Bari and other Southerners.

In spite of these disruptions, the Bari of 1979 remained intact as a social entity, with a strong social organisation based on patrilineal, exogamous clans whose active networks spanned the socio-economic and geographical divides within modern Southern Sudan.

Drinking, and the violence associated with drinking, should not be assumed to be signs that the Bari community of the late 1970s and early 1980s was disintegrating or somehow producing a large number of socially maladapted individuals. Rather, alcohol production, drinking and the definition and containment of drink problems must be seen as integral aspects of the dynamics of Bari life. To make this clearer, I shall just outline a few aspects of Bari social organisation in the context of the economic and political realities of modern Sudan.

Bari Social Organisation

The Bari are divided into patrilineal, exogamous clans. A clan is a collection of people who recognise a common ancestor – in the case of a patrilineal clan, this ancestor is a man, the forefather. The clans have different names, and members of the same clan cannot marry.

For the purposes of the exchange of women in marriage and the regulation of domestic affairs, the operational units of clans are called 'doors' in Bari parlance. A 'door' consists of a group of brothers, their sons and grandsons. These groups of male relatives give away their sisters and daughters in marriage to members of other 'doors' of different clans. In return, they are given bridewealth, which the brothers and fathers exchange for wives and daughters-in-law from other 'doors'.

This process of exchange of women for bridewealth between units of kinsmen is an important and central activity. The whole process of exchange is controlled by the senior, male members of 'doors'. The status of an elder, or 'big man', is conferred by a combination of age, lineage seniority and proven ability to negotiate in marriage and kinship affairs.

The Bari were known as an acephalous (literally 'headless') tribe on contact with British colonial powers. Their 'chiefs' wielded little or no real power. Political power, together with economic power, in the ownership of land, lay with the lineage elders. Today, younger, educated men and women with well-paid and influential jobs within the Sudanese administration and government have greater earning power and more political influence than their elders. However, the old men have retained their control over marriage and bridewealth negotiations, by virtue of the strict control they exert over their daughters and sisters.

A Bari girl is under the guardianship of her father, father's brother or own brother until she marries. Her movements are strictly controlled, for she must be a virgin and maintain a good reputation in order to marry a respectable Bari. And marry she must, in return for good bridewealth, otherwise her brothers cannot, in turn, get the bridewealth they need to bring the women into the lineage who will bear the next generation.

Marriage, family and tribal matters remain important concerns of one who feels herself or himself to be a true Bari, no matter what his or her career, occupation or success in modern Sudanese political and economic life. The community of kin and fellow Bari channels competition towards investment in the collectivity. A man's or woman's reputation and income are converted into social currency only if they are shared by a large number of kinsmen. The lineage and clan, not the individual, are what matters here.

A true Bari remains an active member of an extensive kinship network wherever he or she goes. The Bari's most significant social contacts remain other Bari with whom they interact as kinsmen or in-laws. These kinship networks span geographical and socio-economic divides within the Southern Sudan. For example, the Bari do not emphasise a sharp division between Juba and the rural villages. Juba grew up around a Bari settlement. 'Juba is the village of the Bari,' I was told when I tried to elicit opinions about the differences between town and country. 'There is no difference.' Of course, the town is different from the village in that there are, for example, more people, more temptations, the town is dirtier, the women wear smart clothes and so on, but since the Bari operate within kinship networks which cross and weaken the urban-rural divide, Juba remains 'the village of the Bari'. The kinship networks extend into other towns in the Southern and Northern Sudan, even outside Sudan's borders.

It follows that escape from the Bari world is very difficult. Wherever a Bari goes, the control of the kinship and clan networks follow. Moving to Juba or other urban centres does not necessarily mean freedom from the obligations and duties of being a Bari. Few realistic alternatives exist to membership in clan or kin networks. 'The people without tribe' is a phrase used to describe the true urbanites, for whom clan or kin allegiance is of little importance. They are looked down on by the majority of Juba citizens.

Contemporary Bari women are therefore destined to marry and have children, while men feel a pressure to invest in their careers to influential elder status, with power and authority in marriage and kinship affairs.

The Bari of 1979 constituted a stable and self-consciously cohesive social colony, with a high degree of social control over its members. Gender, age and genealogical seniority were the main criteria for the distribution of power and authority. Old men controlled both women and younger men through their positions as fathers and 'door' elders exerting strict control over their daughters, their marriages and the marriage and bridewealth negotiations.

Bari dependence on the modern Sudanese economy represents a potential threat to the power of the old men. Money, not land and cattle, has become the most important economic asset. The people with least influence in Bari affairs are the ones with easiest access to money: women, by virtue of their monopoly of brewing and distilling, and young people, both men and women, through education and jobs within the Sudanese administration and bureaucracy. However, at the time of my fieldwork the new classes of high-income Bari posed no challenge to the gerontocracy. Young men investing their money in the lineage – in the form of bridewealth for younger brothers and cousins and payment for young kinsmen's education – were also building up their position as the most powerful elders and lineage heads. The term 'big person' refers to both old people, men and women, and to men with power and influence in modern State politics and affairs.

Women's high earning power compared with that of their husbands causes tensions for which no solution exists, however, and these tensions are linked to Bari patterns of drinking and violence. Interestingly, these patterns reflect the divisions among the Bari based on gender, age and socio-economic status within the modern Sudanese cash economy. With the exception of children and young girls, all categories of Bari drink alcohol. Violence and drinking occur together in men and women of lower to middle income, while old people and the Bari with a good income from jobs in the Sudanese bureaucracy and government drink, but do not become violent. To explain these patterns, we shall look at the Bari domestic arena as one where the discrepancy between, on the one hand, men's authority and power and, on the other, their poor earning ability compared to that of their wives, causes tensions and conflict.

Bari Domestic Structure

To fulfil the expectations and obligations of a true Bari, both men and women must marry and establish their own independent households so that they can have and rear children. However, the household and family take on different meaning and significance for the two: for the man the position of a household head is an entry to the extra-domestic arena where he is expected to take part in the management of kinship and tribal affairs together with other men. For a woman, her children are her main responsibility and also her main source of power, prestige and security in old age. A man thus needs to invest resources beyond the household, while the woman needs to retain resources within it. When household income is insufficient, conflicts inevitably erupt over its use.

Ideally, a Bari man has supreme authority over the household. He derives this authority mainly from his membership of the lineage which paid the bridewealth for his wife. The lineage traditionally owns the economic asset from which the household makes a living: land. A man's authority in household matters is thus linked to obligations to provide for his wife (or wives), their children and other household members. His wife or wives grow the food the household needs, using his land and his help in the heavy tasks of cultivation.

In town, these obligations have been rewritten to fit the realities of a cash economy. Husbands in town are supposed to provide their wives with a sack of grain per month, from which they will brew beer and supplement the husbands' usually insufficient wages for the feeding of the household. In the countryside, wives grow and sell cash crops, and may use some of the money to brew and distill. In effect, then, women contribute to the household maintenance using capital, which is sometimes given to them by their husbands, but which can be, and often is, their own.

The average Bari household has an income which barely covers what are seen to be essential expenditures, such as food, fuel, clothes and medicines. The husband also has financial obligations to a number of his own and his wife's relatives. Fulfilling these obligations is a vital part of building a reputation as an influential elder to whom people will turn in kinship matters.

Young and middle-aged men of medium to lower socio-economic standing thus face social obligations they cannot fulfil. They do not earn enough money to provide adequately for their households, to help out both their own and their wives' relatives who have legitimate claims on their support, and to show proper hospitality. Their wives carry much of the burden of supporting the household, through their brewing.

Men of this category lack the financial means to back up and confirm their authority in the home. They face an impossible task: they have to act the part of the undisputed household head, while at the same time refusing their wives' legitimate requests for money for food, medicines and clothes for a growing number of household members. The role of the aggressive drunk offers a way out of this dilemma. By appearing aggressive in front of his wife, in a way which drunkenness here allows, a man can brush aside her demands for money, while at the same time emphasise his legitimate authority over her as her husband and household head.

A Bari married woman faces more manageable obligations than her husband. She must cook, clean, fetch water and bear children and look after them. She is expected to contribute to household income, but not to provide for it entirely, and she has no absolute obligation to support relatives outside the household. Running the household on a tight budget is difficult, and the physical work of household management, which includes brewing, distilling and in some cases paid work, is extremely hard, but it is within most women's means to fulfil the social expectations of a good wife. This is also in most women's interest. Staying within a marriage, no matter how unsatisfactory, is often the only option for a woman. Her future lies with her children, and her children belong to the husband's 'door' as the kin group which provided the bridewealth for her marriage.

Women need to fight off their husbands' attempts at diverting household resources to extra-domestic kinship matters, and to create space and freedom to invest in their own future through the children. This involves striking a delicate balance between self-assertion and recognition of the husband's authority and power. This balance is often achieved in situations which involve alcohol and drinking. It is possible to see some of the most typical drinking behaviour among women as a response to their husbands' aggressive drinking, in the face of which they are by no means passive victims.

A wife's most effective response to a husband's displays of authority is to provoke him into overdoing the act in a way which makes him lose face in public. Such acts of provocation often take place when both husband and wife have been drinking and when quarrels and aggression are expected and excused. Women inflict injuries, as well as receive them, in domestic fights. If the cause of the quarrel is deemed to be the husband's inability to exert his domestic authority appropriately, the wife will have gained the sympathy of her neighbours, kinsmen and in-laws. The husband will refrain from ill-founded displays of power and leave his wife alone for a while.

Not all domestic conflicts are seen to be caused by the husbands' inability or unwillingness to meet the challenges of household management. Wives are also blamed for marital conflicts, and a common stereotype of a bad wife is of one who spends all morning in the beer-house, rushing home late to prepare a quick and unsubstantial meal for her husband when he comes home from work.

Men and women with a good education, and influential, well-paid jobs in the government and administration, have the resources to meet both domestic and extra-domestic kinship obligations. They drink, but their drunkenness does not tend to include violence. The men of this category have no need of displays of aggression in order to confirm their authority.

Old men also drink, but without displays of aggression. Overt aggression does not accord with the dignity of an elder, and they, too, have no need for such displays of authority. Their influence and power rest on non-material assets: the control they exert over their daughters, together with their skills in negotiating marriage settlements and kinship affairs. In older women, displays of drunkenness are tolerated as harmless. These women are reaping the reward of years of hard child-rearing work by demanding the financial support, help and reverence of their grown sons, daughters-in-law, and daughters. They can become demanding, morose or merry under the influence of alcohol, but are generally humoured, and a certain distance is maintained until they sober up.

The drinking behaviour of some Bari, particularly of middle-aged men and women of middle to lower socio-economic status, is so stereotyped that it is possible to describe it as an institutional form of dealing with an impossible technical task of role performance. Similar interpretations of stereotyped drunken behaviour come from studies of Truk society (Marshall 1979), for example, where it is the young, unmarried men who ritually 'run amok' when drinking alcohol.

Anthropological studies of drinking and drunken behaviour emphasise the symbolic properties of alcohol (e.g. Mandelbaum 1965, MacAndrew and Edgerton 1969, Douglas 1987). MacAndrew and Edgerton suggest that drinking behaviour is learned behaviour subject to rules and norms, just as sober comportment is. Drinking, and overt shows of the effects of alcohol, give the drinker a licence to engage in 'time-out' behaviour, in which everyday norms and rules can be broken with impunity.

Hill (1978) has gone further than this and suggested that drinking and the show of intoxication are a means of changing the boundaries of social interaction, of establishing a new 'situational definition' (e.g. Goffman 1959). The effects of drunken aggression, and the interpretation and reaction to such behaviour, will vary with the relationships of the drunk person to the people around him or her, and the focus for interaction. Thus, when a Bari husband comes home drunk and acts aggressively, he switches the focus of interaction from his obligations to provide money for his wife, to his authority over her. A similar process takes place in other, non-domestic situations in which alcohol is seen to precipitate fights. For example, in social gatherings where drinking takes place, apparent intoxication is often used to turn trivial incidents into the reason for inter-tribal or inter-clan fights.

The reaction to incidents of drunken aggression will vary with the severity of damage caused, together with the kind of defence the injured parties can put together in a forum of arbitration. If somebody is killed in a drunken fight, the police and courts will be involved. However, injuries sustained or inflicted in a fight to defend the reputation of clan or lineage can add to a man's claims to strength and manliness. In many such cases of inter-tribal rivalries, and also in cases of domestic violence, incidents are gently smoothed over unless drinking openly prevents a person from marrying or functioning in a marriage. Action would then be taken by the person's or couple's elders.

Continued drinking and drunken, aggressive behaviour suggest here an avoidance of domestic responsibilities and a shying away from recognised and common problems of household management. Drinking can thus become perceived as a 'problem' when it prevents the drinker from marrying and facing domestic responsibilities, or when it threatens an established marriage. In severe cases of excessive drinking and/or domestic violence, on the part of the husband, the wife or both, the Bari believe that the drinker has to be made to give up drinking.

Bari Management of Drink Problems

It is the elders' main responsibility, and in their interest, to keep their younger kinsmen's marriages together. Divorce among the Bari is extremely rare. It would mean the dissolution of in-law ties and the return of a substantial bridewealth which has been distributed among the woman's kinsmen as a symbol of the new family bonds. Complaining to the elders of her own lineage is, for a Bari woman, the main redress from an unsatisfactory marriage. Physical escape is a rare option because of the close-knit networks which bridge the physical and social distance between different parts of the country. This network helps a woman's kinsmen to find her and bring her –

by force, if necessary – back to the protection and control of her own and of her husband's family.

The Bari way of managing drink problems is part of the Bari elders' way of managing and controlling the affairs of their younger kinsmen. A complaint about excessive drinking will usually be brought before them as part of a complaint about domestic mismanagement. The complaint can be put by the husband or the wife. If a wife feels she is being mistreated, she can leave her husband for a while, asking for her elders' protection. Also, if a man has serious complaints to make against his wife, he might send her home. The elders may decide the matter is not serious enough for their intervention, in which case they will tell the parties to pull themselves together, go home and behave. If they decide the matter merits negotiations between the two families, both husband's and wife's elders will meet, discuss the matter and decide a settlement.

If drink is thought to be the problem, the elders will try to persuade the drinker to take part in a ceremony where the culprit swears by the spear never to touch alcohol (or 'black beer', which is distilled alcohol) again. Disease is thought to befall anyone who breaks this most solemn of Bari oaths. Some do break it, with impunity, it would seem, but most stick to their promise.

It is difficult to say what makes a Bari keep or break the oath; the economic and social sanctions the elders can levy against a drinker certainly play a part. I do not have quantitative material on the Bari 'success' rate in managing drink problems, but my material indicates that their approach works most easily and quickly in cases where the drinkers clearly have a vested interest in the support and approval of their kin group.

Conclusion: The Bari 'Problem Drinker'

This chapter has suggested some of the ways in which the production and consumption of alcohol, and the definition and containment of drink problems, articulate aspects of gender and kinship identity in Bari society. Drinking and violence, while expected patterns of behaviour in certain situations, become a problem when they put a person's marriage at risk and challenge ideas about who a true Bari man or woman is, or how they should behave.

From an anthropological perspective, a man's or a woman's drinking among the Bari becomes a problem not simplistically because of their personal inability to cope. The way alcohol becomes a problem, and when and how this happens, is negotiated in a wider social setting. This process is intimately linked to dimensions of power and authority, and to the social enforcement of values concerning the 'good woman' and the 'worthy man'. These values are articulated and enforced in a lineage context, through older men exerting their authority as fathers and guardians of sons and daughters.

Alcohol problems are defined and managed as aspects of interpersonal conflict, with the 'person' constructed through kin and lineage ties and investments. Resolution of such conflicts is the responsibility of old men as lineage heads. Their reaction to problem drinking is to pull the culprit even closer into the controlling social networks. In this sense, the social identity of a 'Bari alcoholic drop-out' does not exist.

References

Douglas, M. (1987), 'A distinctive anthropological perspective' in M. Douglas (ed.) *Constructive Drinking. Perspectives on Drink from Anthropology*. Cambridge: Cambridge University Press.

Field, P.B. (1962), 'A New Cross-Cultural Study of Drunkenness' in D.J. Pittman and C.R. Snyder (eds) *Society, Culture and Drinking Patterns*. New York: John Wiley and Sons.

Goffman, E. (1959), *The Presentation of Self in Everyday Life*. New York: Anchor Books.

Hill, T.W. (1978), 'Drunken Comportment of Urban Indians: Time Out Behaviour?' *Journal of Anthropological Research*, vol. 34, No. 3.

Horton, D. (1943), 'The Function of Alcohol in Primitive Societies: A Cross-Cultural Study', *Quarterly Journal of Studies on Alcohol*, vol. 4, pp.199–320.

Huby, G. (1981), 'Big Men and Old Men – and Women. Social Organisation and Urban Adaptation of the Bari, Southern Sudan'. Unpublished MA Thesis, University of Trondheim, Norway.

MacAndrew, C. and Edgerton, R.B. (1969), *Drunken Comportment: A Social Explanation*. Chicago: Aldine Publishing Co.

Mandelbaum, D.G. (1965), 'Alcohol and Culture', *Current Anthropology*, vol. 6, No. 3.

Marshall, M. (1979), *Weekend Warriors. Alcohol in a Micronesian Culture*. Palo Alto: Mayfield Publishing Company.

12

Women, Moral Virtue and *Tchat*-chewing

Astier M. Almedom and Sembatu Abraham

Introduction: Men, Women and *Tchat*

The chewing of the leaves and young shoots of the shrub *Catha edulis* (Qat or Khat, known in Ethiopia as *tchat*) is widespread in parts of central and eastern Ethiopia, particularly among the Gurage of the Shoa region and the Qotu (Oromo) and Adare of the Harrar region. The Qotu, a large sub-group of the Oromo ethnic group, are subsistence farmers in the Harrar region while the Adare, a separate ethnic group, are merchants and owners of *tchat* plantations. The Adare are predominantly Muslim as are also the Gurage, another ethnic group who live in Shoa and parts of the Arsi regions. *Tchat* has been widely cultivated and used by Muslims in the Horn of Africa (mainly Ethiopia, Somalia, Djibouti and the ethnic Somali areas of Kenya) and in Southern Arabia (particularly Yemen) for many centuries. The crop spreads as far down the east coast as Madagascar where it is cultivated for local consumption as well as for export.

In Ethiopia, it is said that the spread of *tchat* was at first heavily and jealously guarded by the Muslims. For instance, in Harrar, a heavy penalty was imposed by the Adare on anyone who gave a *tchat* plant to a Qotu (Oromo) farmer to grow. *Tchat* was a highly sought-after crop for a long time until the battle of Chellenko in 1887, when many Adare lost their lives fighting against Emperor Menelik. Their widows, unable to tend the *tchat* plantations, took the Qotus as tenants. Thereafter, the Qotus were responsible for spreading the crop rapidly among non-Muslims (Getahun and Krikorian 1973).

Tchat is considered 'holy' by devout Muslims who refer to it as the 'flower of paradise', and often offer prayers before they begin to chew it. Unlike alcohol consumption, the use of *tchat* is not banned

249

by the Qur'an. Indeed, accepted histories suggest that, originally, 'Chat was used only by older men in connection with religious rites. They chewed chat and drank coffee in order to stay awake and pray. Later its use was extended to non-religious activities such as attending the sick, weddings, or funerals, and business gatherings' (Getahun and Krikorian 1973:370). Among Christians in Ethiopia, the use of *tchat* is generally regarded as evil. It is said to defile a person by inviting demons. Chewing *tchat* makes people 'behave like goats' according to the Christians. Goats are 'evil' creatures that eat any plant (and indeed anything else) they come across. Goats represent sin in biblical imagery (as opposed to sheep that symbolise innocence and righteousness). However, some Christians are said to accept *tchat* as a medicinal plant, in which case they would chew it on the prescription of local healers in the belief that it will cure specific ailments. Many Muslims attribute medicinal qualities to *tchat*. Getahuna and Krikorian (1973) relate that in Harrar *tchat* is believed to effect 501 different kinds of cures which correspond to the numerical value of the letters of its Arabic name *Ga-a-t* (400+100+1).

The cultivation of *tchat* is done by men and is not considered illegal in any way. *Tchat* is a very important cash crop for the farmers who grow it, and its cultivation makes efficient use of land. *Tchat* seedlings are planted several metres apart so that other crops such as sorghum, maize and sweet potatoes can be grown in the space between. It takes about five years for a *tchat* tree to grow before its leaves can be harvested. The men harvest *tchat* by trimming off the new leaves and shoots from the tips of the branches. They do this either very early in the mornings or late in the evenings in order to minimize evaporation and wilting of the leaves. The freshly cut *tchat* is sprinkled with water and carefully wrapped up in *ensete* (false banana) leaves or castor bean leaves and transported. *Tchat* must be consumed while still fresh, and transporting it rapidly to market is a lucrative business.

In the towns of central and south-eastern Ethiopia, men (and sometimes women too) sell *tchat* in the markets as well as in small shops where it is placed on the open shelves next to coffee, sugar and other foodstuffs. The women we studied could identify at least seven kinds of *tchat* in the market, according to the colour of the leaves (and stems), morphology and method of cultivation. 'White' *tchat* is deemed superior to 'red' *tchat* in quality, and it costs more. Men, among whom are the connoisseur users, are further able to distinguish *tchat* that is grown on irrigated fields from that which is grown on rain-fed fields. If the *tchat* is of the best quality, both the stems and leaves may be chewed; otherwise, only the leaves are chewed, by both men and women alike.

The practice of *tchat*-chewing cuts across many faiths, social levels and age-groups. In the rural areas, men have *tchat* for breakfast. The farmer is said to be unable to think straight and to be unhappy in the early mornings. By mid-morning, he enters the state of *mirkana* (mild euphoria) when he begins to smile and is said to forget all his troubles, having chewed a quarter to three-quarters of a kilogram of *tchat*. Thereafter, it is said, 'he may work for 2–3 hours continuously without any sign of fatigue' (Getahun and Krikorian 1973:374).

In urban centres, civil servants and businessmen take time to chew *tchat* as a normal social habit. Some may chew it occasionally while others chew it frequently. The number of schoolboys who use *tchat* is said to be high in the major towns of central and southern Ethiopia. In the city of Addis Ababa, *tchat*-chewing is also popular among university students, both men and women, who claim that it improves their ability to concentrate, making them more alert, especially when preparing for examinations. *Tchat*-chewing is a fairly common, public and visible social habit among men in Addis Ababa, and it remains predominantly a habit of the Gurage and the Qotu Oromo.

The Qotu Oromo of Harrar cultivate the shrub and provide fresh *tchat* supplies to the Harrar Region more generally. They may also export it to Djibouti, Somalia and Addis Ababa, although it is the Gurage of Shoa region who produce most of the *tchat* which makes its way to the markets and shops of Addis Ababa. The most common occupation of Gurage men in Addis Ababa is in trade – usually shop-keeping. Gurage men usually chew *tchat* in the afternoons or evenings while minding their shops. Chewing *tchat* in this setting resembles in some ways a 'coffee break' with *tchat* rather than coffee. The men claim that *tchat* helps them to put in extra hours of work by providing them with extra energy. *Tchat*-chewing in public is perceived by the Gurage men as an activity that constitutes them as 'real men' in the sense that it makes them hard-working and successful traders. A Gurage man who does not chew *tchat* would be considered lazy and incompetent among his peers. By contrast, it is strictly unacceptable for Gurage women to chew *tchat* in public in the same way.

The Gurage ethnicity consists of several sub-groups, the most well-known of which in Addis Ababa is the *Sebat-beit*. Among these people, gender relations are organized according to constructs of 'man' and 'woman' in which the ideal man is responsible for earning his income in order to support his wife and family both economically and morally, and the woman is responsible for caring for her husband and her children within the domain of the home. Women do not usually take part in 'public' life. For Gurage Muslim women, this means that they are not expected to engage in employed work, for example. However, women may play important roles in making decisions that affect the wider community, and they also decide on how to allocate resources between household members. During social gatherings and feasts, the sexes are segregated: the men and the women occupy separate rooms and socialize only with people of the same sex. Such arrangements are felt to be natural and traditional. This visible segregation can only be properly understood, however, in relation to other aspects of gender. It is not segregation _tout court_. For instance, during childbirth, it is customary for the properly supportive Gurage husband to be present while the woman is in labour and to help along the way by massaging her back and abdomen. This is particularly true for the Muslim Gurages who constitute the majority of Gurages. Marriage between two partners is arranged by the heads of households, the men of the respective parties. Marriage between first or second cousins is common and is felt to strengthen kinship and economic ties. Young girls and women are expected to become good wives and good mothers, and older women play an important role in reinforcing the sanctions of marriage. In contrast to those of the Oromo and the Amhara, the other two major ethnic groups in and around Addis Ababa, Gurage marriages are relatively stable, with low rates of divorce.

To a large extent, the Gurage have not succumbed to the ideals of 'Ethiopianization' or 'Amharization' that have prevailed in central and southern Ethiopia over the last hundred years. The process of Ethiopianization involved conversion to Orthodox Christianity, the adoption of an Amharic name by getting baptized, and the use of Amharic as an everyday language. This was the route by which 'peripheral' peoples could gain access to the 'core' of the Ethiopian Empire (Donham 1986). A very limited number of Gurages have undergone this process of Ethiopianization. The majority have self-consciously maintained their own 'traditional' values and practices. The majority have remained Muslim and their language, Guraginya, is widely spoken. Women play an important part in the maintenance of these and other self-consciously traditional values. One involves the ritual chewing of *tchat*. Women chew *tchat* in the privacy of their own homes or in the homes of their friends. Among Gurage Muslim women, *tchat*-chewing sessions take the form of a religious ceremony. The following paragraphs describe such ceremonies among Gurage Muslim mothers in urban low-income households in Addis Ababa.

Tchat-chewing Ceremonies

The material presented here was gained during a longitudinal study of infant health and growth in urban low-income households in Ethiopia. A selected sample of 113 mother-infant pairs (infants aged below two years) was studied over a period of six months during 1987–8 in an area known as *Kebele* 11, *Keftegna* 24, in the western part of the city of Addis Ababa. Mothers were interviewed on their health, lactation and menses status, their infant's health and weaning status, and other relevant matters during monthly visits to their homes. Discussions took place in Amharic and involved informal conversations rather than strict question-answer sessions. The research was conducted by a principal investigator and a research assistant – both women and both fluent in Tigrinya and Amharic. (For further comment on the methods used in this study, see Almedom 1991a and 1991b.)

Early on in this research, one of the mothers visited explained that she was preparing to host a *tchat*-chewing ceremony. This was going to be attended by a couple of her friends from the neighbourhood. The living-room area was clean with seating mats and cushions arranged neatly in a circle. A bunch of fresh *tchat* leaves, a bowl of sugar, a jar of drinking water and some glasses were placed in the middle. The woman stated that she was expecting her friends to arrive any minute for the *tchat*-chewing ceremony. 'You two may join us, if you are clean,' she added. Further investigation revealed that a woman was considered 'clean', and therefore fit to partake of *tchat*, if she had taken a bath the previous night and slept on her own (i.e. not with her husband). This was all part of a ritual cleansing to be undergone prior to chewing *tchat*.

Tchat-chewing commenced when everyone had arrived and settled down on the mats. The women helped themselves to the bunch of *tchat* leaves that had been placed in the middle. No conversations were allowed whilst actually chewing the *tchat*. The women were said to be entertaining 'good' thoughts and meditating over them. 'Bad' thoughts were discouraged from occupying the mind, and no exchange of news was allowed. Sometimes the women muttered prayers and verses from the Qur'an that they had memorized, but usually the ceremony was conducted in silence. 'Good' thoughts, we learnt, should ideally consist of thoughts of generosity towards needy neighbours and relations, and of caring for one's husband and children. It was also important to express good wishes for the house where the ceremony was held. 'Bad' thoughts consisted of the opposite. The conduct and atmosphere of *tchat*-chewing sessions was solemn, with a mood of reflective quietude (periodically interrupted by infants demanding a feed). The women were engaged in quiet contemplation while chewing *tchat* and breast-feeding at the same time. These sessions normally lasted for three to four hours. *Tchat* is allowed a long time to take effect. The women chew for hours before they begin to achieve the state of *mirkana* (a term that probably derives from Arabic). The women describe this state as one in which their worries disappear and they feel happy and at peace with the world.

The chewing of *tchat* in such ceremonies involves the following steps. A few leaves at a time are placed in the mouth and chewed long and hard. The juice is swallowed and the remains are spat out discreetly on to the palm of the hand each time and put away into a waste-container. We learned that when the *tchat* is fresh and of good quality, it is chewed long and hard and everything is swallowed. However, the women we encountered could only afford *dimma* (red *tchat*) which is deemed inferior in quality and often not very fresh, so they could not swallow everything. *Tchat* is perceived to be bitter and some women like to consume granulated sugar while they chew the leaves. By contrast, men do not take sugar with *tchat*, as doing so would disrobe them of their adult manhood and make them boyish. Schoolboys are said to consume sugar with *tchat* while they are novices, until they get used to the taste. It is not customary for girls to consume *tchat*; they start only after they both reach womanhood (after menstruation) and are married. The consumption of sugar is perceived to cause constant thirst and so a substantial amount of water is also drunk during the *tchat*-chewing ceremony. No hot drinks are taken with *tchat* and Gurage women do not smoke (unlike the men, who often smoke cigarettes while chewing *tchat*). *Tchat*-chewing sessions are held twice a week by the devout Muslim Gurage women, on Tuesdays ('Nur-Hussein's Day') and Thursdays ('Muhammad's Day'). Sessions start soon after midday and go on until late afternoon or early evening. At the end of the ceremony, when all the *tchat* had been consumed, the guests leave the room looking happy and somewhat detached, uttering barely audible words of thanks and blessings.

The women we encountered who chewed *tchat* together were all of similar socio-economic status and often related by kinship or marriage ties. The ceremonies rotate among kin, friends and neighbours. The hostess is normally expected to provide enough *tchat* for everyone, drawing participants into a system of reciprocity. In some circumstances, a woman may not be expected to provide the *tchat* for the ceremony – if her husband had died, for example, or if she is a newly delivered mother; in such cases, her friends, neighbours or kin would arrive with their own *tchat* and share it with her. Sometimes these women were invited to better-off houses where *tchat* was provided by wealthy women in the belief that their homes would be 'blessed' by these ceremonies. All these *tchat*-chewing ceremonies were held by Gurage Muslim women who reported that they would never chew *tchat* otherwise, simply as a social activity. For them, *tchat*-chewing is a strictly religious activity which simultaneously constitutes them as good wives, mothers, neighbours and kin.

Tchat and Health

The nature of the study from which this material is taken meant that common biomedical notions of 'health' were imported into these women's homes and could have been linked in a predictable way. However, the women did not perceive the practice of *tchat*-chewing as detrimental to their health in any way. On the contrary, *tchat*-chewing was regarded as a beneficial practice from the moral as well as physiological points of view. The women felt that they could derive strength from *tchat* through rest and refreshment. They also believed that *tchat* was 'good for the soul': it helped to erase 'bad' thoughts from the mind and brought about blessings not only for the chewers but also for the household hosting the ceremony. In some cases, *tchat* was said to relieve pain and even cure common ailments such as backache and upset stomachs.

These women's views stand in sharp contrast to 'Western' and 'biomedical' views of *tchat*-chewing as a health hazard (see for example, United Nations 1981; Gough and Cookson 1984; Kristiansson 1987; Abdul Ghani et al. 1987; Kristiansson et al. 1987). These works associate *tchat*-chewing with gastritis, anorexia, constipation, insomnia, headaches and with emotional disturbances as well as urinary and liver diseases. They also suggest that female chewers may be more vulnerable to ill-health than male chewers. In one of these studies, the average birthweight of full-term babies born to a sample of chewers was significantly lower than that of babies born to a sample of non-chewers (Abdul Ghani et al. 1987). Biomedical evidence suggests that the chewing of *tchat* suppresses hunger and results in the undernourishment of pregnant women. A preliminary study of the use of *tchat* by lactating women also traced the active ingredients of *tchat* in the urine of one breast-fed infant (Kristiansson et al. 1987), with the possible implication that *tchat* may suppress the baby's appetite and cause undernourishment and subsequently propensity to illness. The medical evidence against *tchat* draws on observations of small samples (see Gough and Cookson 1984). In one study where relatively large samples of Yemeni *tchat*-users were investigated using methods of blind physical examination and extensive interviews, 'remarkably few of the allegations regarding the direct effects of qat use on health by western visitors to Yemen were supported' (Kennedy et al. 1980; 1983). Inevitably, bio-medical studies focusing on *tchat* have carried with them a variety of biologically-based notions of 'health' as well as moral assumptions about 'substance' and 'drug' use which are very different from the assumptions in operation locally, and which cannot take into account the moral considerations and the perceived personal and social beliefs involved.

Previous studies of the Gurage peoples in Ethiopia do not mention *tchat*-chewing among rural women (Shack 1966; Shack 1969). The reason for this may be that these researchers did not gain access to the ceremonies as we did. The *tchat*-chewing ceremonies described above are not normally open to 'outsiders'. We were invited to join probably because we were not deemed foreign, and we had the advantage of being women. The women in our study explicitly mentioned that their rural kin conducted similar ceremonies. In their own perceptions, these women's use of *tchat* is not a question of health and disease. *Tchat*-chewing is part and constitutive of ritual purity and an affirmation of their social selves as good Muslim women. As in other countries around the Red Sea, *tchat*-chewing in central and eastern Ethiopia has a very different reality among men, for whom it is a public part of their manly vigour, responsibilities and workaday activities.

Conclusion

The significance of chewing *tchat* is gender-specific. While the men chew *tchat* in order to be real men, to socialize and to derive extra energy for their work, women use it as a means of achieving religious fellowship and womanly fulfilment.

Tchat is socially and economically important to the populations of large areas of the Horn of Africa and Southern Arabia. The people who use it in these parts of the world regard it highly, both morally and socially. However, for Westerners, *tchat* is a sort of 'drug'. The significance of *tchat* in the lives of peoples such as the Gurage is little understood by outsiders. For instance, the *tchat* ceremonies described in this paper might easily be misinterpreted by a tabloid newspaper in the UK which might refer to the women as 'drug-dazed', from an unreflecting, ethnocentric point of view. *Tchat*-chewing could, in the west, easily be assimilated to 'drug-taking'. This paper endeavours to present the women's own perceptions, and these do not equate *tchat* with 'drug' – a harmful or dangerous substance. There is no moral danger here on which to build a secure pharmacology of harm. The persuasiveness of western biomedical models of danger and harm in drug use often relies heavily on historically constructed notions of moral and social threat (cf. McDonald, Introduction and chapter 4, this volume). Here, *tchat* use fits ill with such models; it is morally and socially constitutive of virtue and propriety. Any simplistic, biomedical 'health' intervention programmes would therefore be doomed to failure.

Tchat-chewing may have possible long-term adverse physiological consequences, particularly in the case of undernourished women who may put the lives of their offspring at risk before as well as after birth. Since such women, for instance the urban Gurage mothers studied in Addis Ababa, regard *tchat*-chewing ceremonies as important events that constitute them as good wives, mothers, neighbours and kin, any medical intervention aimed at discouraging them from using *tchat* would have to be sensitive to the culture of *tchat* use. One sensible aim might be to improve the women's access to adequate nutrition to prevent *tchat* from replacing the nutrients required during pregnancy and lactation. However, 'food' and 'nutrition' are, it should be borne in mind, no less cultural than anything else.

Acknowledgements

Field research for this study was financed by the Wenner-Gren Foundation for Anthropological Research and by the Royal Anthropological Institute. Constructive comments on earlier drafts of this paper from Maryon McDonald and Alexander de Waal are gratefully acknowledged. We would also like to thank the women who participated in this study.

References

Abdul Ghani, N., Eriksson, M., Kristiansson, B., Qirbi, A. (1987), 'The influence of Khat-chewing on birth-weight in full-term infants', *Social Science and Medicine*, vol. 24, pp.625–7.

Almedom, A.M. (1991a), 'Infant weaning among urban low-income households in Ethiopia: I. The Weaning Process', *Ecology of Food and Nutrition*, vol. 25, pp.97–109.

Almedom, A.M. (1991b), 'Aspects of the growth and health of the suckling and weanling infant in Ethiopia'. Unpublished D.Phil. Thesis, University of Oxford.

Donham, D. (1986), 'Old Abyssinia and the New Ethiopian Empire: Themes in Social History' in D. Donham and W. James (eds) *The Southern Marches of Imperial Ethiopia*. African Studies Series, vol. 51, Cambridge.

Donham, D. and James W. (eds) (1986), *The Southern Marches of Imperial Ethiopia*. African Studies Series, vol. 51, Cambridge.

Getahun, A. and Krikorian, A.D. (1973), 'Chat: Coffee's rival from Harrar, Ethiopia: I. Botany, Cultivation and Use', *Economic Botany*, vol. 27, pp.353–377.

Gough, S.P. and Cookson, I.B. (1984), 'Khat-induced schizophreniform psychosis in the U.K.', *Lancet* i, p.455.

Kennedy, J.G., Teague, J., Fairbanks, L. (1980), 'Qat use in north Yemen and the problem of addiction: a study in Medical Anthropology', *Culture, Medicine and Psychiatry*, vol. 4, pp.311–344.

Kennedy, J.G., Teague, J., Rockaw, W., Cooney, E. 'A medical evaluation of the use of qat in North Yemen', *Social Science and Medicine*, vol. 17, pp.783–793.

Kristiansson, B. (1987), 'Position paper on Khat and its effects during pregnancy and lactation.' University of Gothenburg, Department of Pediatrics, Mimeo.

Kristiansson, B., Abdul Ghani, N., Eriksson, M., Garle, M., Qirbi, A. (1987), 'Use of Khat in lactating women: A pilot study on breast-milk secretion', *Journal of Ethnopharmacology*, vol. 21, pp.85–90.

Shack, D.N. (1969), 'Nutritional processes and personality development among the Gurage of Ethiopia', *Ethnology*, vol. 8, pp.292–300.

Shack, W.A. (1966), *The Gurage: A People of the Ensete Culture.* London: Oxford University Press.

United Nations (1981), *Bulletin on Narcotics* (Special Issue Devoted to *Catha edulis* (*Khat*)), vol. 32, United Nations Division of Narcotic Drugs, New York.

Notes on Contributors

Astier Almedom is a Research Fellow in Medical Anthropology, London School of Hygiene and Tropical Medicine. She has carried out fieldwork in Ethiopia, Eritrea and Kenya and is author of a number of articles on infant-feeding, morbidity and growth.

Sembatu Abraham worked as Research Assistant on a project with Astier Almedom in Ethiopia and is currently working at the Nutrition Institute, Addis Ababa.

Tamara Dragadze is Research Associate at the School of Slavonic and East European Studies, University of London.

Penny Harvey is Lecturer in Social Anthropology at the University of Manchester. She has carried out research in the Southern Peruvian Andes and is co-author of *Researching Language: Issues of Power and Method* (Routledge, 1992) (with D. Cameron, E. Frazer, M. Rampton and K. Richardson).

Joy Hendry is Lecturer in Social Anthropology at Oxford Brook's University and has been Reader at the Scottish Centre for Japanese Studies, University of Stirling. She is author of *Marriage in Changing Japan* (Tuttle, 1987), *Becoming Japanese* (Manchester University Press, 1986), *Understanding Japanese Society* (Routledge, 1987) and *Wrapping Culture* (Oxford University Press, 1993).

Guro Huby is a Social Anthropologist and Research Associate, Department of General Practice, University of Edinburgh. Apart from her research among the Bari in the Sudan, she has worked on inner city projects in Britain concerned with the provision of services for problem drinkers, and self-help groups in primary health care. She is currently conducting research on the management of HIV and AIDS in the community, and is the author of several papers on social and medical service provision.

Roland Littlewood is a consultant psychiatrist and Reader in Psychiatry and Anthropology at University College London, and Joint Director of the UCL Centre for Medical Anthropology. He has carried out fieldwork in Trinidad and London, and is author of *Aliens and Alienists* (with Maurice Lipsedge, revised edition 1989, Unwin Hyman) and *Pathology and Identity: The teachings of Mother Earth in Trinidad* (Cambridge University Press, 1993) and co-editor (with Jafar Kareem) of *Intercultural Therapy: Themes, Theories and Practices* (Blackwell, 1992).

Maryon McDonald is Senior Lecturer in Social Anthropology at Brunel University. She has carried out research in France and Britain and has more recently been engaged in ethnographic research and fieldwork in the European Parliament and in the European Commission. She is author of *'We are not French!' Language, Culture and Identity in Brittany* (Routledge, 1989) and co-editor (with Malcolm Chapman and Elizabeth Tonkin) of *History and Ethnicity* (Routledge, 1989).

Sharon Macdonald is Lecturer in Social Anthropology at Keele University. She has carried out ethnographic fieldwork in the Scottish Highlands and the Science Museum, London. She is editor of *Inside European Identities* (Berg, 1993).

Nicholas Purcell is Fellow and Tutor in Ancient History, St John's College, Oxford. He has published widely on ancient Mediterranean social and cultural history.

Betsy Thom is Lecturer in Drug and Alcohol Studies, Centre for Research on Drugs and Health Behaviour, Charing Cross and Westminster Medical School, London. She has carried out research in the use and problem use of alcohol and drugs and has a particular interest in women's substance use. She has published a number of articles on issues in health and welfare.

Christina Toren is Lecturer in Social Anthropology at Brunel University. She has carried out extensive fieldwork in Fiji, and is the author of *Making Sense of Hierarchy* (Athlone Press, London, 1990) and of several articles bringing together the insights of psychology and social anthropology.

Malcolm Young joined the Newcastle Police Force in 1955 as a sixteen-year-old cadet. In the ensuing thirty-three years, he rose to become a police superintendent and gained a doctorate in Social Anthropology. For seven years, he ran the first drugs squad in the north-east of England. He is the author of *An Inside Job* (Oxford University Press, 1991) and *In the Sticks* (Oxford University Press, 1993).

Name Index

Subject Index